EARTH BEFORE US

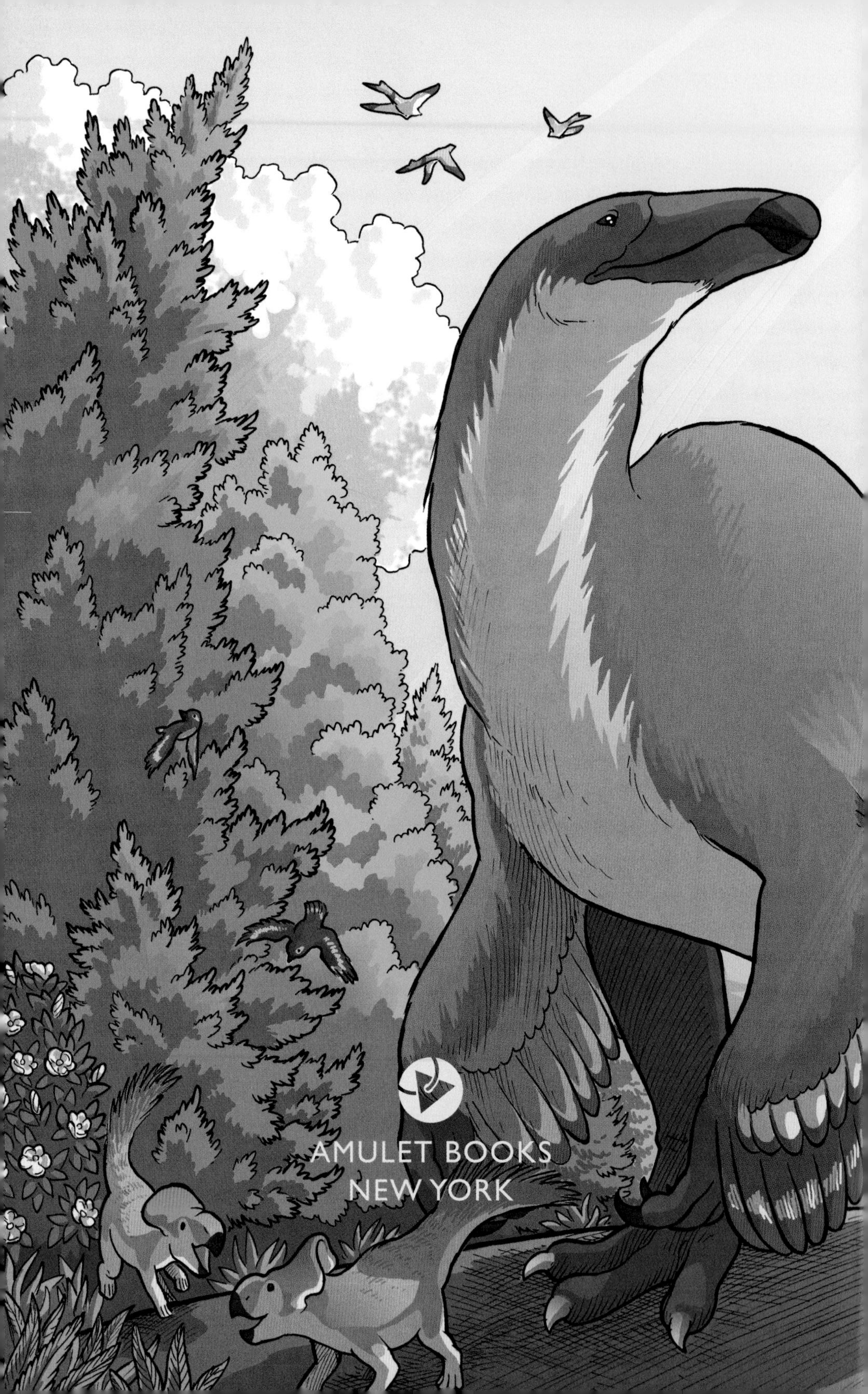

AMULET BOOKS
NEW YORK

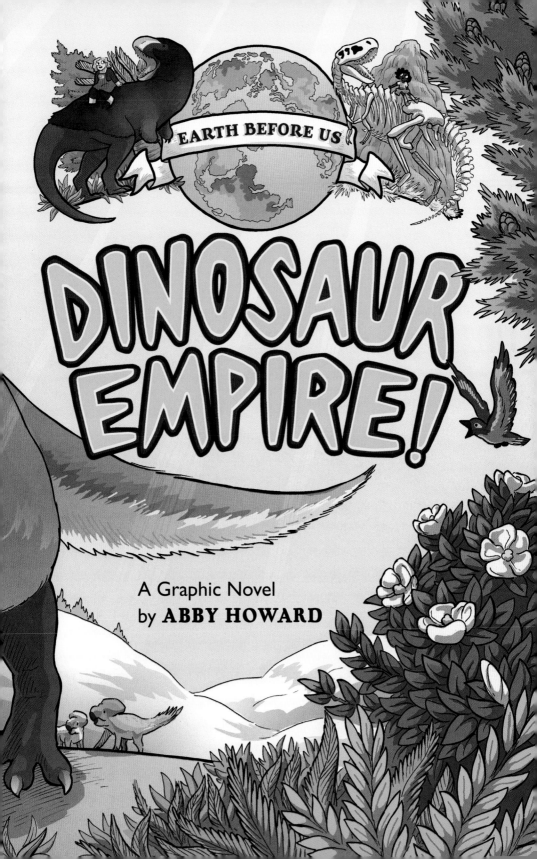

EARTH BEFORE US

DINOSAUR EMPIRE!

A Graphic Novel
by **ABBY HOWARD**

DEDICATED TO ALL
THE MUSEUMS IN WHICH
I HAVE CRIED

Cataloging-in-Publication Data has been applied for and may be obtained from the Library of Congress.
ISBN 978-1-4197-2306-3

Text and illustrations copyright © 2017 Abby Howard
Book design by Pamela Notarantonio

Amulet Books and Amulet Paperbacks are registered trademarks of Harry N. Abrams, Inc.

Printed and bound in China
10 9 8 7 6 5 4 3 2 1

Amulet Books are available at special discounts when purchased in quantity for premiums and promotions as well as fundraising or educational use. Special editions can also be created to specification. For details, contact specialsales@abramsbooks.com or the address below.

ABRAMS The Art of Books
115 West 18th Street, New York, NY 10011
abramsbooks.com

ACKNOWLEDGMENTS

Thank you to Scott Hartman, Darren Naish, and Mark Witton for providing up-to-date information and resources for anyone and everyone.

Thanks to Professor Hans Larsson and the Redpath Museum.

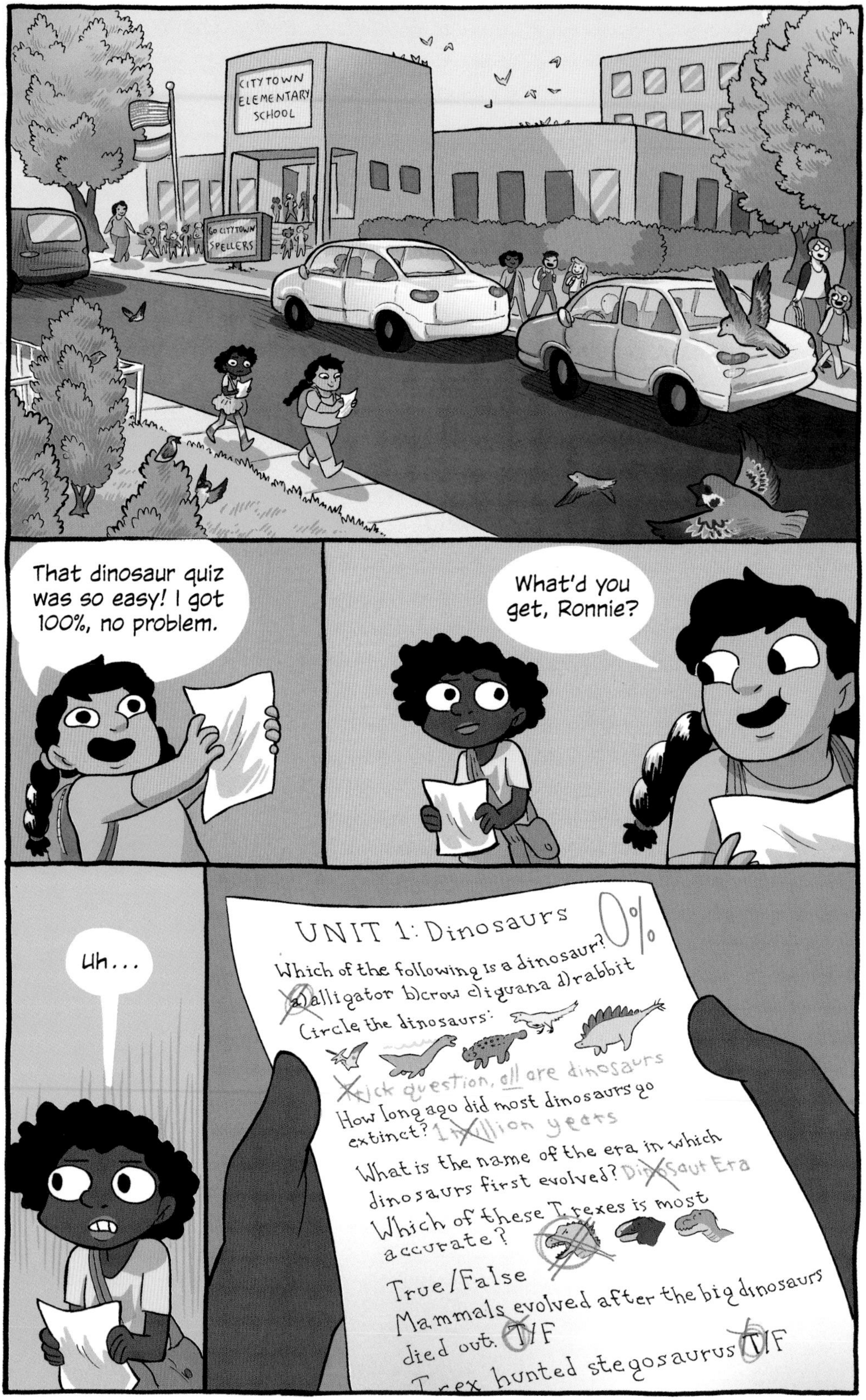
CITYTOWN ELEMENTARY SCHOOL
GO CITYTOWN SPELLERS
That dinosaur quiz was so easy! I got 100%, no problem.
What'd you get, Ronnie?
Uh...
UNIT 1: Dinosaurs
0%
Which of the following is a dinosaur?
a) alligator b) crow c) iguana d) rabbit
Circle the dinosaurs:
trick question, all are dinosaurs
How long ago did most dinosaurs go extinct? 1 million years
What is the name of the era in which dinosaurs first evolved? Dinosaur Era
Which of these T. rexes is most accurate?
True/False
Mammals evolved after the big dinosaurs died out. T/F
T. rex hunted stegosaurus T/F

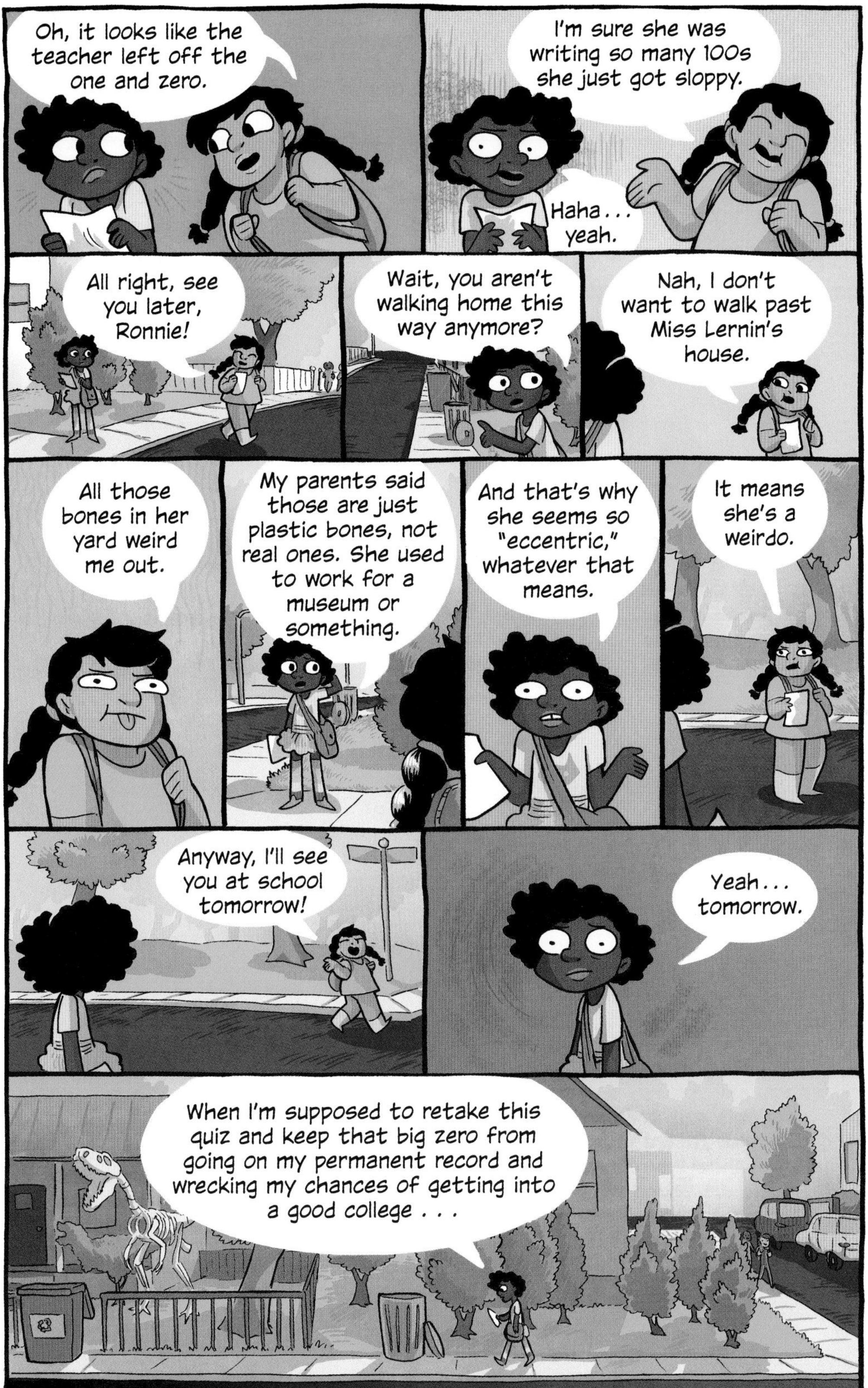
Oh, it looks like the teacher left off the one and zero.
I'm sure she was writing so many 100s she just got sloppy.
Haha . . . yeah.
All right, see you later, Ronnie!
Wait, you aren't walking home this way anymore?
Nah, I don't want to walk past Miss Lernin's house.
All those bones in her yard weird me out.
My parents said those are just plastic bones, not real ones. She used to work for a museum or something.
And that's why she seems so "eccentric," whatever that means.
It means she's a weirdo.
Anyway, I'll see you at school tomorrow!
Yeah . . . tomorrow.
When I'm supposed to retake this quiz and keep that big zero from going on my permanent record and wrecking my chances of getting into a good college . . .

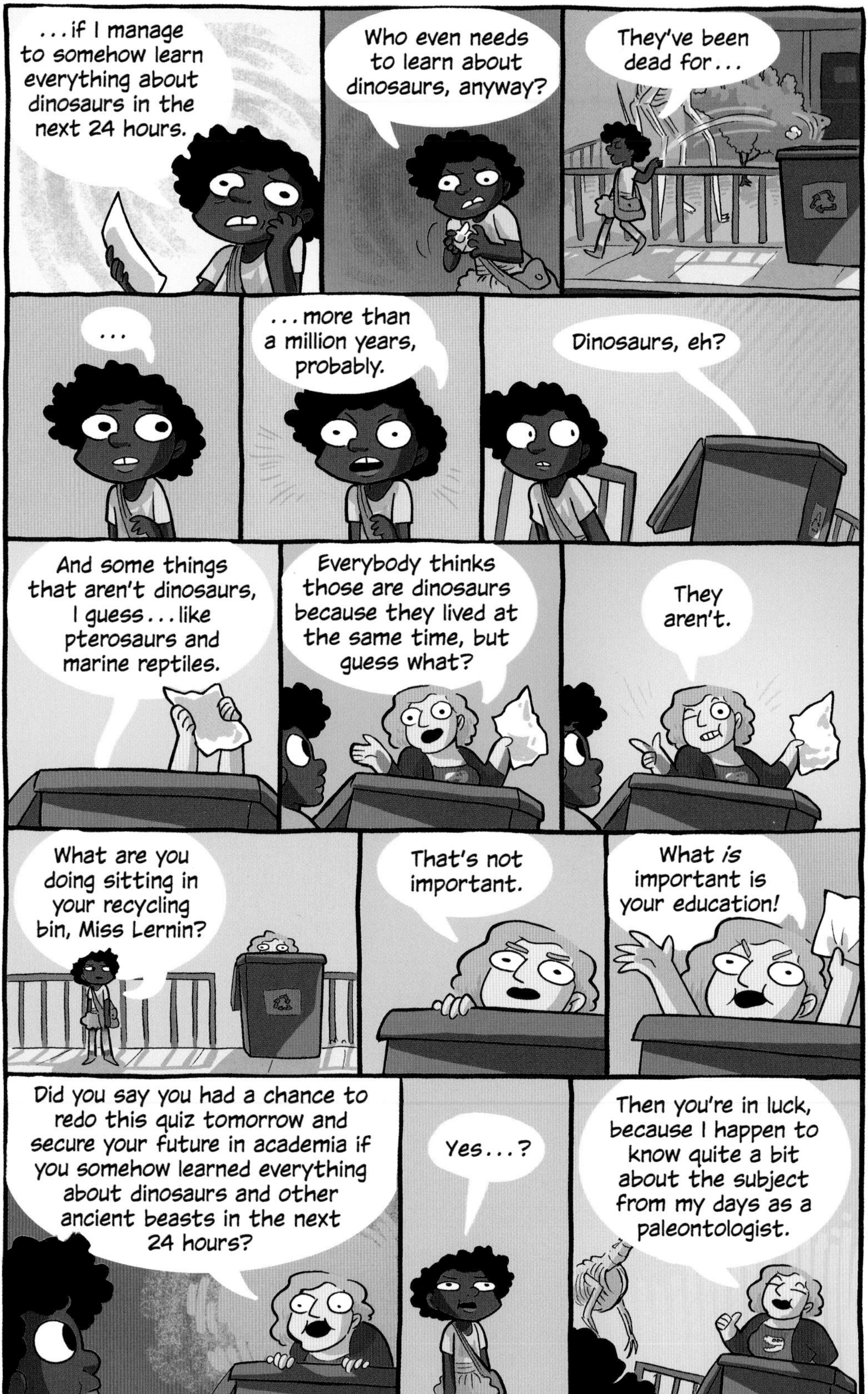

...if I manage to somehow learn everything about dinosaurs in the next 24 hours.
Who even needs to learn about dinosaurs, anyway?
They've been dead for...
...
...more than a million years, probably.
Dinosaurs, eh?
And some things that aren't dinosaurs, I guess...like pterosaurs and marine reptiles.
Everybody thinks those are dinosaurs because they lived at the same time, but guess what?
They aren't.
What are you doing sitting in your recycling bin, Miss Lernin?
That's not important.
What *is* important is your education!
Did you say you had a chance to redo this quiz tomorrow and secure your future in academia if you somehow learned everything about dinosaurs and other ancient beasts in the next 24 hours?
Yes...?
Then you're in luck, because I happen to know quite a bit about the subject from my days as a paleontologist.

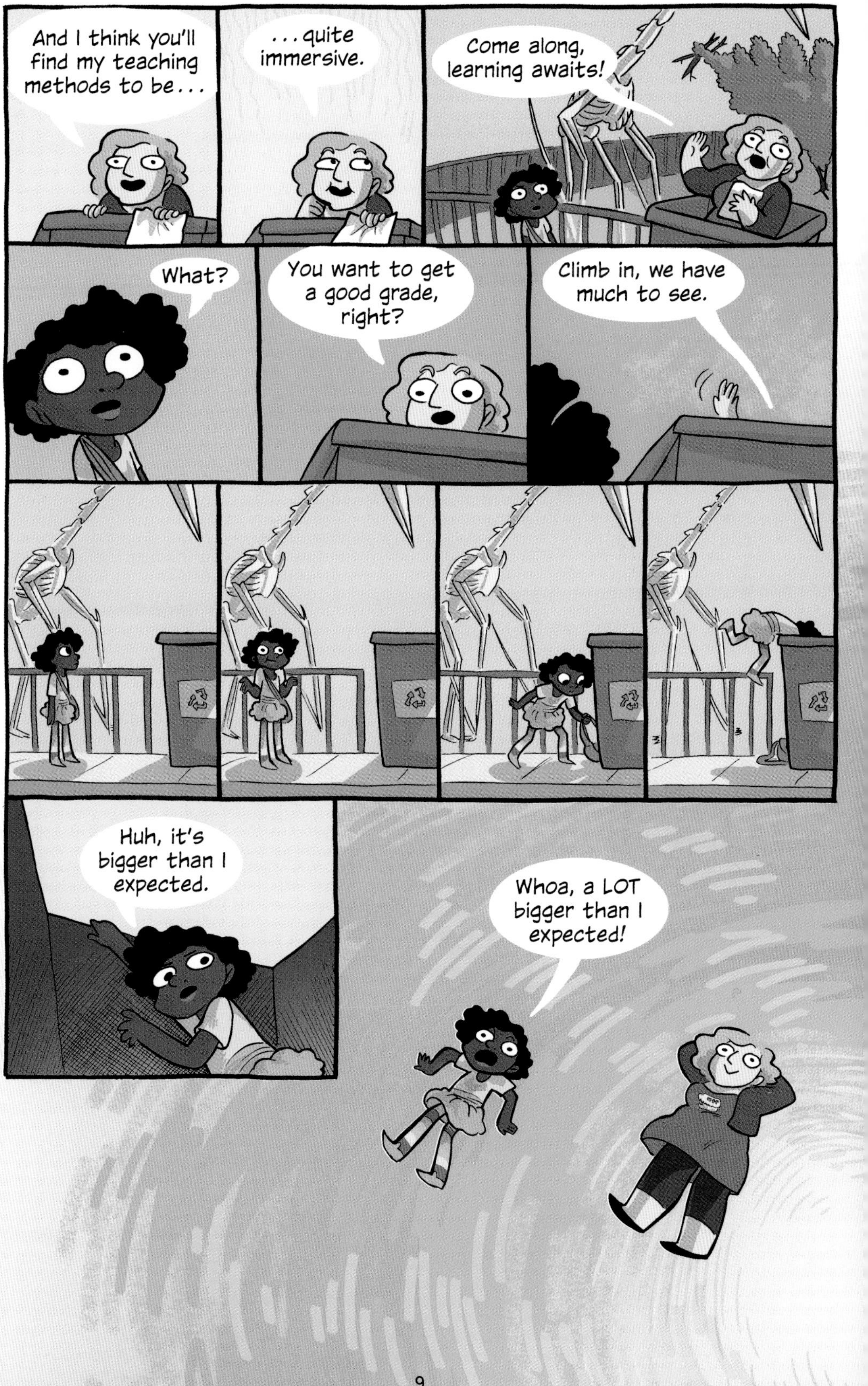
And I think you'll find my teaching methods to be...
...quite immersive.
Come along, learning awaits!
What?
You want to get a good grade, right?
Climb in, we have much to see.
Huh, it's bigger than I expected.
Whoa, a LOT bigger than I expected!

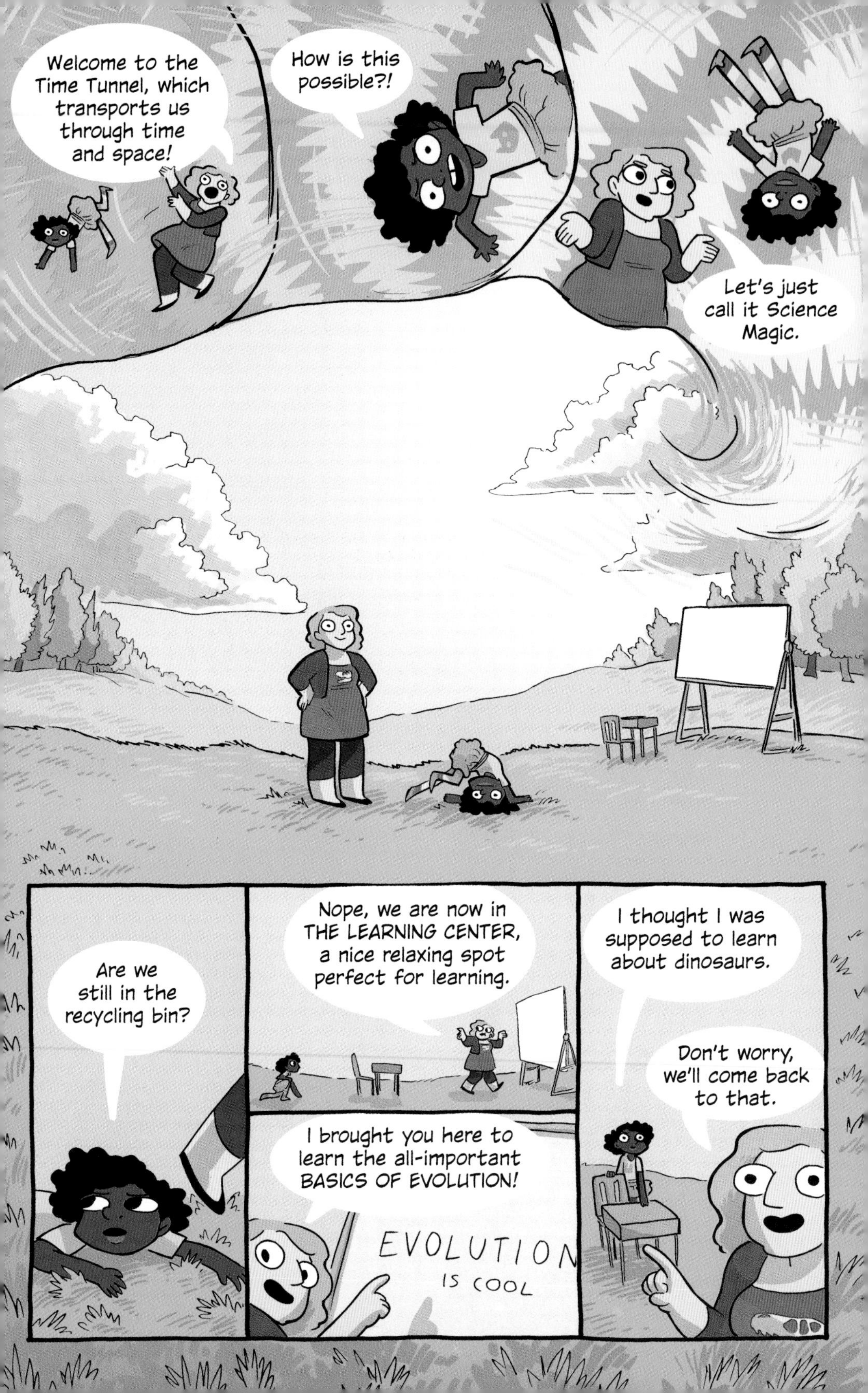
Welcome to the Time Tunnel, which transports us through time and space!
How is this possible?!
Let's just call it Science Magic.
Are we still in the recycling bin?
Nope, we are now in THE LEARNING CENTER, a nice relaxing spot perfect for learning.
I brought you here to learn the all-important BASICS OF EVOLUTION!
EVOLUTION IS COOL
I thought I was supposed to learn about dinosaurs.
Don't worry, we'll come back to that.

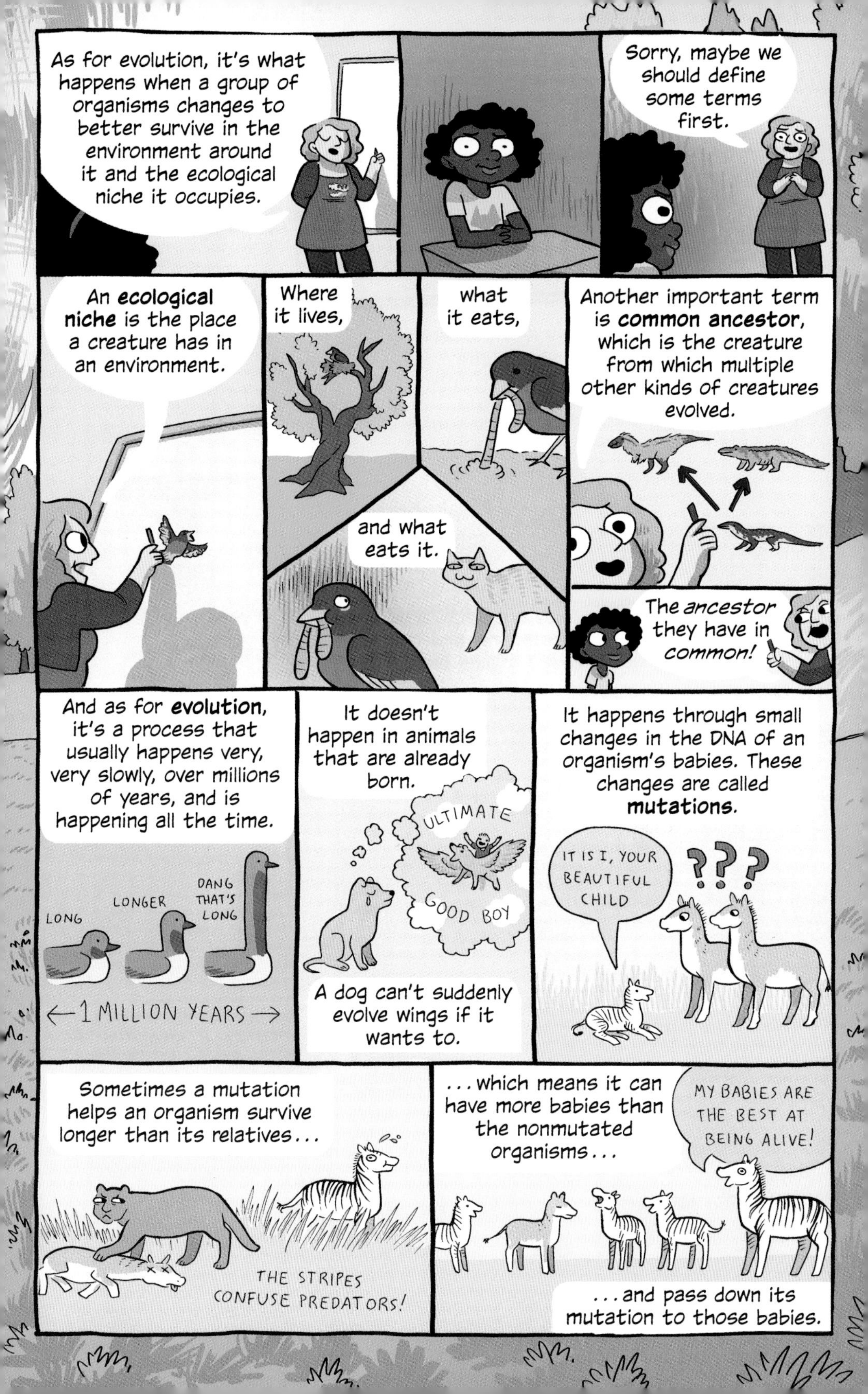
As for evolution, it's what happens when a group of organisms changes to better survive in the environment around it and the ecological niche it occupies.
Sorry, maybe we should define some terms first.
An **ecological niche** is the place a creature has in an environment.
Where it lives,
what it eats,
and what eats it.
Another important term is **common ancestor**, which is the creature from which multiple other kinds of creatures evolved.
The *ancestor* they have in *common!*
And as for **evolution**, it's a process that usually happens very, very slowly, over millions of years, and is happening all the time.
LONG
LONGER
DANG THAT'S LONG
← 1 MILLION YEARS →
It doesn't happen in animals that are already born.
ULTIMATE
GOOD BOY
A dog can't suddenly evolve wings if it wants to.
It happens through small changes in the DNA of an organism's babies. These changes are called **mutations**.
IT IS I, YOUR BEAUTIFUL CHILD
???
Sometimes a mutation helps an organism survive longer than its relatives...
THE STRIPES CONFUSE PREDATORS!
...which means it can have more babies than the nonmutated organisms...
MY BABIES ARE THE BEST AT BEING ALIVE!
...and pass down its mutation to those babies.

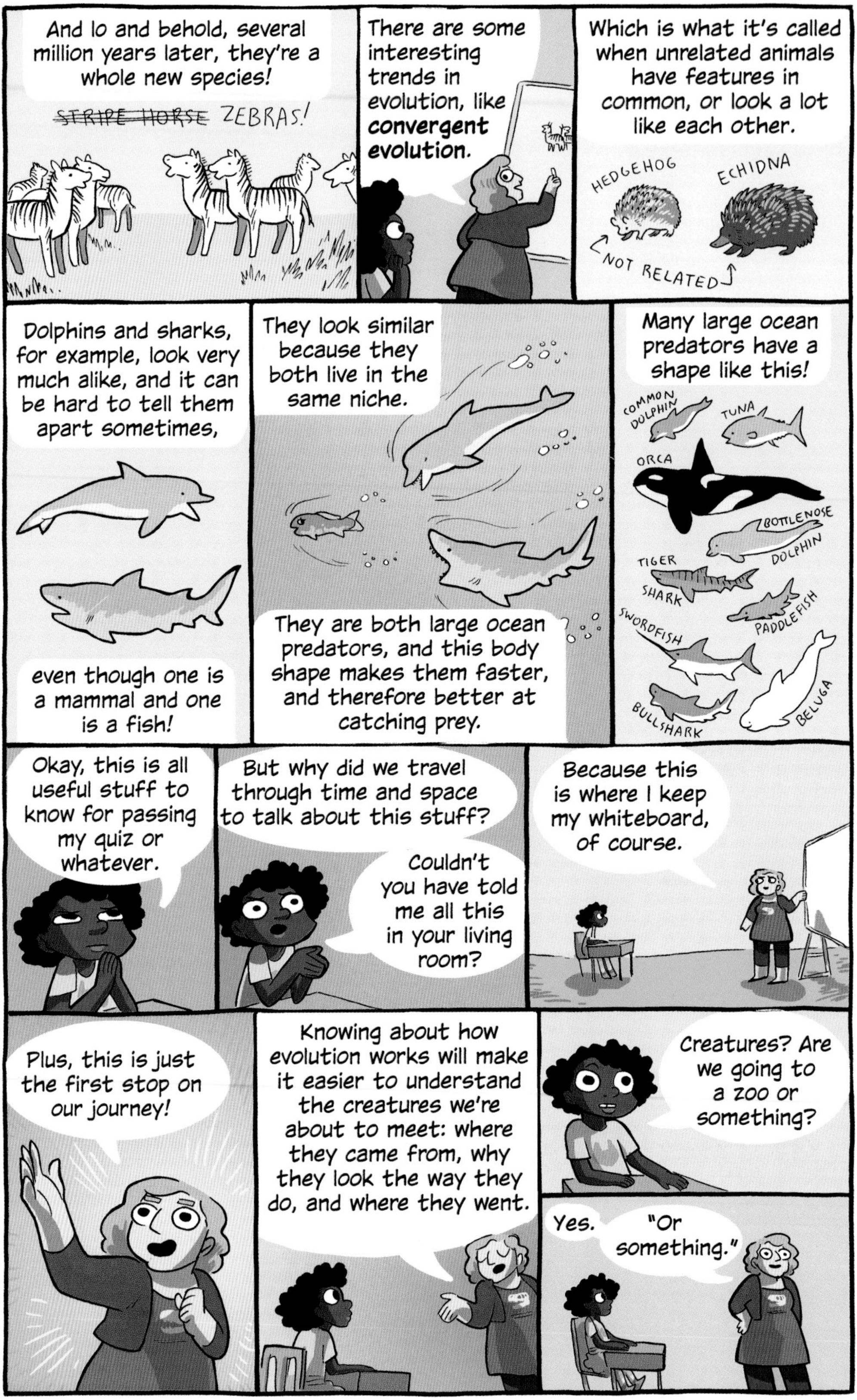
And lo and behold, several million years later, they're a whole new species!
STRIPE HORSE ZEBRAS!
There are some interesting trends in evolution, like **convergent evolution**.
Which is what it's called when unrelated animals have features in common, or look a lot like each other.
HEDGEHOG
ECHIDNA
NOT RELATED
Dolphins and sharks, for example, look very much alike, and it can be hard to tell them apart sometimes,
even though one is a mammal and one is a fish!
They look similar because they both live in the same niche.
They are both large ocean predators, and this body shape makes them faster, and therefore better at catching prey.
Many large ocean predators have a shape like this!
COMMON DOLPHIN
TUNA
ORCA
BOTTLENOSE DOLPHIN
TIGER SHARK
PADDLEFISH
SWORDFISH
BULL SHARK
BELUGA
Okay, this is all useful stuff to know for passing my quiz or whatever.
But why did we travel through time and space to talk about this stuff?
Couldn't you have told me all this in your living room?
Because this is where I keep my whiteboard, of course.
Plus, this is just the first stop on our journey!
Knowing about how evolution works will make it easier to understand the creatures we're about to meet: where they came from, why they look the way they do, and where they went.
Creatures? Are we going to a zoo or something?
Yes.
"Or something."

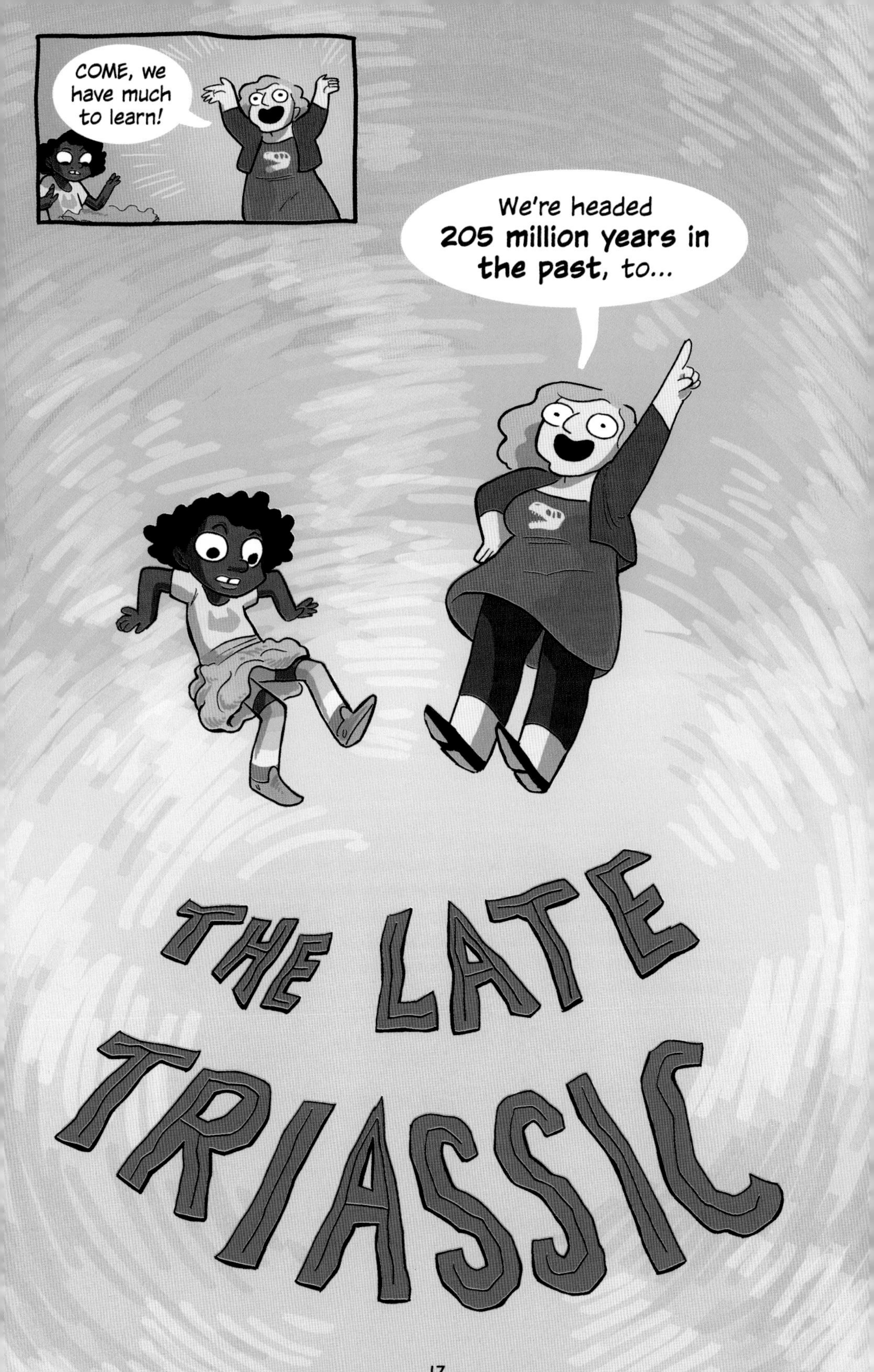
COME, we have much to learn!
We're headed **205 million years in the past**, to...
THE LATE TRIASSIC

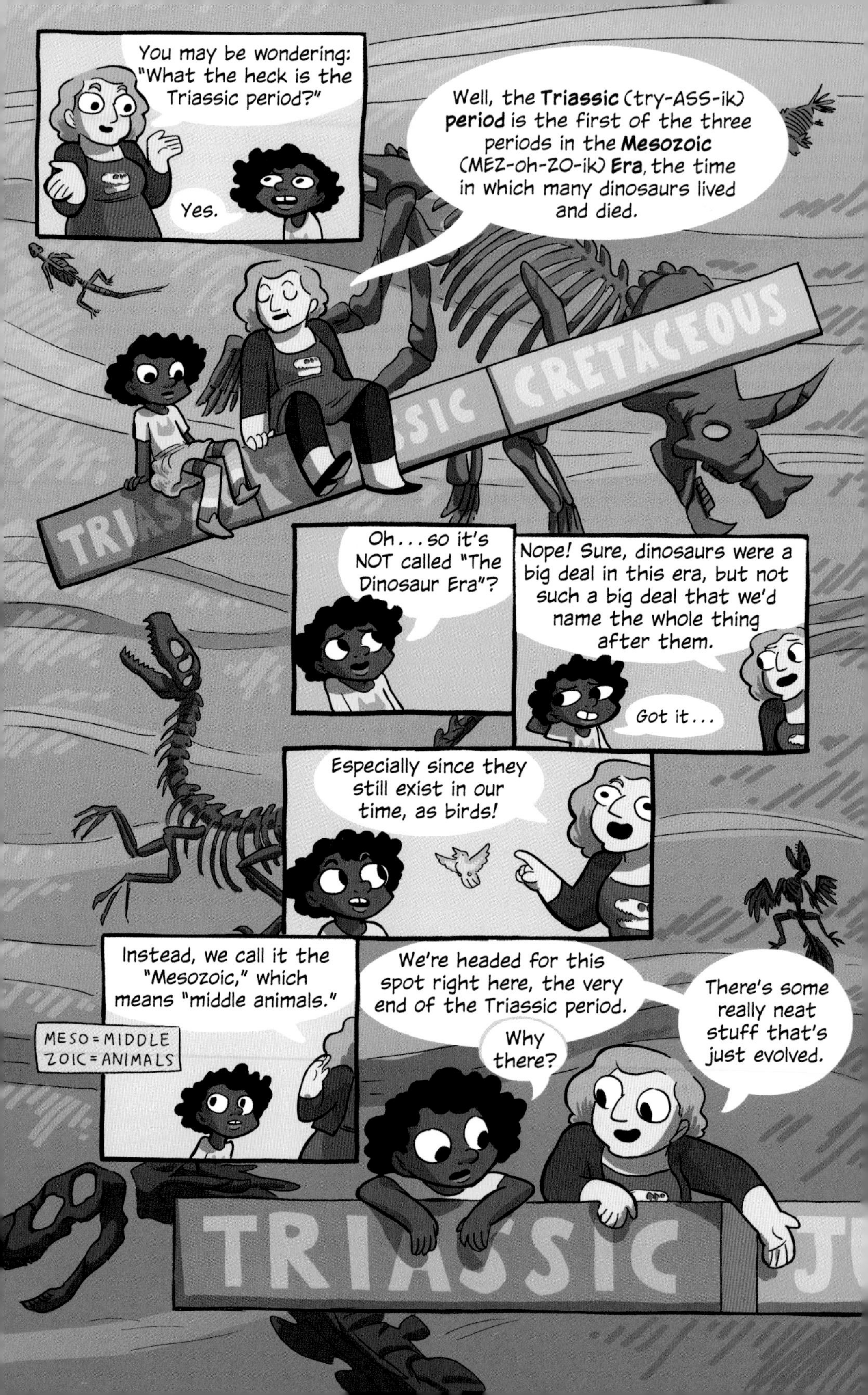
You may be wondering: "What the heck is the Triassic period?"
Yes.
Well, the **Triassic** (try-ASS-ik) **period** is the first of the three periods in the **Mesozoic** (MEZ-oh-ZO-ik) **Era**, the time in which many dinosaurs lived and died.
TRIASSIC
CRETACEOUS
Oh . . . so it's NOT called "The Dinosaur Era"?
Nope! Sure, dinosaurs were a big deal in this era, but not such a big deal that we'd name the whole thing after them.
Got it . . .
Especially since they still exist in our time, as birds!
Instead, we call it the "Mesozoic," which means "middle animals."
MESO = MIDDLE
ZOIC = ANIMALS
We're headed for this spot right here, the very end of the Triassic period.
Why there?
There's some really neat stuff that's just evolved.
TRIASSIC

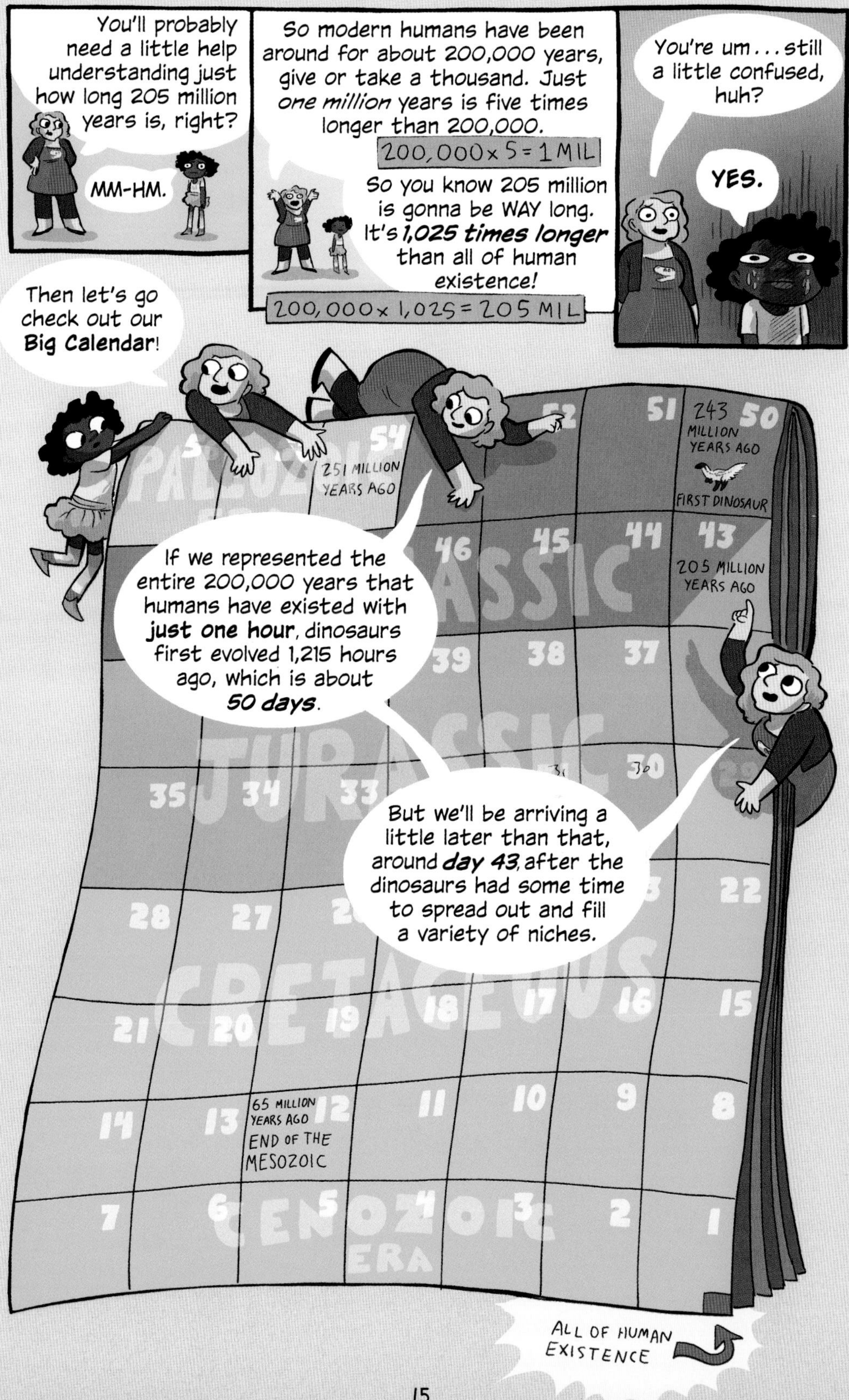

You'll probably need a little help understanding just how long 205 million years is, right?
MM-HM.
So modern humans have been around for about 200,000 years, give or take a thousand. Just *one million* years is five times longer than 200,000.
200,000 x 5 = 1 MIL
So you know 205 million is gonna be WAY long. It's ***1,025 times longer*** than all of human existence!
200,000 x 1,025 = 205 MIL
You're um . . . still a little confused, huh?
YES.
Then let's go check out our **Big Calendar**!
251 MILLION YEARS AGO
243 MILLION YEARS AGO
FIRST DINOSAUR
205 MILLION YEARS AGO
If we represented the entire 200,000 years that humans have existed with **just one hour**, dinosaurs first evolved 1,215 hours ago, which is about ***50 days***.
But we'll be arriving a little later than that, around ***day 43***, after the dinosaurs had some time to spread out and fill a variety of niches.
TRIASSIC
JURASSIC
CRETACEOUS
CENOZOIC ERA
65 MILLION YEARS AGO END OF THE MESOZOIC
ALL OF HUMAN EXISTENCE

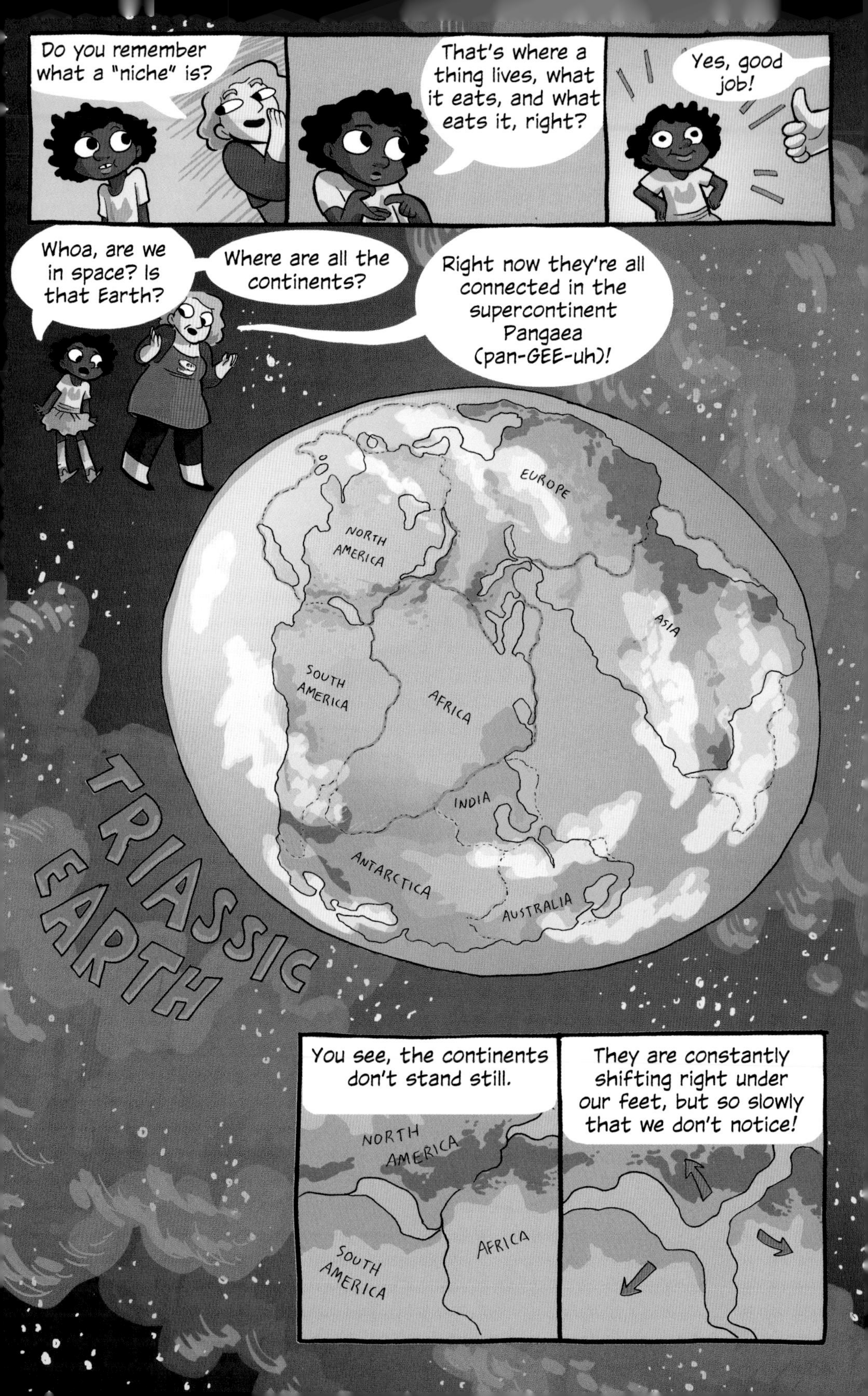

Do you remember what a "niche" is?
That's where a thing lives, what it eats, and what eats it, right?
Yes, good job!
Whoa, are we in space? Is that Earth?
Where are all the continents?
Right now they're all connected in the supercontinent Pangaea (pan-GEE-uh)!
EUROPE
NORTH AMERICA
ASIA
SOUTH AMERICA
AFRICA
INDIA
ANTARCTICA
AUSTRALIA
TRIASSIC EARTH
You see, the continents don't stand still.
NORTH AMERICA
AFRICA
SOUTH AMERICA
They are constantly shifting right under our feet, but so slowly that we don't notice!

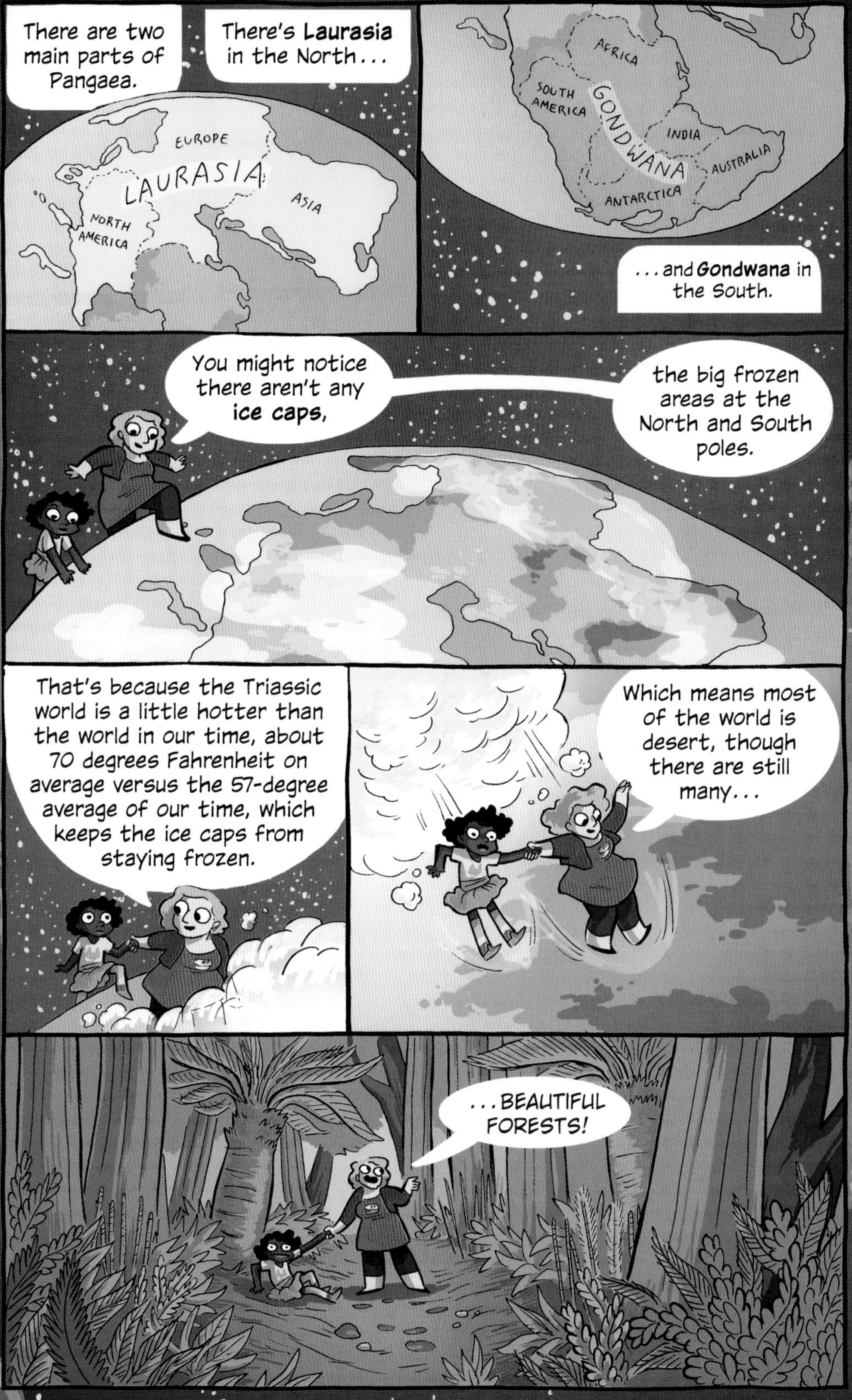
There are two main parts of Pangaea.
There's **Laurasia** in the North...
EUROPE
LAURASIA
ASIA
NORTH AMERICA
AFRICA
SOUTH AMERICA
GONDWANA
INDIA
AUSTRALIA
ANTARCTICA
...and **Gondwana** in the South.
You might notice there aren't any **ice caps**,
the big frozen areas at the North and South poles.
That's because the Triassic world is a little hotter than the world in our time, about 70 degrees Fahrenheit on average versus the 57-degree average of our time, which keeps the ice caps from staying frozen.
Which means most of the world is desert, though there are still many...
...BEAUTIFUL FORESTS!

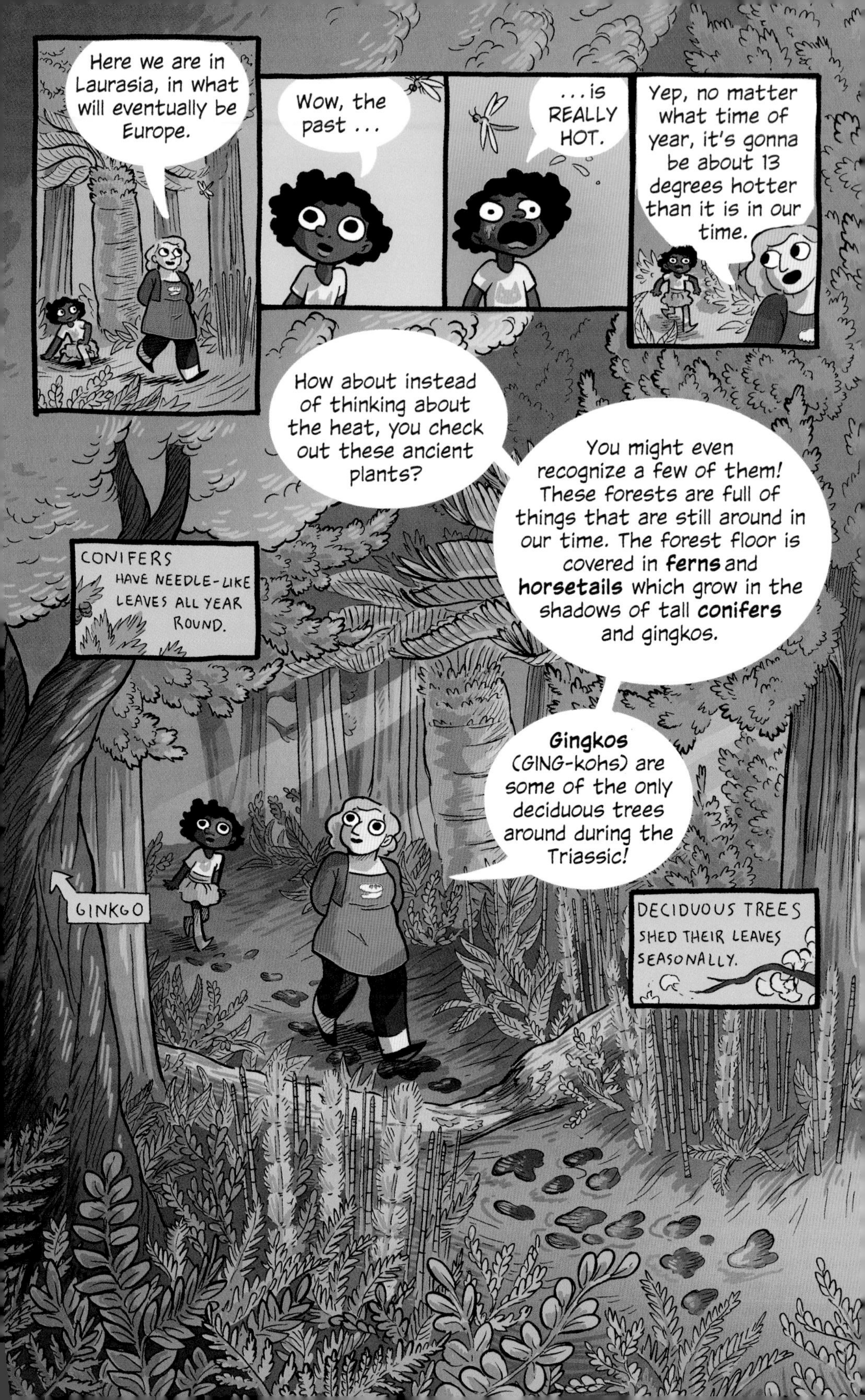
Here we are in Laurasia, in what will eventually be Europe.
Wow, the past . . .
. . . is REALLY HOT.
Yep, no matter what time of year, it's gonna be about 13 degrees hotter than it is in our time.
How about instead of thinking about the heat, you check out these ancient plants?
You might even recognize a few of them! These forests are full of things that are still around in our time. The forest floor is covered in **ferns** and **horsetails** which grow in the shadows of tall **conifers** and gingkos.
CONIFERS HAVE NEEDLE-LIKE LEAVES ALL YEAR ROUND.
Gingkos (GING-kohs) are some of the only deciduous trees around during the Triassic!
GINKGO
DECIDUOUS TREES SHED THEIR LEAVES SEASONALLY.

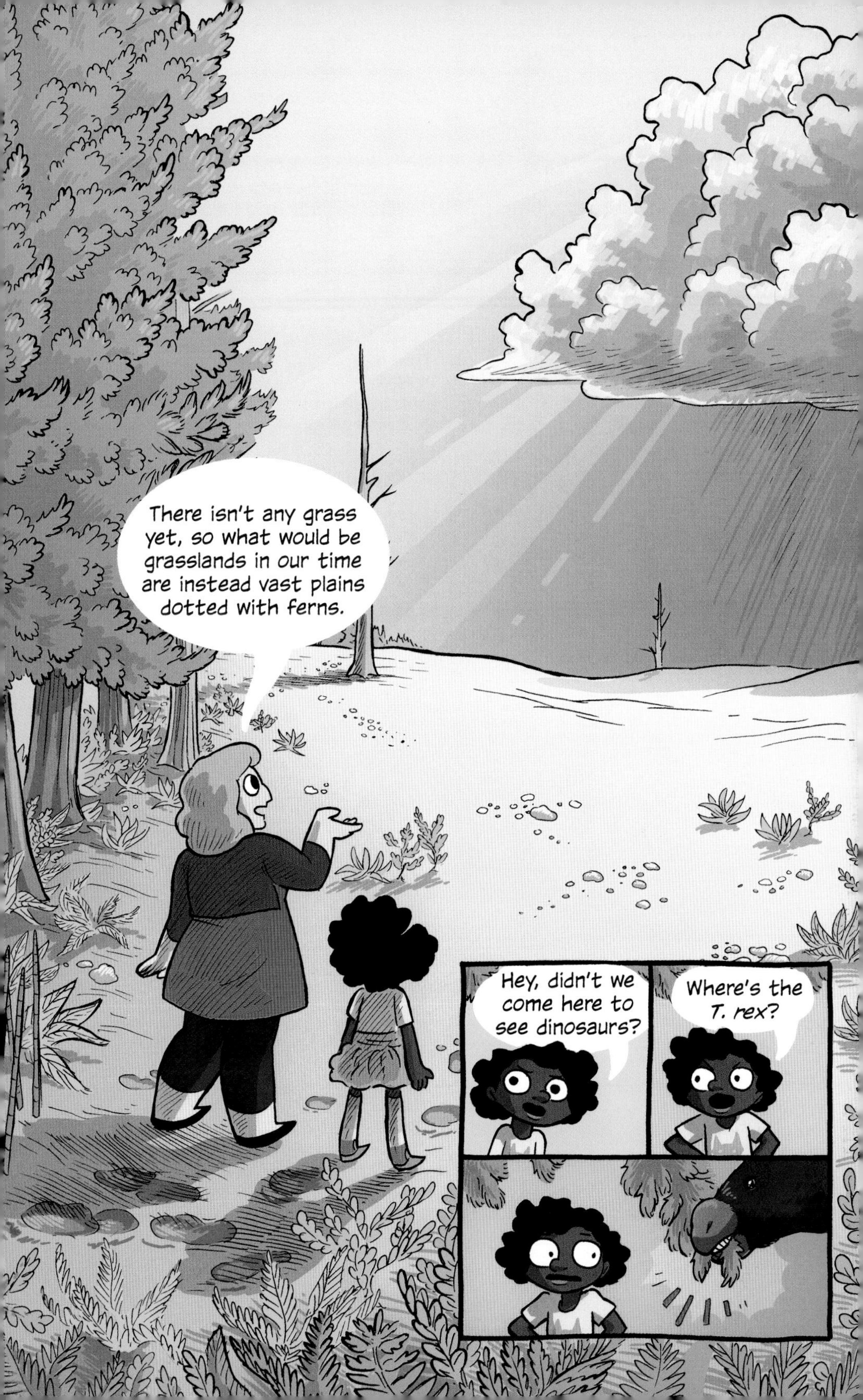
There isn't any grass yet, so what would be grasslands in our time are instead vast plains dotted with ferns.
Hey, didn't we come here to see dinosaurs?
Where's the *T. rex*?

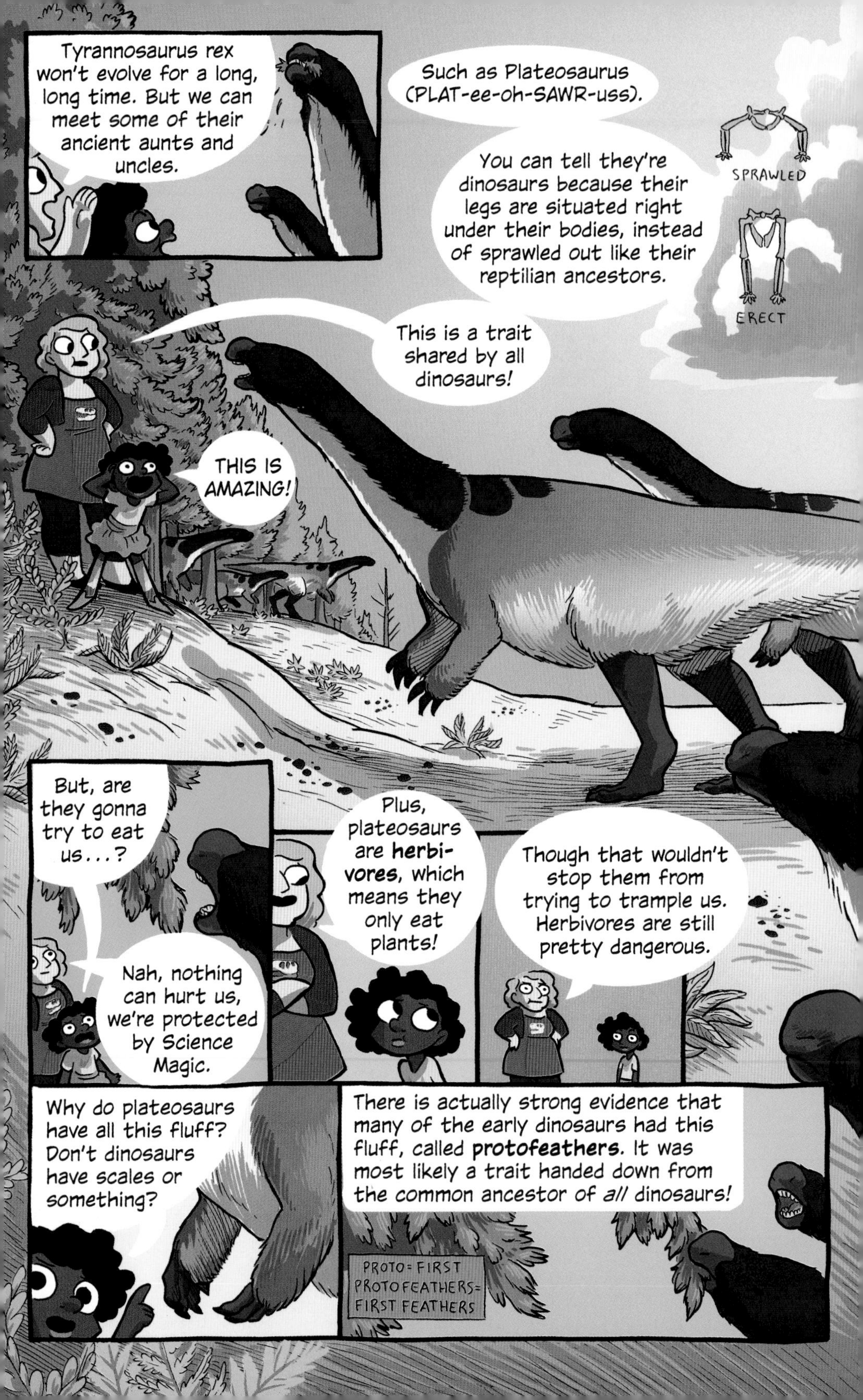
Tyrannosaurus rex won't evolve for a long, long time. But we can meet some of their ancient aunts and uncles.
Such as Plateosaurus (PLAT-ee-oh-SAWR-uss).
You can tell they're dinosaurs because their legs are situated right under their bodies, instead of sprawled out like their reptilian ancestors.
SPRAWLED
ERECT
This is a trait shared by all dinosaurs!
THIS IS AMAZING!
But, are they gonna try to eat us . . . ?
Nah, nothing can hurt us, we're protected by Science Magic.
Plus, plateosaurs are **herbivores**, which means they only eat plants!
Though that wouldn't stop them from trying to trample us. Herbivores are still pretty dangerous.
Why do plateosaurs have all this fluff? Don't dinosaurs have scales or something?
There is actually strong evidence that many of the early dinosaurs had this fluff, called **protofeathers**. It was most likely a trait handed down from the common ancestor of *all* dinosaurs!
PROTO = FIRST
PROTOFEATHERS = FIRST FEATHERS

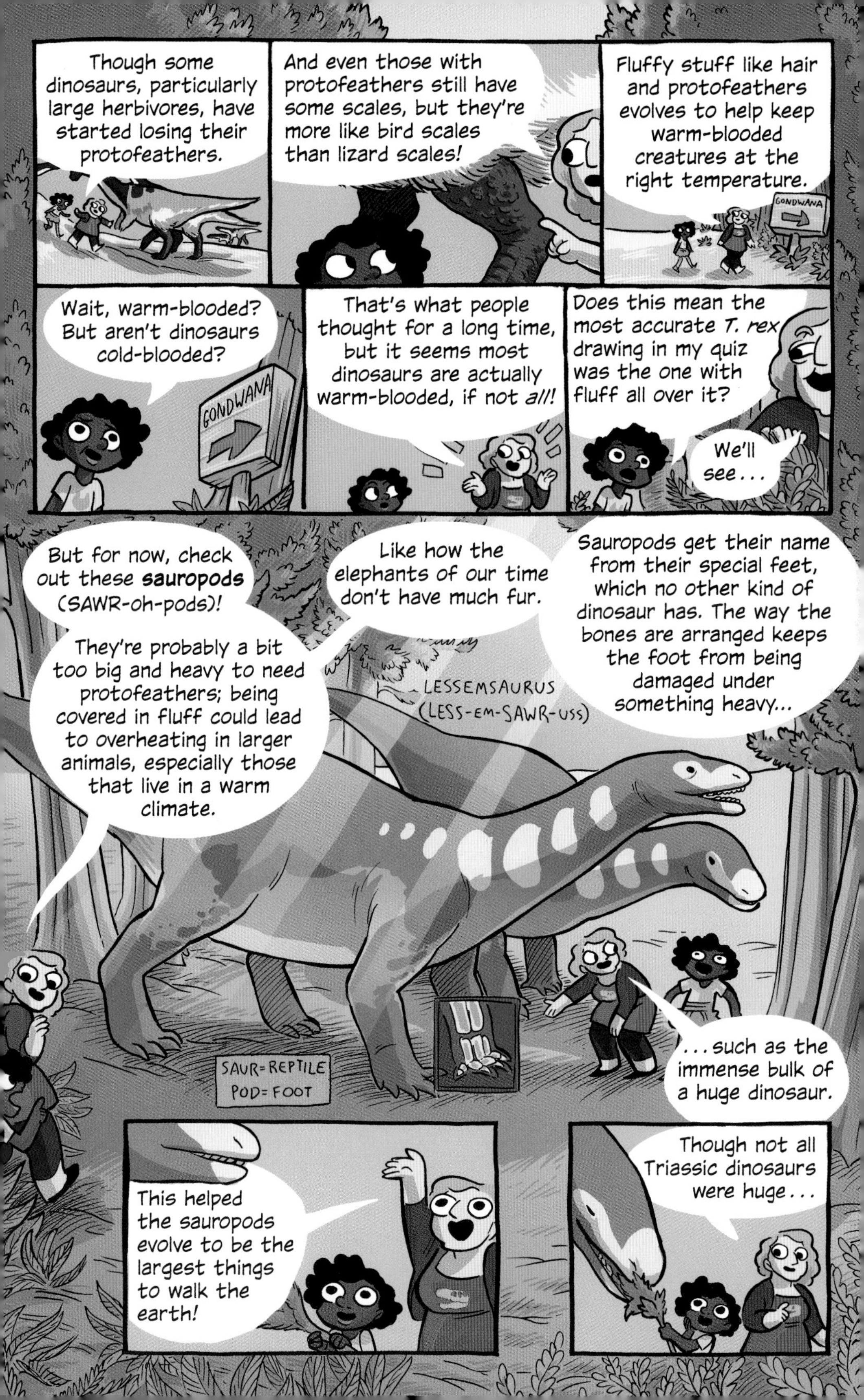
Though some dinosaurs, particularly large herbivores, have started losing their protofeathers.
And even those with protofeathers still have some scales, but they're more like bird scales than lizard scales!
Fluffy stuff like hair and protofeathers evolves to help keep warm-blooded creatures at the right temperature.
GONDWANA
Wait, warm-blooded? But aren't dinosaurs cold-blooded?
GONDWANA
That's what people thought for a long time, but it seems most dinosaurs are actually warm-blooded, if not *all*!
Does this mean the most accurate *T. rex* drawing in my quiz was the one with fluff all over it?
We'll see...
But for now, check out these **sauropods** (SAWR-oh-pods)!
They're probably a bit too big and heavy to need protofeathers; being covered in fluff could lead to overheating in larger animals, especially those that live in a warm climate.
Like how the elephants of our time don't have much fur.
Sauropods get their name from their special feet, which no other kind of dinosaur has. The way the bones are arranged keeps the foot from being damaged under something heavy...
LESSEMSAURUS (LESS-EM-SAWR-USS)
SAUR=REPTILE
POD=FOOT
...such as the immense bulk of a huge dinosaur.
This helped the sauropods evolve to be the largest things to walk the earth!
Though not all Triassic dinosaurs were huge...

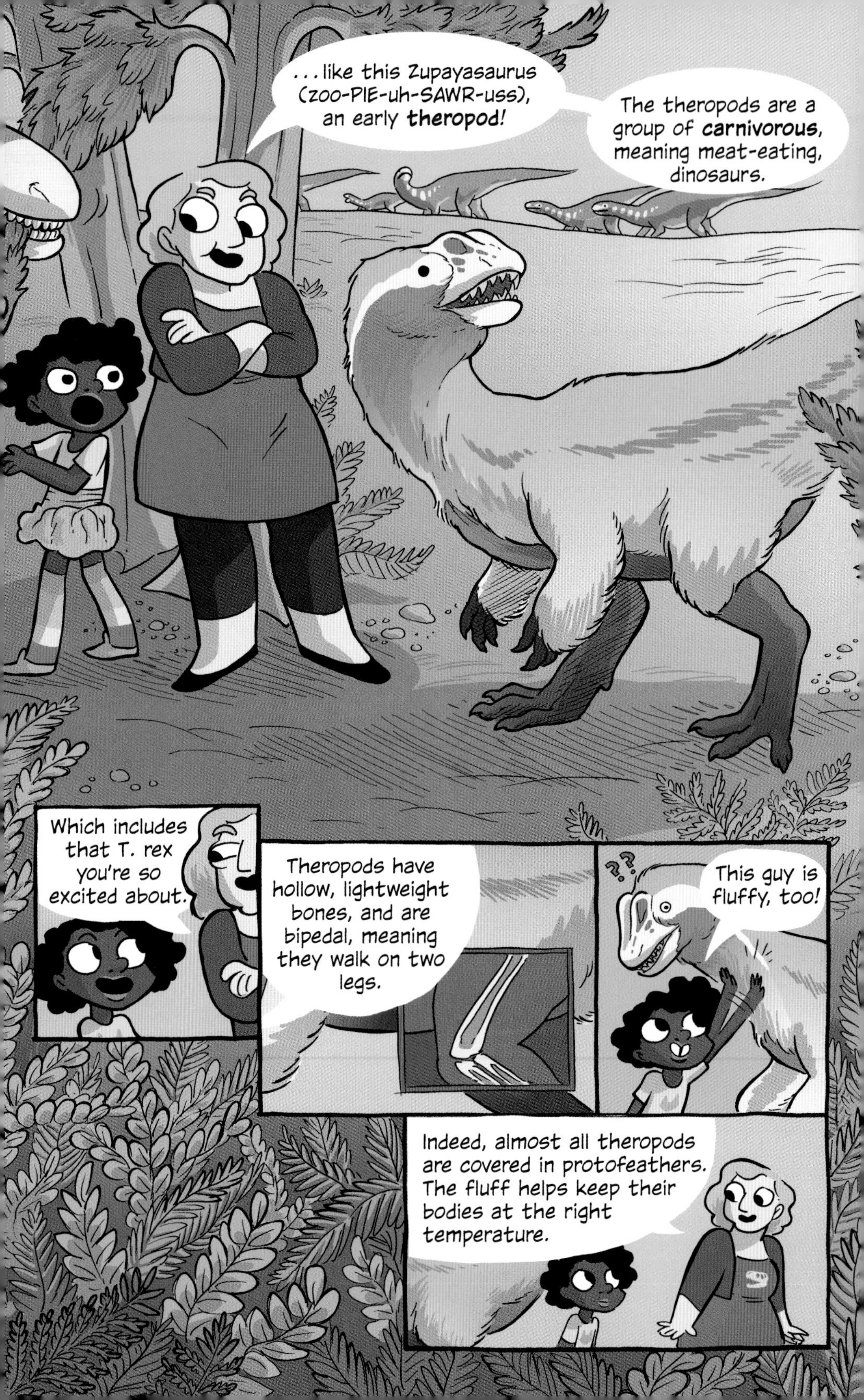
. . . like this Zupayasaurus (zoo-PIE-uh-SAWR-uss), an early **theropod**!
The theropods are a group of **carnivorous**, meaning meat-eating, dinosaurs.
Which includes that T. rex you're so excited about.
Theropods have hollow, lightweight bones, and are bipedal, meaning they walk on two legs.
??
This guy is fluffy, too!
Indeed, almost all theropods are covered in protofeathers. The fluff helps keep their bodies at the right temperature.

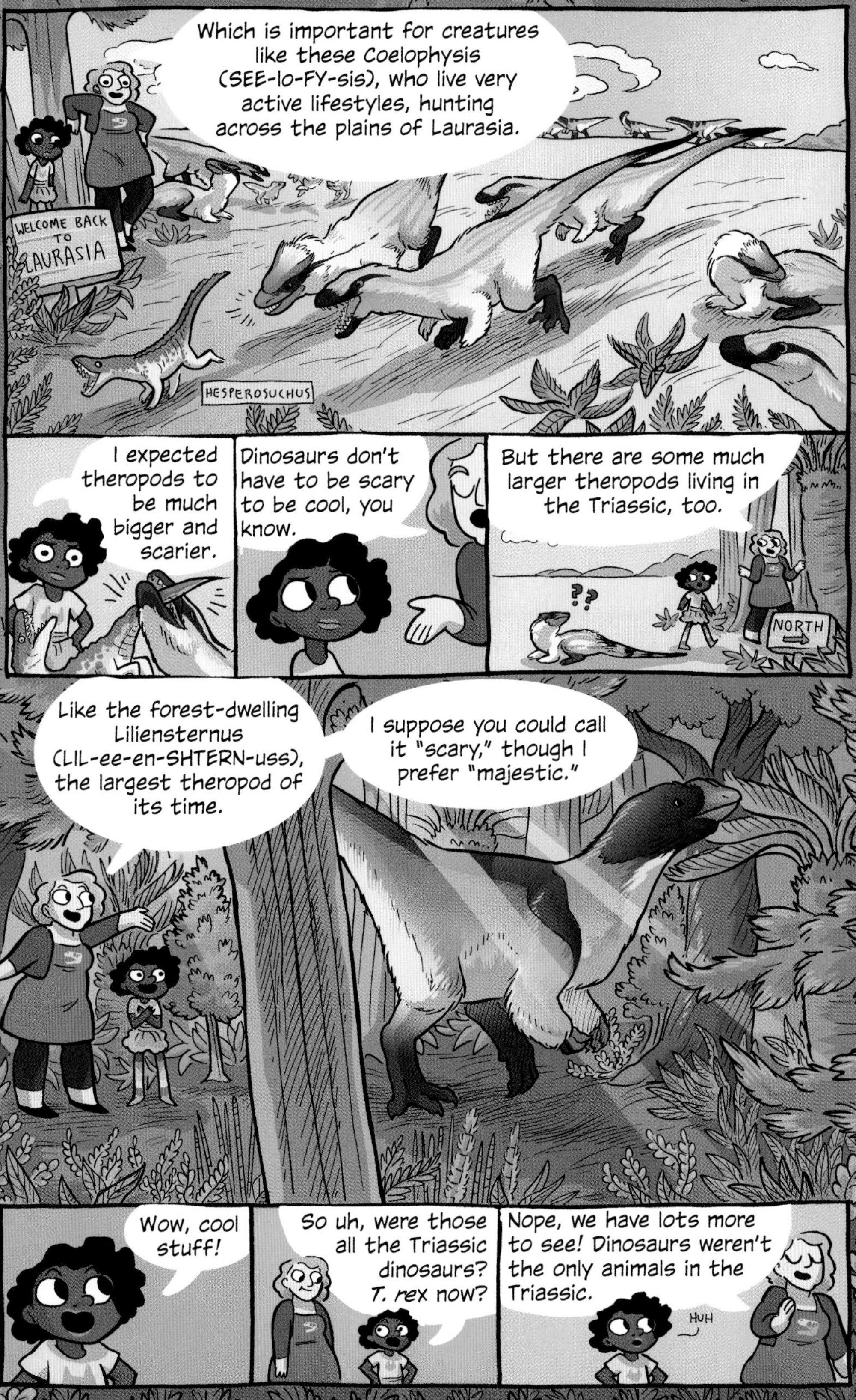
Which is important for creatures like these Coelophysis (SEE-lo-FY-sis), who live very active lifestyles, hunting across the plains of Laurasia.
WELCOME BACK TO LAURASIA
HESPEROSUCHUS
I expected theropods to be much bigger and scarier.
Dinosaurs don't have to be scary to be cool, you know.
But there are some much larger theropods living in the Triassic, too.
??
NORTH
Like the forest-dwelling Liliensternus (LIL-ee-en-SHTERN-uss), the largest theropod of its time.
I suppose you could call it "scary," though I prefer "majestic."
Wow, cool stuff!
So uh, were those all the Triassic dinosaurs? *T. rex* now?
Nope, we have lots more to see! Dinosaurs weren't the only animals in the Triassic.
HUH

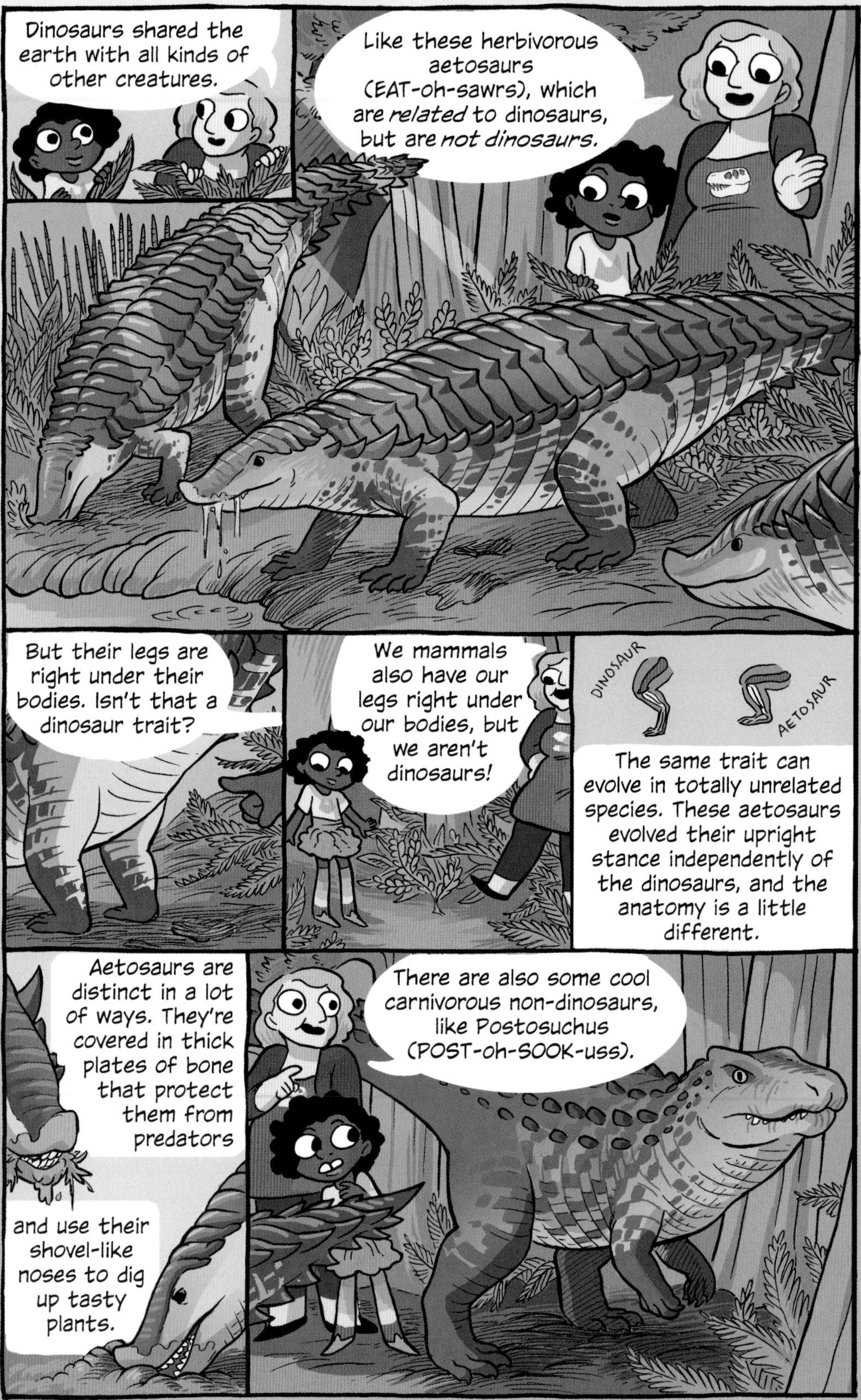
Dinosaurs shared the earth with all kinds of other creatures.
Like these herbivorous aetosaurs (EAT-oh-sawrs), which are *related* to dinosaurs, but are *not dinosaurs.*
But their legs are right under their bodies. Isn't that a dinosaur trait?
We mammals also have our legs right under our bodies, but we aren't dinosaurs!
DINOSAUR
AETOSAUR
The same trait can evolve in totally unrelated species. These aetosaurs evolved their upright stance independently of the dinosaurs, and the anatomy is a little different.
Aetosaurs are distinct in a lot of ways. They're covered in thick plates of bone that protect them from predators
and use their shovel-like noses to dig up tasty plants.
There are also some cool carnivorous non-dinosaurs, like Postosuchus (POST-oh-SOOK-uss).

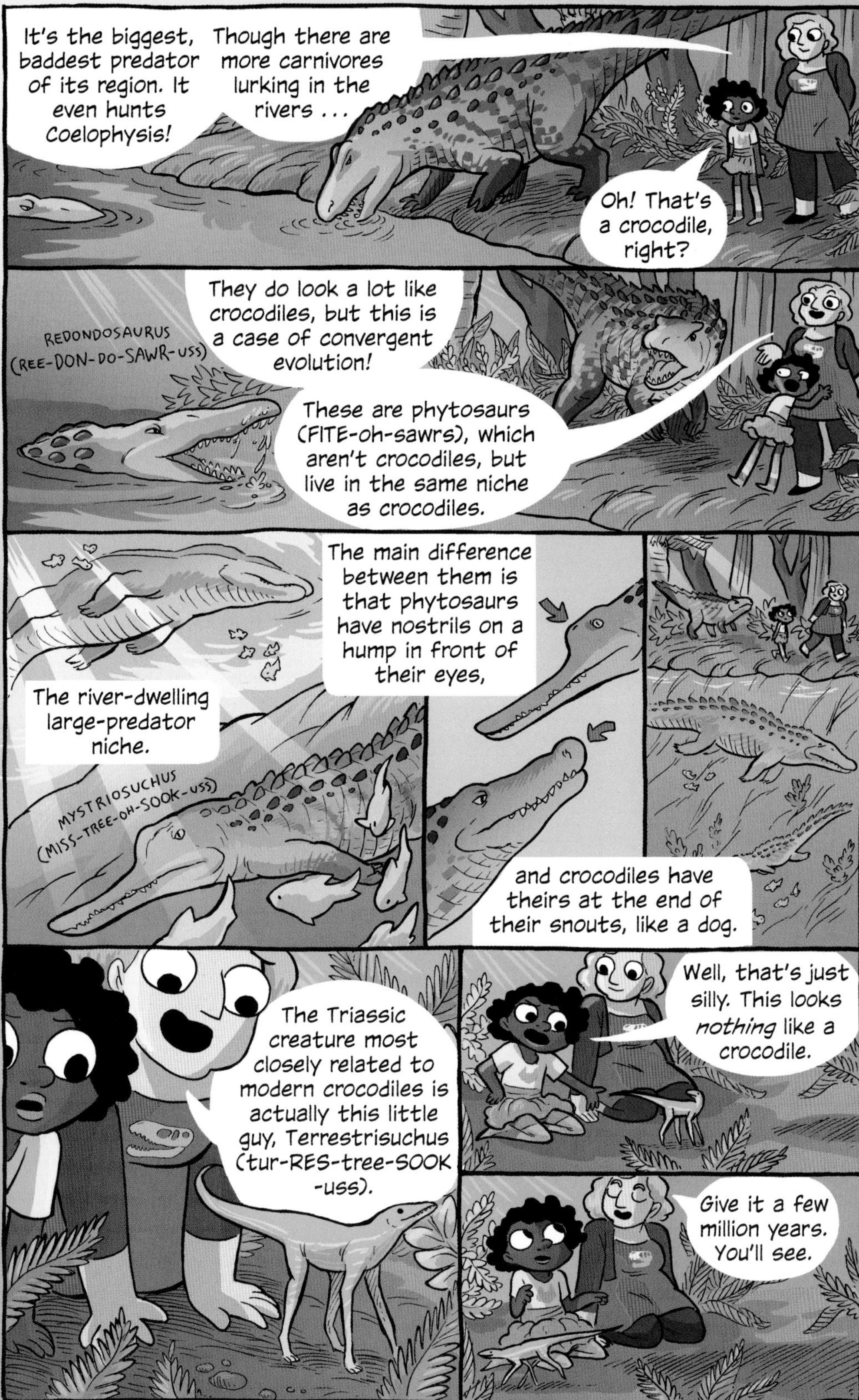

It's the biggest, baddest predator of its region. It even hunts Coelophysis!
Though there are more carnivores lurking in the rivers . . .
Oh! That's a crocodile, right?
REDONDOSAURUS (REE-DON-DO-SAWR-USS)
They do look a lot like crocodiles, but this is a case of convergent evolution!
These are phytosaurs (FITE-oh-sawrs), which aren't crocodiles, but live in the same niche as crocodiles.
The river-dwelling large-predator niche.
MYSTRIOSUCHUS (MISS-TREE-OH-SOOK-USS)
The main difference between them is that phytosaurs have nostrils on a hump in front of their eyes,
and crocodiles have theirs at the end of their snouts, like a dog.
The Triassic creature most closely related to modern crocodiles is actually this little guy, Terrestrisuchus (tur-RES-tree-SOOK -uss).
Well, that's just silly. This looks *nothing* like a crocodile.
Give it a few million years. You'll see.

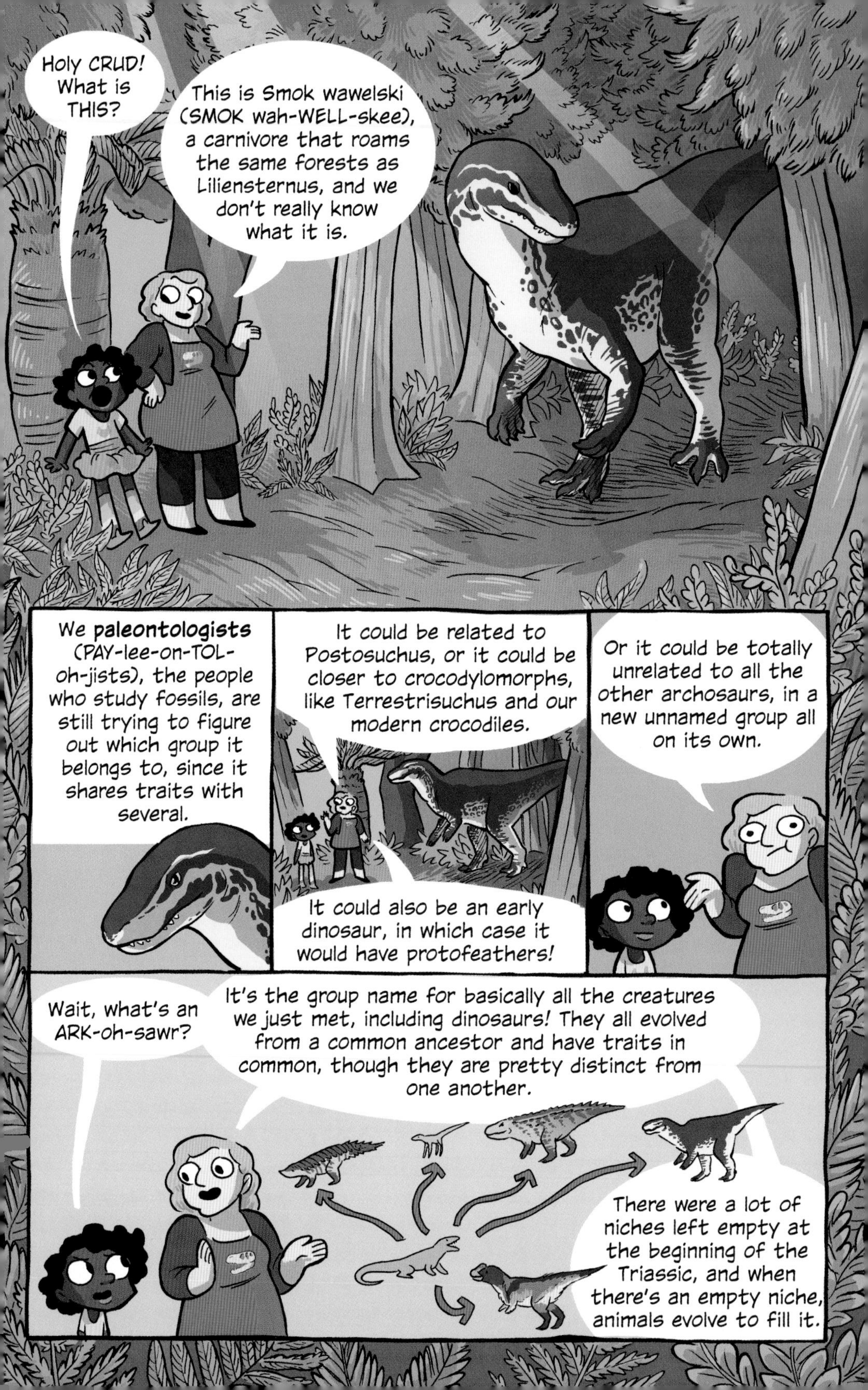
Holy CRUD! What is THIS?
This is Smok wawelski (SMOK wah-WELL-skee), a carnivore that roams the same forests as Liliensternus, and we don't really know what it is.
We **paleontologists** (PAY-lee-on-TOL-oh-jists), the people who study fossils, are still trying to figure out which group it belongs to, since it shares traits with several.
It could be related to Postosuchus, or it could be closer to crocodylomorphs, like Terrestrisuchus and our modern crocodiles.
It could also be an early dinosaur, in which case it would have protofeathers!
Or it could be totally unrelated to all the other archosaurs, in a new unnamed group all on its own.
Wait, what's an ARK-oh-sawr?
It's the group name for basically all the creatures we just met, including dinosaurs! They all evolved from a common ancestor and have traits in common, though they are pretty distinct from one another.
There were a lot of niches left empty at the beginning of the Triassic, and when there's an empty niche, animals evolve to fill it.

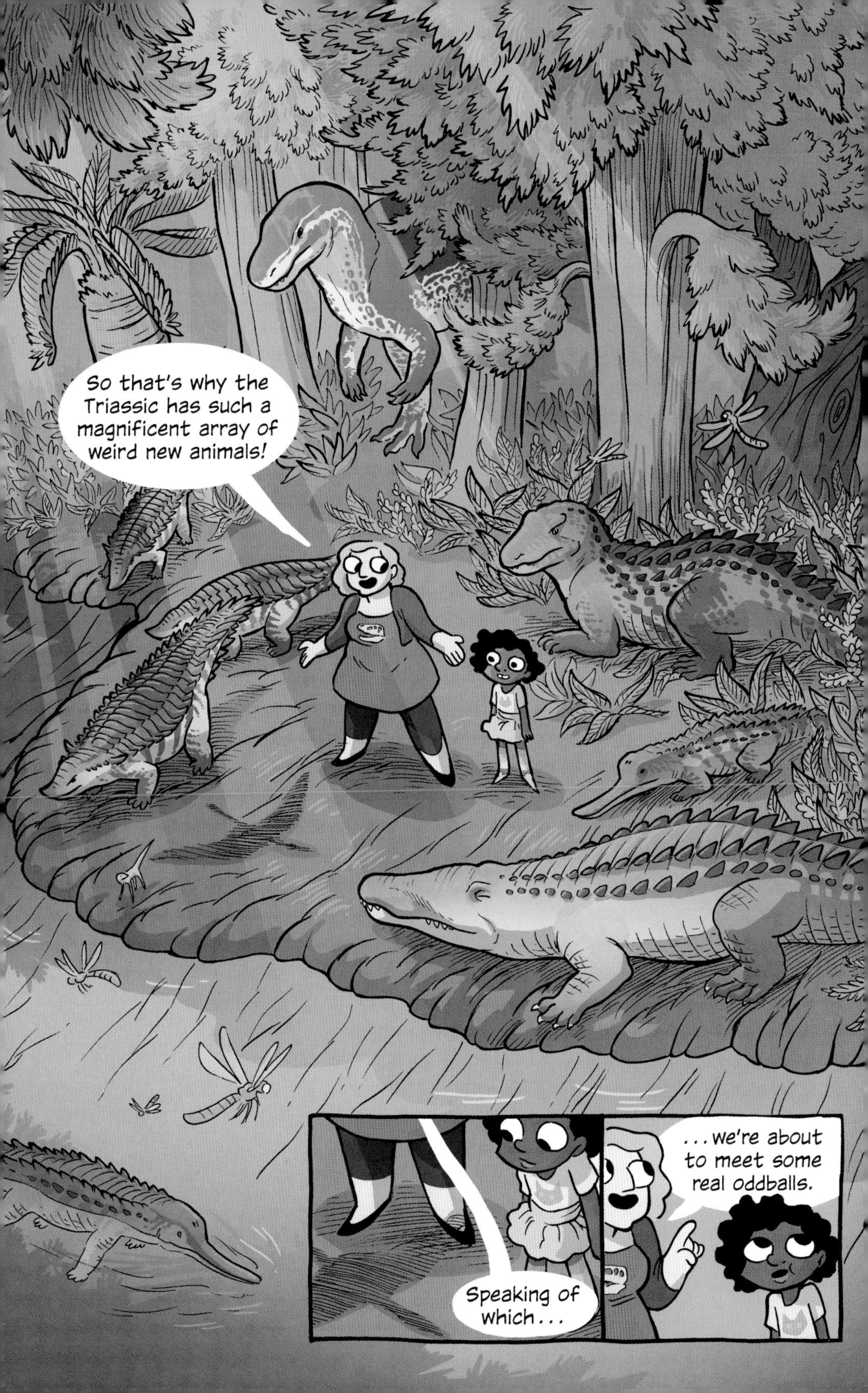
So that's why the Triassic has such a magnificent array of weird new animals!
Speaking of which...
...we're about to meet some real oddballs.

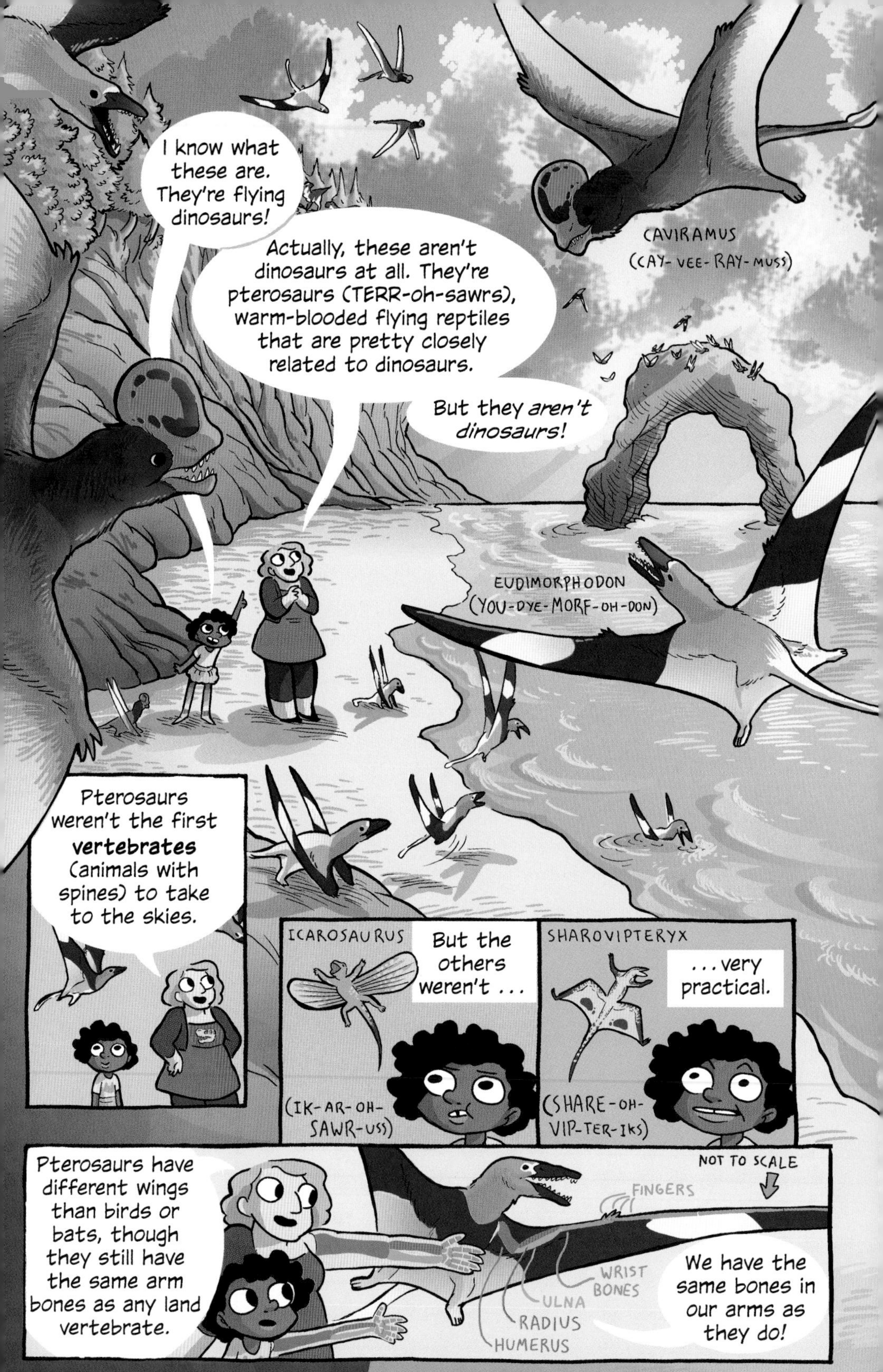
I know what these are. They're flying dinosaurs!
Actually, these aren't dinosaurs at all. They're pterosaurs (TERR-oh-sawrs), warm-blooded flying reptiles that are pretty closely related to dinosaurs.
But they *aren't dinosaurs!*
CAVIRAMUS (CAY-VEE-RAY-MUSS)
EUDIMORPHODON (YOU-DYE-MORF-OH-DON)
Pterosaurs weren't the first **vertebrates** (animals with spines) to take to the skies.
ICAROSAURUS
But the others weren't . . .
(IK-AR-OH-SAWR-USS)
SHAROVIPTERYX
. . . very practical.
(SHARE-OH-VIP-TER-IKS)
Pterosaurs have different wings than birds or bats, though they still have the same arm bones as any land vertebrate.
NOT TO SCALE
FINGERS
WRIST BONES
ULNA
RADIUS
HUMERUS
We have the same bones in our arms as they do!

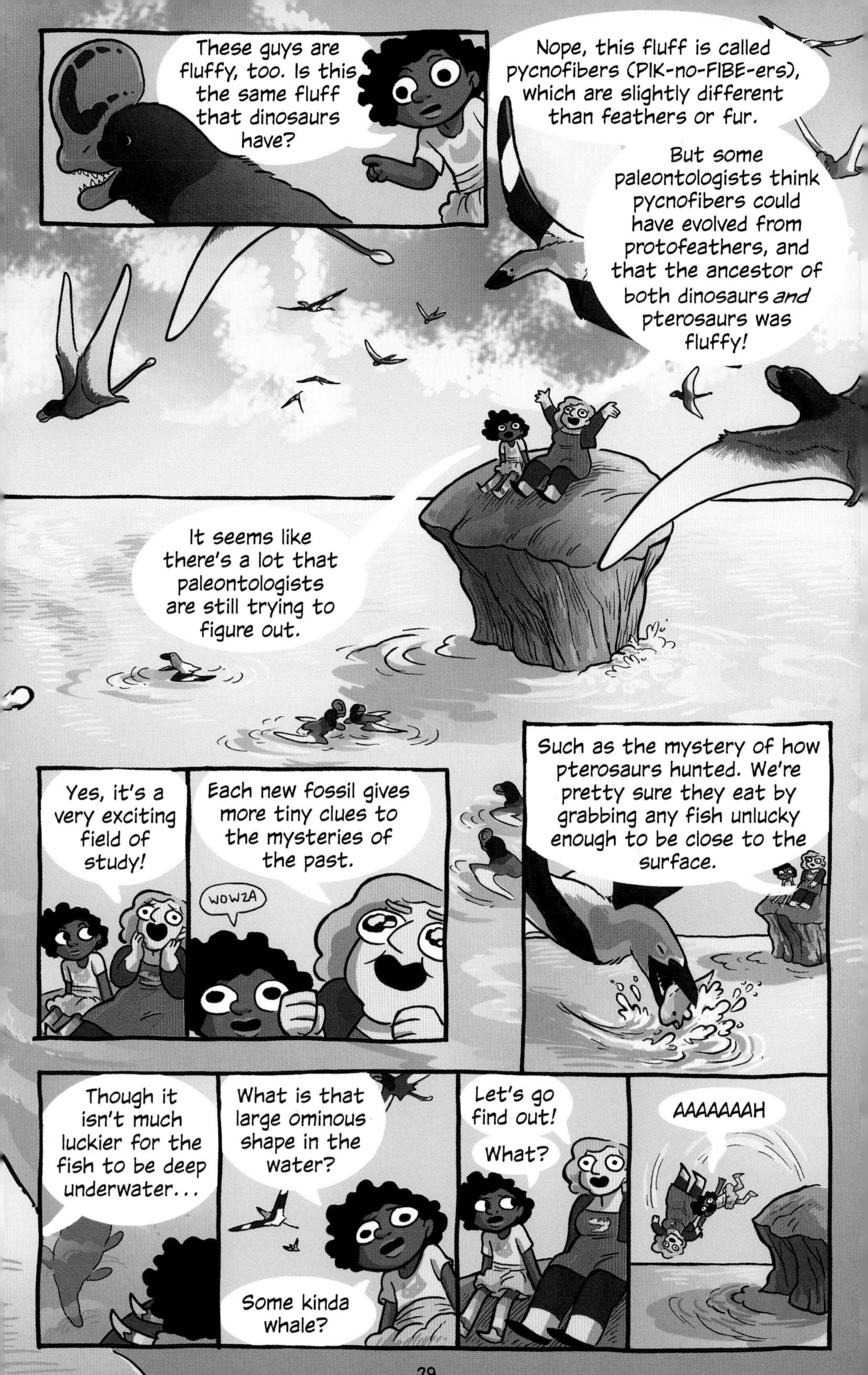
These guys are fluffy, too. Is this the same fluff that dinosaurs have?
Nope, this fluff is called pycnofibers (PIK-no-FIBE-ers), which are slightly different than feathers or fur.
But some paleontologists think pycnofibers could have evolved from protofeathers, and that the ancestor of both dinosaurs *and* pterosaurs was fluffy!
It seems like there's a lot that paleontologists are still trying to figure out.
Yes, it's a very exciting field of study!
Each new fossil gives more tiny clues to the mysteries of the past.
WOWZA
Such as the mystery of how pterosaurs hunted. We're pretty sure they eat by grabbing any fish unlucky enough to be close to the surface.
Though it isn't much luckier for the fish to be deep underwater...
What is that large ominous shape in the water?
Some kinda whale?
Let's go find out!
What?
AAAAAAAH

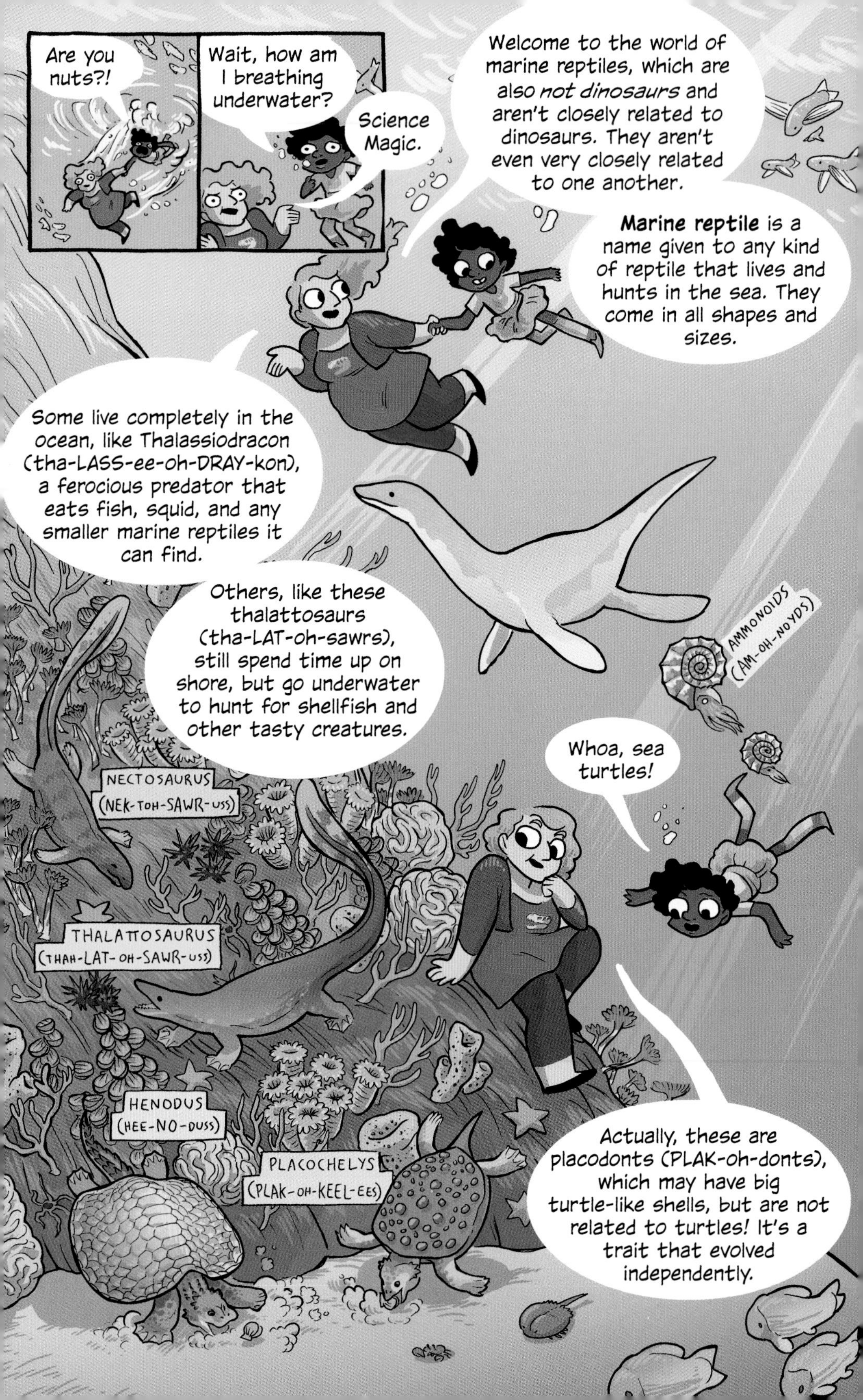
Are you nuts?!
Wait, how am I breathing underwater?
Science Magic.
Welcome to the world of marine reptiles, which are also *not dinosaurs* and aren't closely related to dinosaurs. They aren't even very closely related to one another.
Marine reptile is a name given to any kind of reptile that lives and hunts in the sea. They come in all shapes and sizes.
Some live completely in the ocean, like Thalassiodracon (tha-LASS-ee-oh-DRAY-kon), a ferocious predator that eats fish, squid, and any smaller marine reptiles it can find.
Others, like these thalattosaurs (tha-LAT-oh-sawrs), still spend time up on shore, but go underwater to hunt for shellfish and other tasty creatures.
AMMONOIDS (AM-OH-NOYDS)
NECTOSAURUS (NEK-TOH-SAWR-USS)
THALATTOSAURUS (THAH-LAT-OH-SAWR-USS)
Whoa, sea turtles!
HENODUS (HEE-NO-DUSS)
PLACOCHELYS (PLAK-OH-KEEL-EES)
Actually, these are placodonts (PLAK-oh-donts), which may have big turtle-like shells, but are not related to turtles! It's a trait that evolved independently.

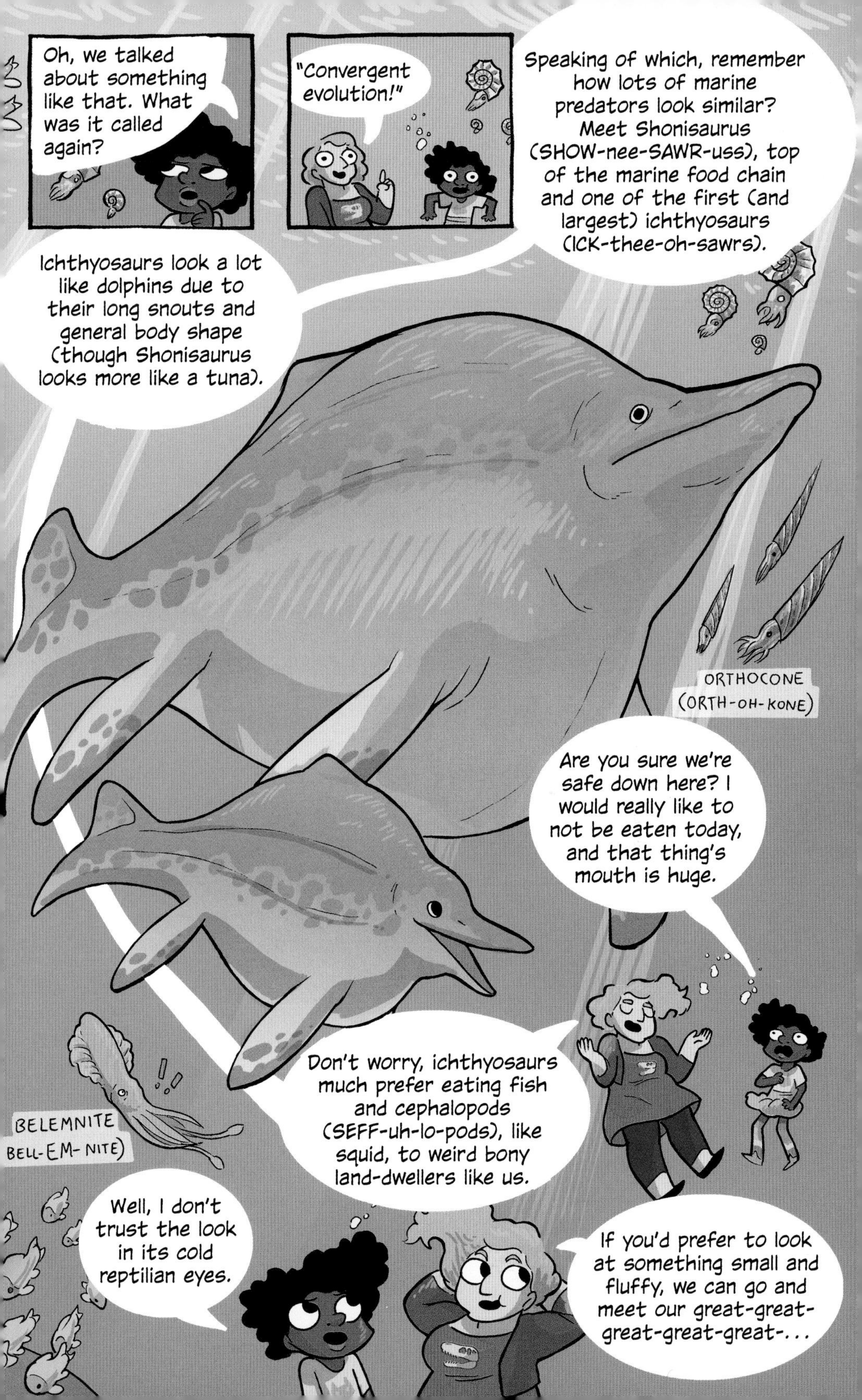
Oh, we talked about something like that. What was it called again?
"Convergent evolution!"
Speaking of which, remember how lots of marine predators look similar? Meet Shonisaurus (SHOW-nee-SAWR-uss), top of the marine food chain and one of the first (and largest) ichthyosaurs (ICK-thee-oh-sawrs).
Ichthyosaurs look a lot like dolphins due to their long snouts and general body shape (though Shonisaurus looks more like a tuna).
ORTHOCONE (ORTH-OH-KONE)
Are you sure we're safe down here? I would really like to not be eaten today, and that thing's mouth is huge.
BELEMNITE BELL-EM-NITE)
!!
Don't worry, ichthyosaurs much prefer eating fish and cephalopods (SEFF-uh-lo-pods), like squid, to weird bony land-dwellers like us.
Well, I don't trust the look in its cold reptilian eyes.
If you'd prefer to look at something small and fluffy, we can go and meet our great-great-great-great-great-. . .

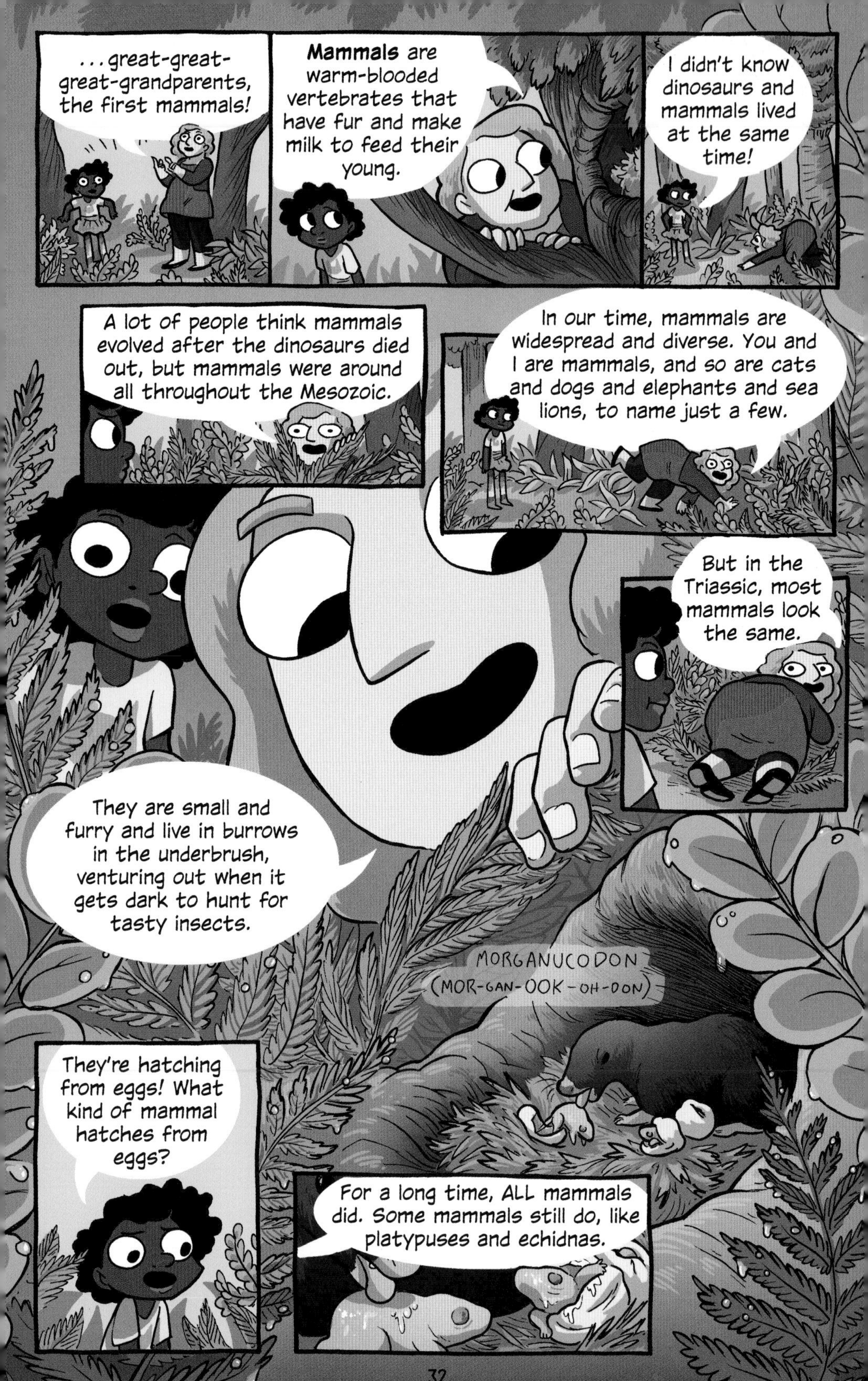

. . . great-great-great-grandparents, the first mammals!
Mammals are warm-blooded vertebrates that have fur and make milk to feed their young.
I didn't know dinosaurs and mammals lived at the same time!
A lot of people think mammals evolved after the dinosaurs died out, but mammals were around all throughout the Mesozoic.
In our time, mammals are widespread and diverse. You and I are mammals, and so are cats and dogs and elephants and sea lions, to name just a few.
But in the Triassic, most mammals look the same.
They are small and furry and live in burrows in the underbrush, venturing out when it gets dark to hunt for tasty insects.
MORGANUCODON (MOR-GAN-OOK-OH-DON)
They're hatching from eggs! What kind of mammal hatches from eggs?
For a long time, ALL mammals did. Some mammals still do, like platypuses and echidnas.

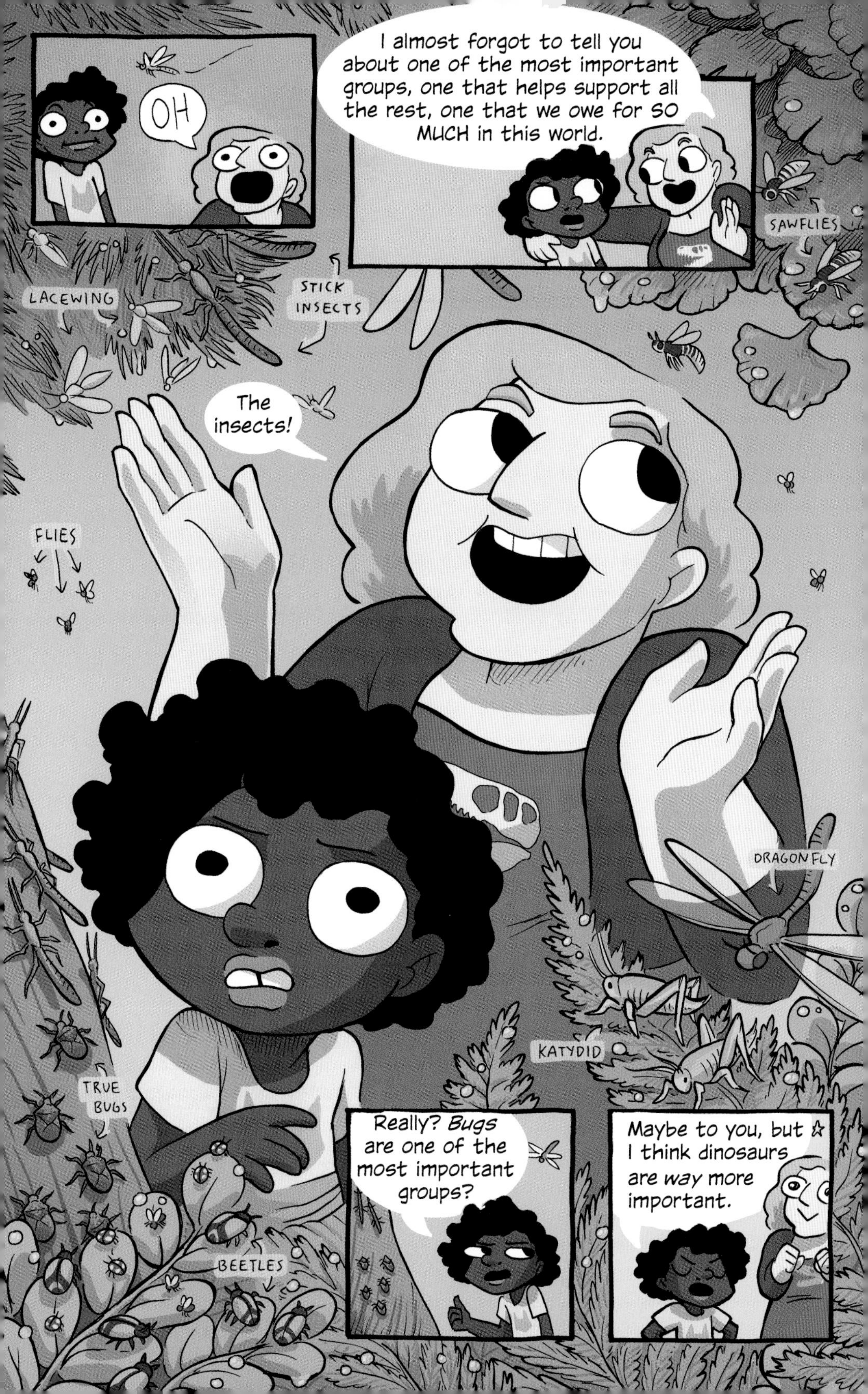
OH
I almost forgot to tell you about one of the most important groups, one that helps support all the rest, one that we owe for SO MUCH in this world.
SAWFLIES
LACEWING
STICK INSECTS
The insects!
FLIES
DRAGONFLY
KATYDID
TRUE BUGS
BEETLES
Really? *Bugs* are one of the most important groups?
Maybe to you, but I think dinosaurs are *way* more important.

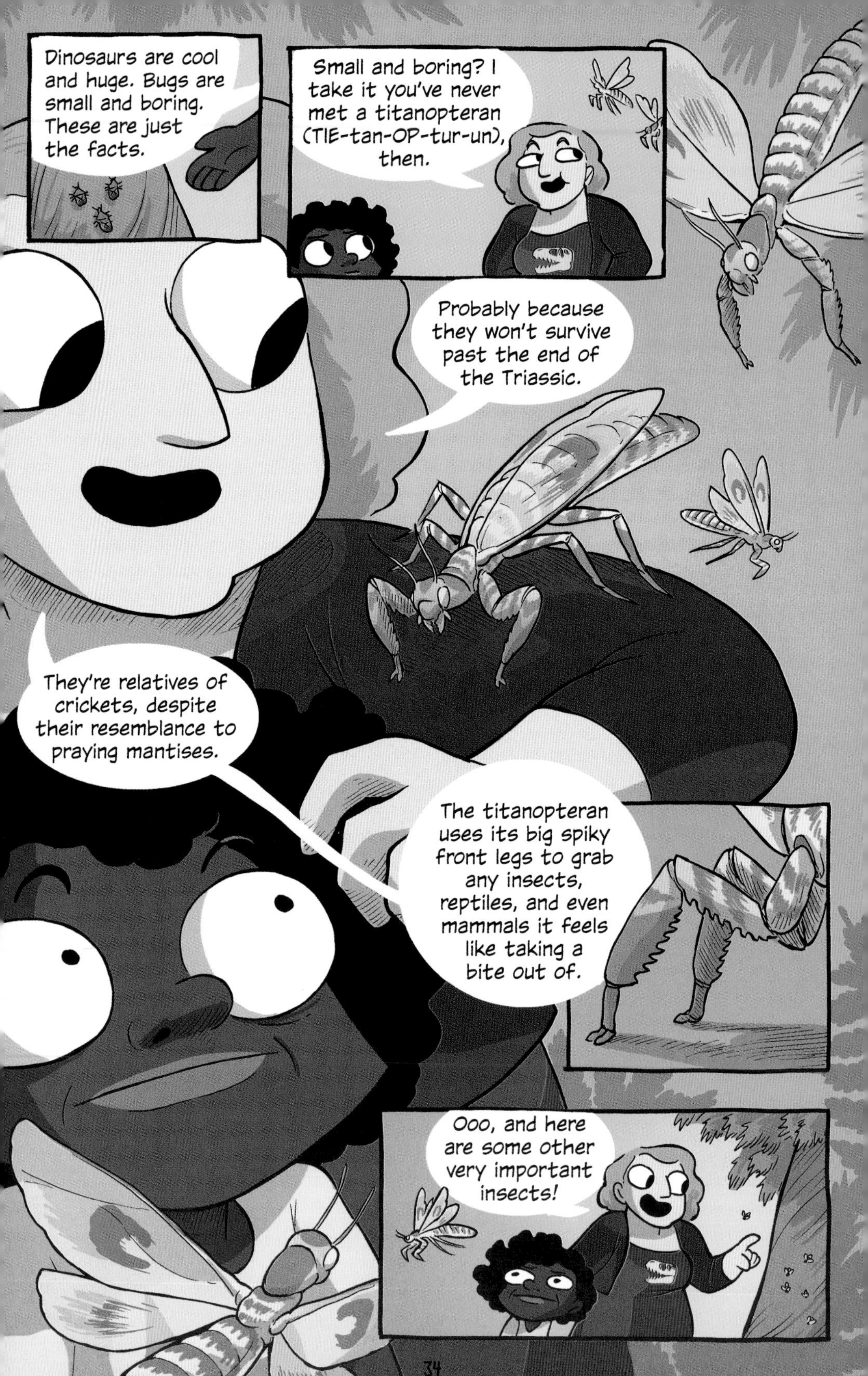
Dinosaurs are cool and huge. Bugs are small and boring. These are just the facts.
Small and boring? I take it you've never met a titanopteran (TIE-tan-OP-tur-un), then.
Probably because they won't survive past the end of the Triassic.
They're relatives of crickets, despite their resemblance to praying mantises.
The titanopteran uses its big spiky front legs to grab any insects, reptiles, and even mammals it feels like taking a bite out of.
Ooo, and here are some other very important insects!

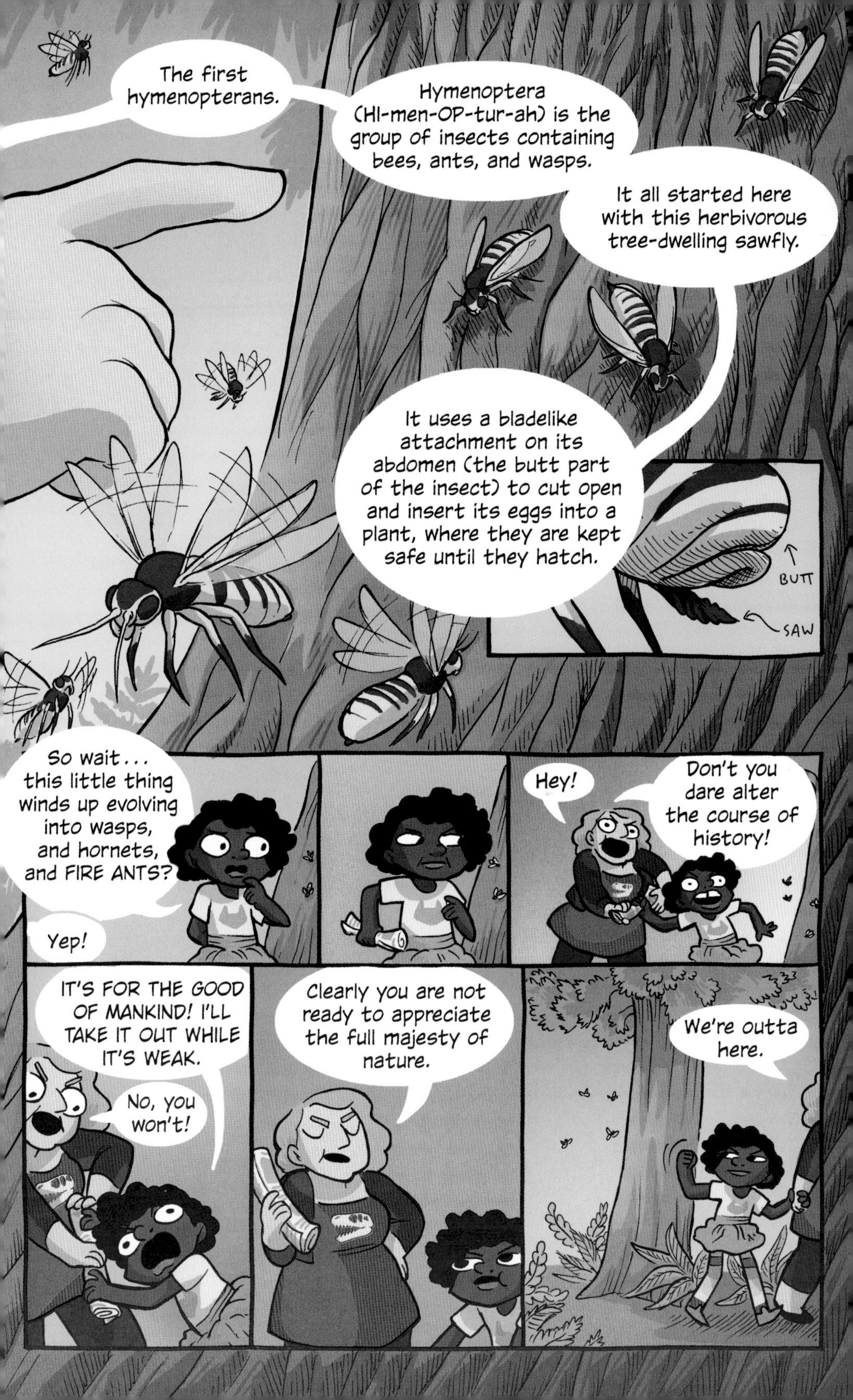
The first hymenopterans.
Hymenoptera (HI-men-OP-tur-ah) is the group of insects containing bees, ants, and wasps.
It all started here with this herbivorous tree-dwelling sawfly.
It uses a bladelike attachment on its abdomen (the butt part of the insect) to cut open and insert its eggs into a plant, where they are kept safe until they hatch.
BUTT
SAW
So wait . . . this little thing winds up evolving into wasps, and hornets, and FIRE ANTS?
Yep!
Hey!
Don't you dare alter the course of history!
IT'S FOR THE GOOD OF MANKIND! I'LL TAKE IT OUT WHILE IT'S WEAK.
No, you won't!
Clearly you are not ready to appreciate the full majesty of nature.
We're outta here.

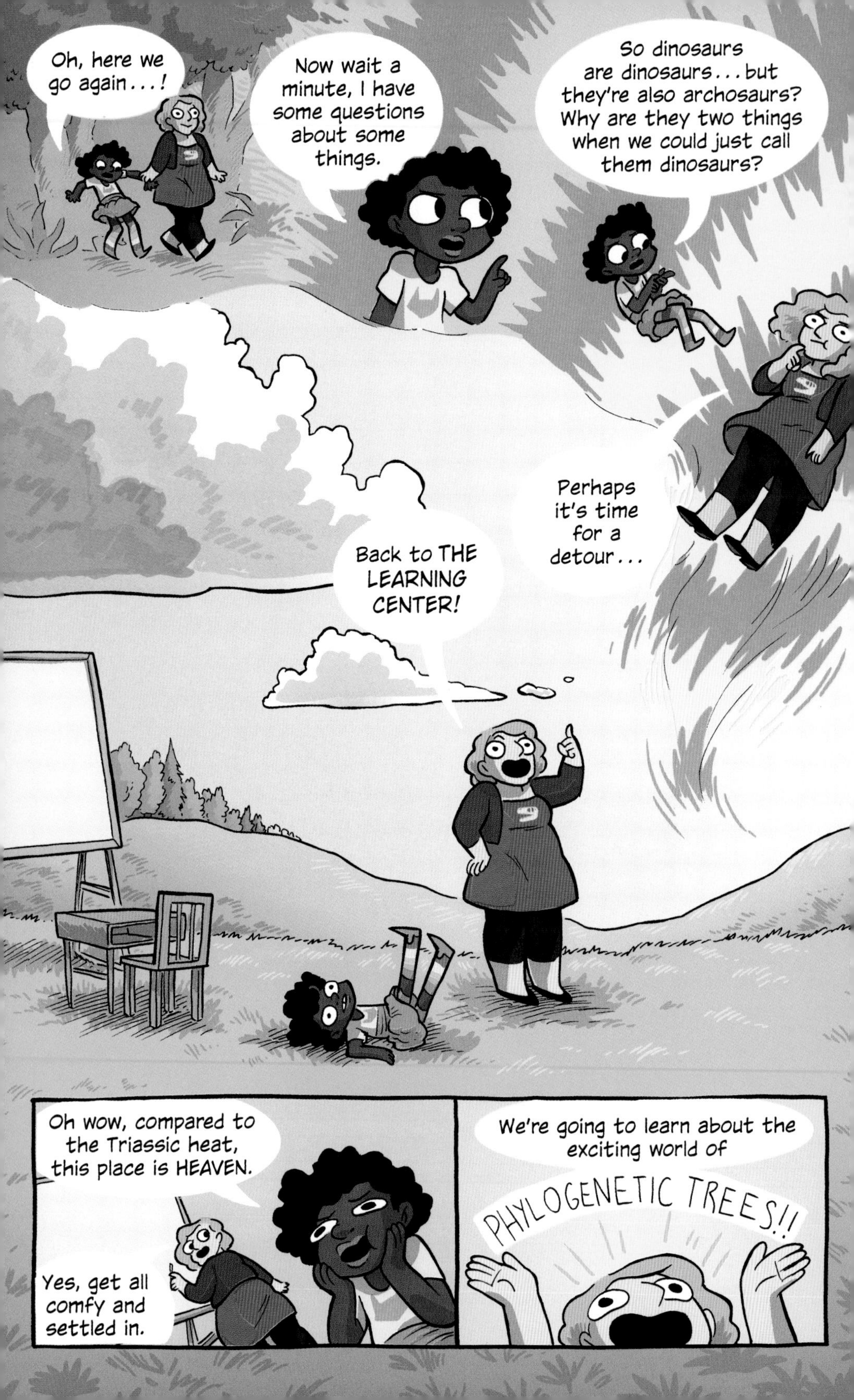
Oh, here we go again...!
Now wait a minute, I have some questions about some things.
So dinosaurs are dinosaurs... but they're also archosaurs? Why are they two things when we could just call them dinosaurs?
Perhaps it's time for a detour...
Back to THE LEARNING CENTER!
Oh wow, compared to the Triassic heat, this place is HEAVEN.
Yes, get all comfy and settled in.
We're going to learn about the exciting world of
PHYLOGENETIC TREES!!

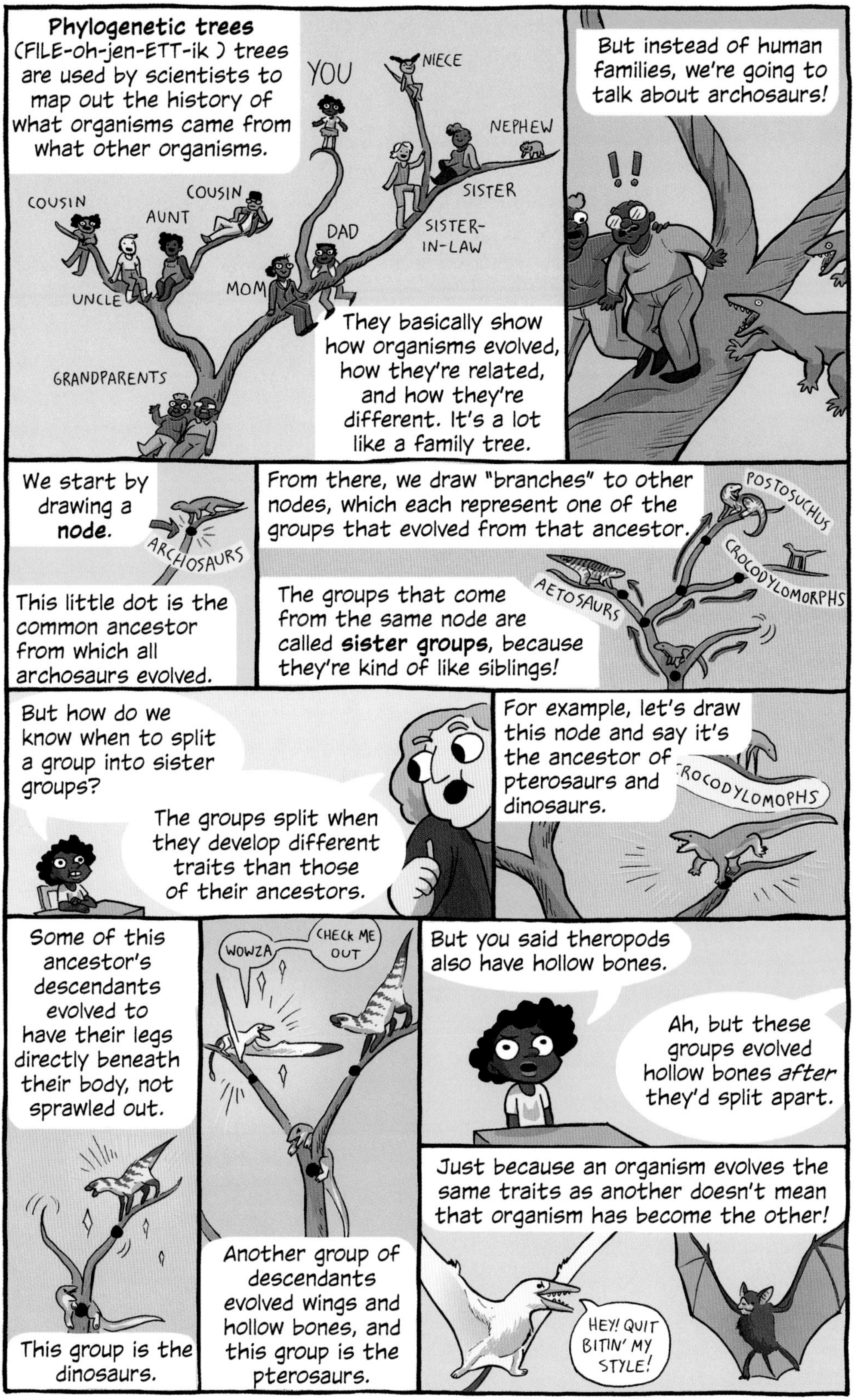
Phylogenetic trees (FILE-oh-jen-ETT-ik) trees are used by scientists to map out the history of what organisms came from what other organisms.
YOU
NIECE
NEPHEW
COUSIN
AUNT
COUSIN
SISTER
DAD
SISTER-IN-LAW
UNCLE
MOM
GRANDPARENTS
They basically show how organisms evolved, how they're related, and how they're different. It's a lot like a family tree.
But instead of human families, we're going to talk about archosaurs!
!!
We start by drawing a **node**.
ARCHOSAURS
This little dot is the common ancestor from which all archosaurs evolved.
From there, we draw "branches" to other nodes, which each represent one of the groups that evolved from that ancestor.
POSTOSUCHUS
CROCODYLOMORPHS
AETOSAURS
The groups that come from the same node are called **sister groups**, because they're kind of like siblings!
But how do we know when to split a group into sister groups?
The groups split when they develop different traits than those of their ancestors.
For example, let's draw this node and say it's the ancestor of pterosaurs and dinosaurs.
CROCODYLOMOPHS
Some of this ancestor's descendants evolved to have their legs directly beneath their body, not sprawled out.
This group is the dinosaurs.
WOWZA
CHECK ME OUT
Another group of descendants evolved wings and hollow bones, and this group is the pterosaurs.
But you said theropods also have hollow bones.
Ah, but these groups evolved hollow bones *after* they'd split apart.
Just because an organism evolves the same traits as another doesn't mean that organism has become the other!
HEY! QUIT BITIN' MY STYLE!

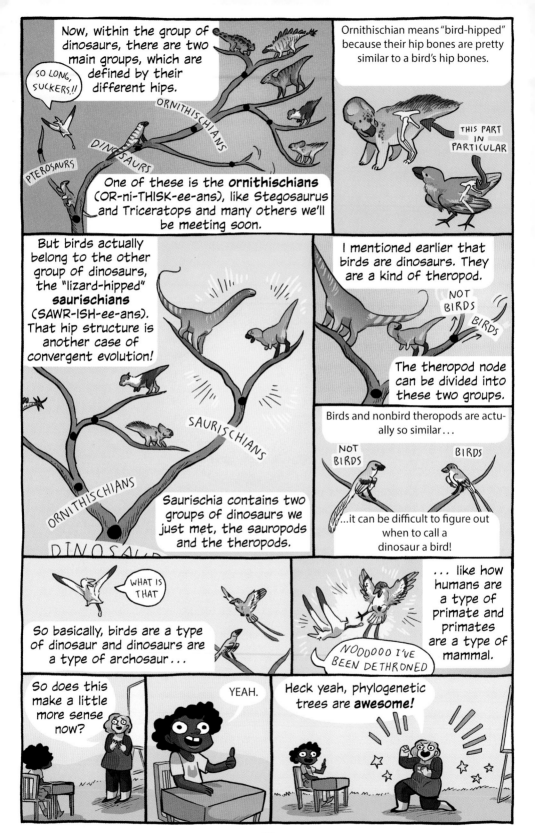

Now, within the group of dinosaurs, there are two main groups, which are defined by their different hips.

SO LONG, SUCKERS!!

ORNITHISCHIANS

DINOSAURS

PTEROSAURS

One of these is the **ornithischians** (OR-ni-THISK-ee-ans), like Stegosaurus and Triceratops and many others we'll be meeting soon.

Ornithischian means "bird-hipped" because their hip bones are pretty similar to a bird's hip bones.

THIS PART IN PARTICULAR

But birds actually belong to the other group of dinosaurs, the "lizard-hipped" **saurischians** (SAWR-ISH-ee-ans). That hip structure is another case of convergent evolution!

SAURISCHIANS

ORNITHISCHIANS

DINOSAUR

Saurischia contains two groups of dinosaurs we just met, the sauropods and the theropods.

I mentioned earlier that birds are dinosaurs. They are a kind of theropod.

NOT BIRDS

BIRDS

The theropod node can be divided into these two groups.

Birds and nonbird theropods are actually so similar...

NOT BIRDS

BIRDS

...it can be difficult to figure out when to call a dinosaur a bird!

WHAT IS THAT

So basically, birds are a type of dinosaur and dinosaurs are a type of archosaur...

... like how humans are a type of primate and primates are a type of mammal.

NOOOOOO I'VE BEEN DETHRONED

So does this make a little more sense now?

YEAH.

Heck yeah, phylogenetic trees are **awesome!**

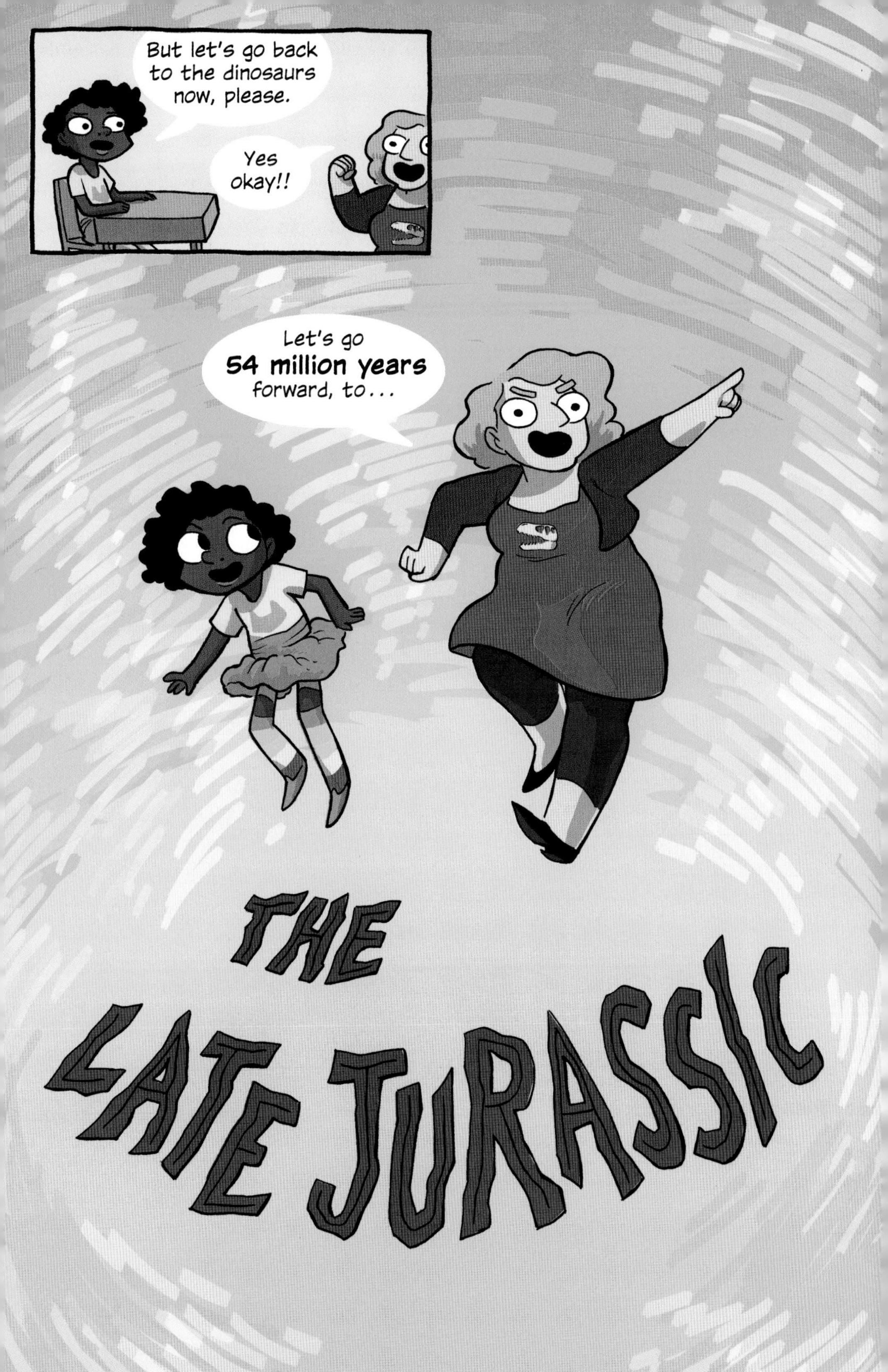
But let's go back to the dinosaurs now, please.
Yes okay!!
Let's go **54 million years** forward, to...
THE LATE JURASSIC

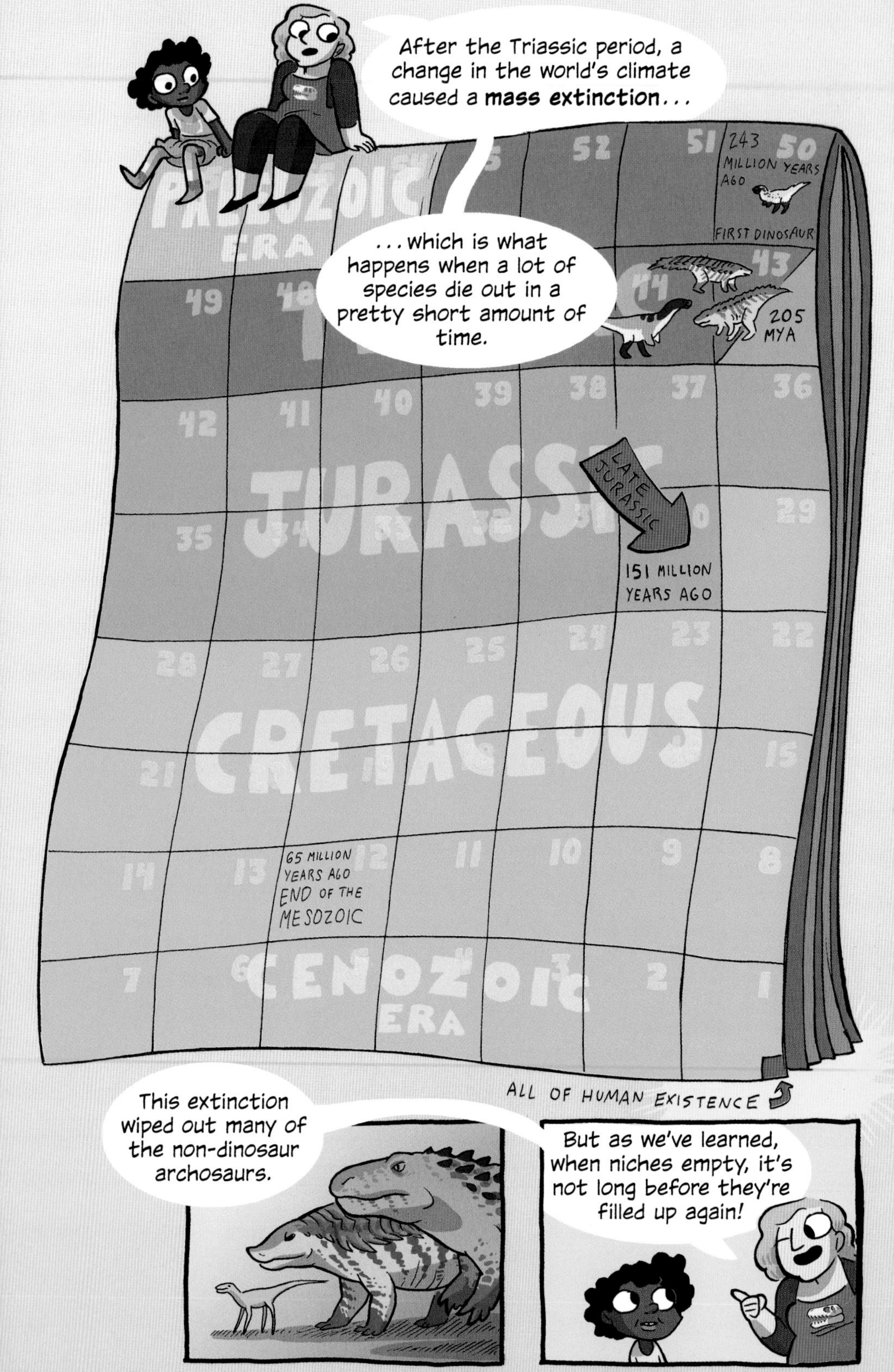

After the Triassic period, a change in the world's climate caused a **mass extinction**...
...which is what happens when a lot of species die out in a pretty short amount of time.
PALEOZOIC ERA
51 243 MILLION YEARS AGO 50
FIRST DINOSAUR
52
49
44
43
205 MYA
42
41
40
39
38
37
36
JURASSIC
LATE JURASSIC
151 MILLION YEARS AGO
35
29
28
27
26
25
24
23
22
CRETACEOUS
21
15
14
13
65 MILLION YEARS AGO END OF THE MESOZOIC
12
11
10
9
8
7
2
1
CENOZOIC ERA
ALL OF HUMAN EXISTENCE
This extinction wiped out many of the non-dinosaur archosaurs.
But as we've learned, when niches empty, it's not long before they're filled up again!

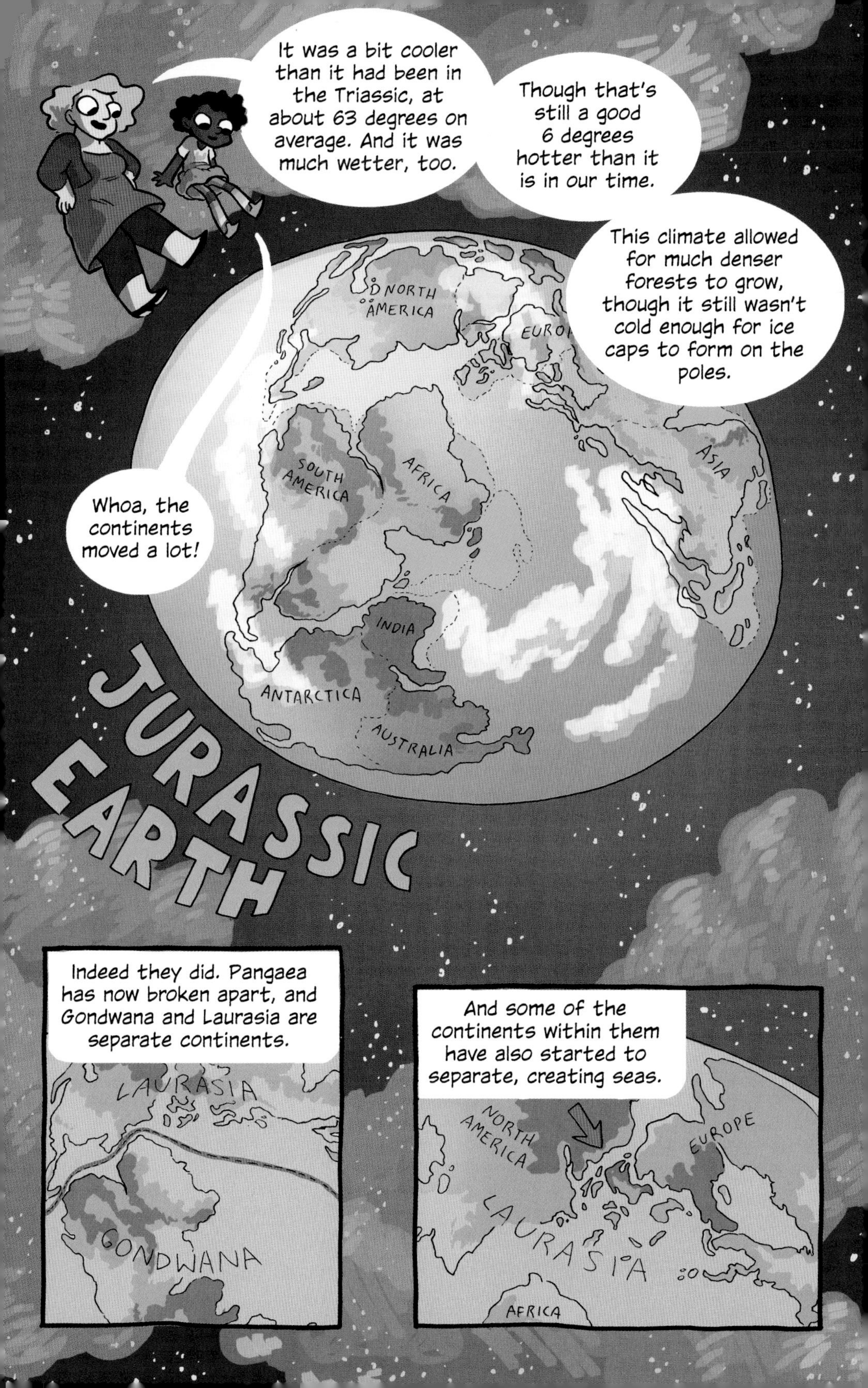
It was a bit cooler than it had been in the Triassic, at about 63 degrees on average. And it was much wetter, too.
Though that's still a good 6 degrees hotter than it is in our time.
This climate allowed for much denser forests to grow, though it still wasn't cold enough for ice caps to form on the poles.
Whoa, the continents moved a lot!
NORTH AMERICA
EUROPE
SOUTH AMERICA
AFRICA
ASIA
INDIA
ANTARCTICA
AUSTRALIA
JURASSIC EARTH
Indeed they did. Pangaea has now broken apart, and Gondwana and Laurasia are separate continents.
LAURASIA
GONDWANA
And some of the continents within them have also started to separate, creating seas.
NORTH AMERICA
EUROPE
LAURASIA
AFRICA

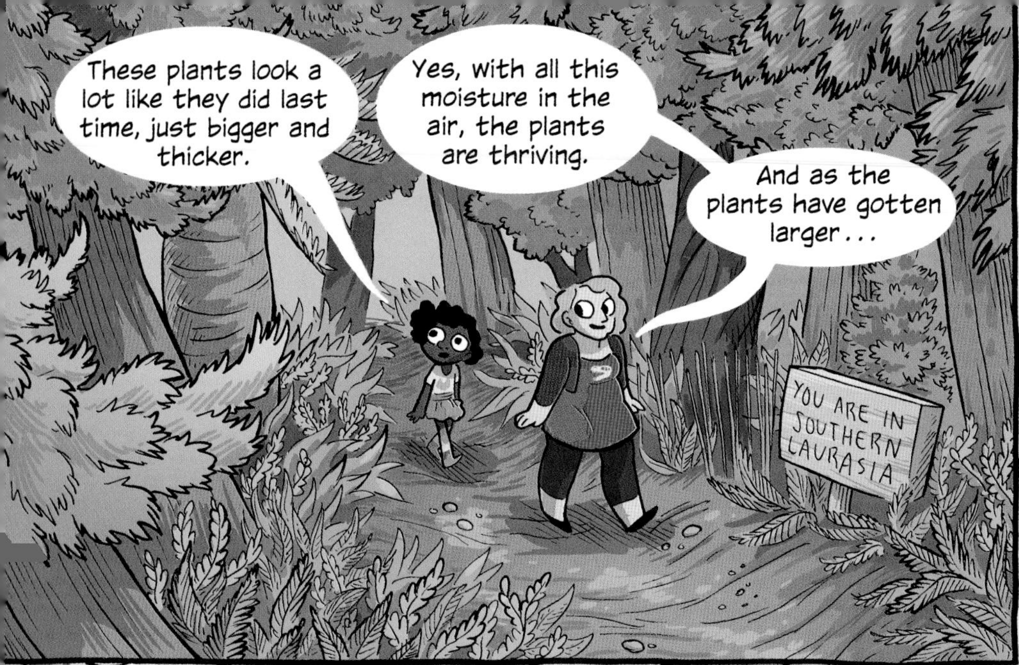
These plants look a lot like they did last time, just bigger and thicker.
Yes, with all this moisture in the air, the plants are thriving.
And as the plants have gotten larger...
YOU ARE IN SOUTHERN LAURASIA

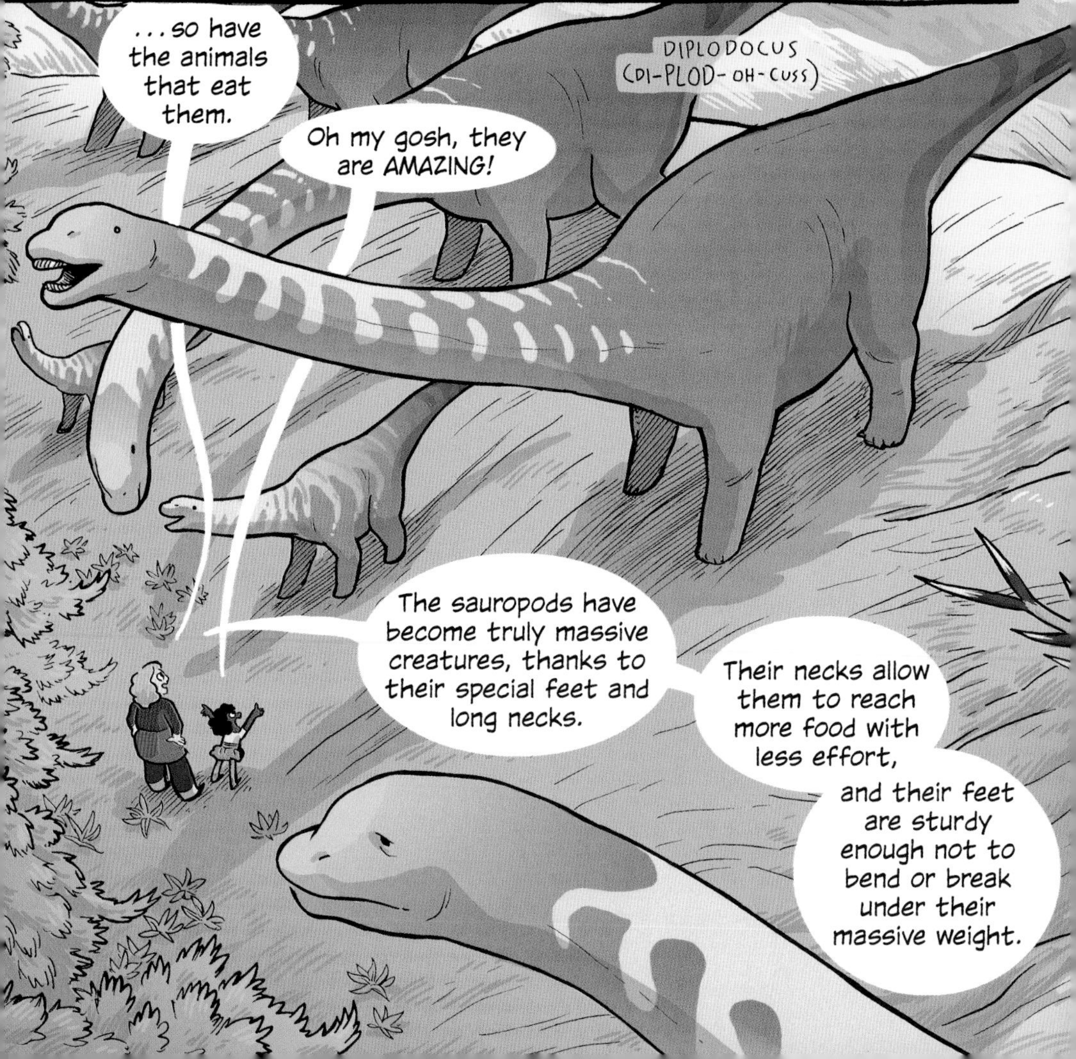
...so have the animals that eat them.
DIPLODOCUS (DI-PLOD-OH-CUSS)
Oh my gosh, they are AMAZING!
The sauropods have become truly massive creatures, thanks to their special feet and long necks.
Their necks allow them to reach more food with less effort,
and their feet are sturdy enough not to bend or break under their massive weight.

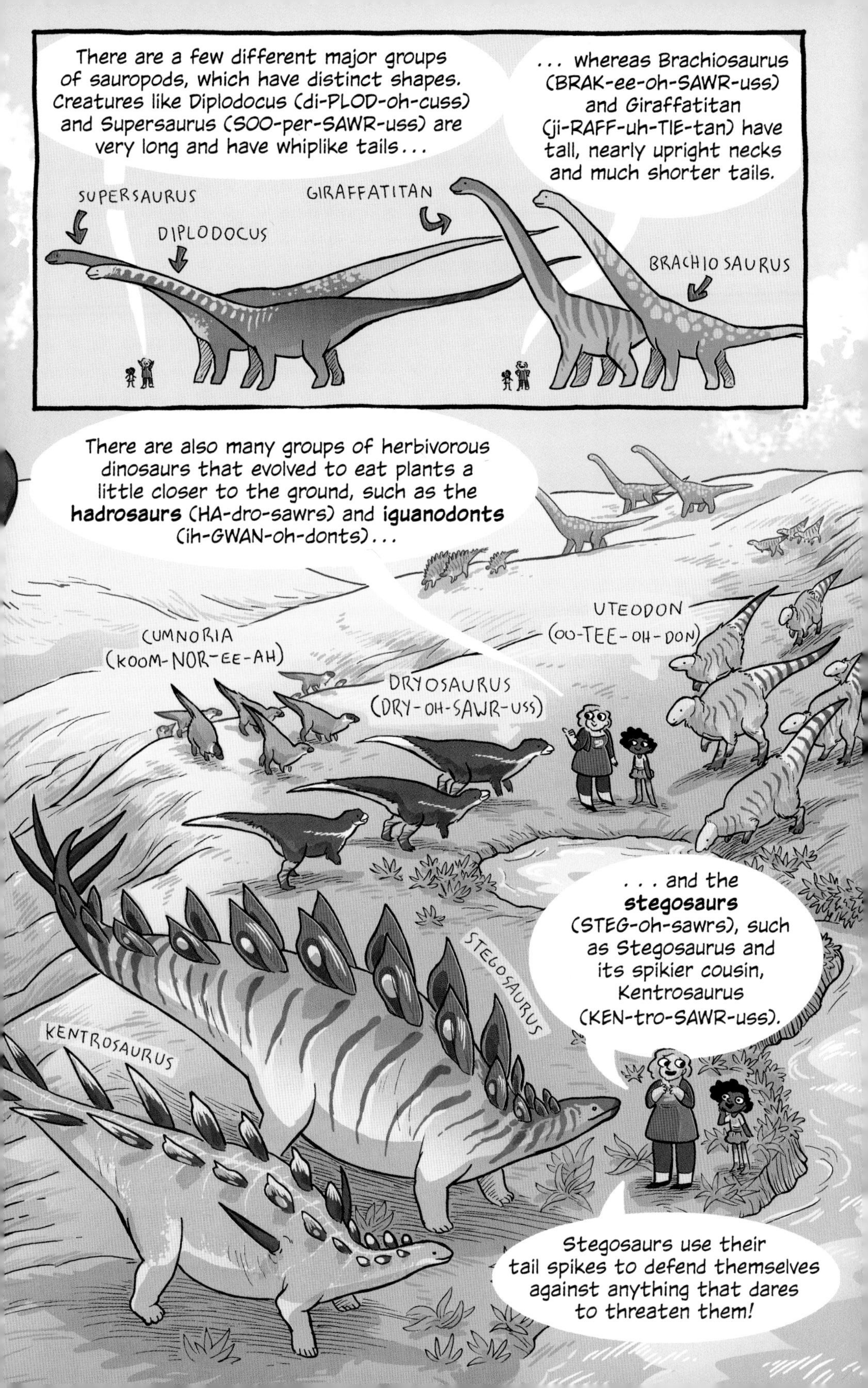

There are a few different major groups of sauropods, which have distinct shapes. Creatures like Diplodocus (di-PLOD-oh-cuss) and Supersaurus (SOO-per-SAWR-uss) are very long and have whiplike tails...
... whereas Brachiosaurus (BRAK-ee-oh-SAWR-uss) and Giraffatitan (ji-RAFF-uh-TIE-tan) have tall, nearly upright necks and much shorter tails.
SUPERSAURUS
DIPLODOCUS
GIRAFFATITAN
BRACHIOSAURUS
There are also many groups of herbivorous dinosaurs that evolved to eat plants a little closer to the ground, such as the **hadrosaurs** (HA-dro-sawrs) and **iguanodonts** (ih-GWAN-oh-donts)...
UTEODON (OO-TEE-OH-DON)
CUMNORIA (KOOM-NOR-EE-AH)
DRYOSAURUS (DRY-OH-SAWR-USS)
... and the **stegosaurs** (STEG-oh-sawrs), such as Stegosaurus and its spikier cousin, Kentrosaurus (KEN-tro-SAWR-uss).
STEGOSAURUS
KENTROSAURUS
Stegosaurs use their tail spikes to defend themselves against anything that dares to threaten them!

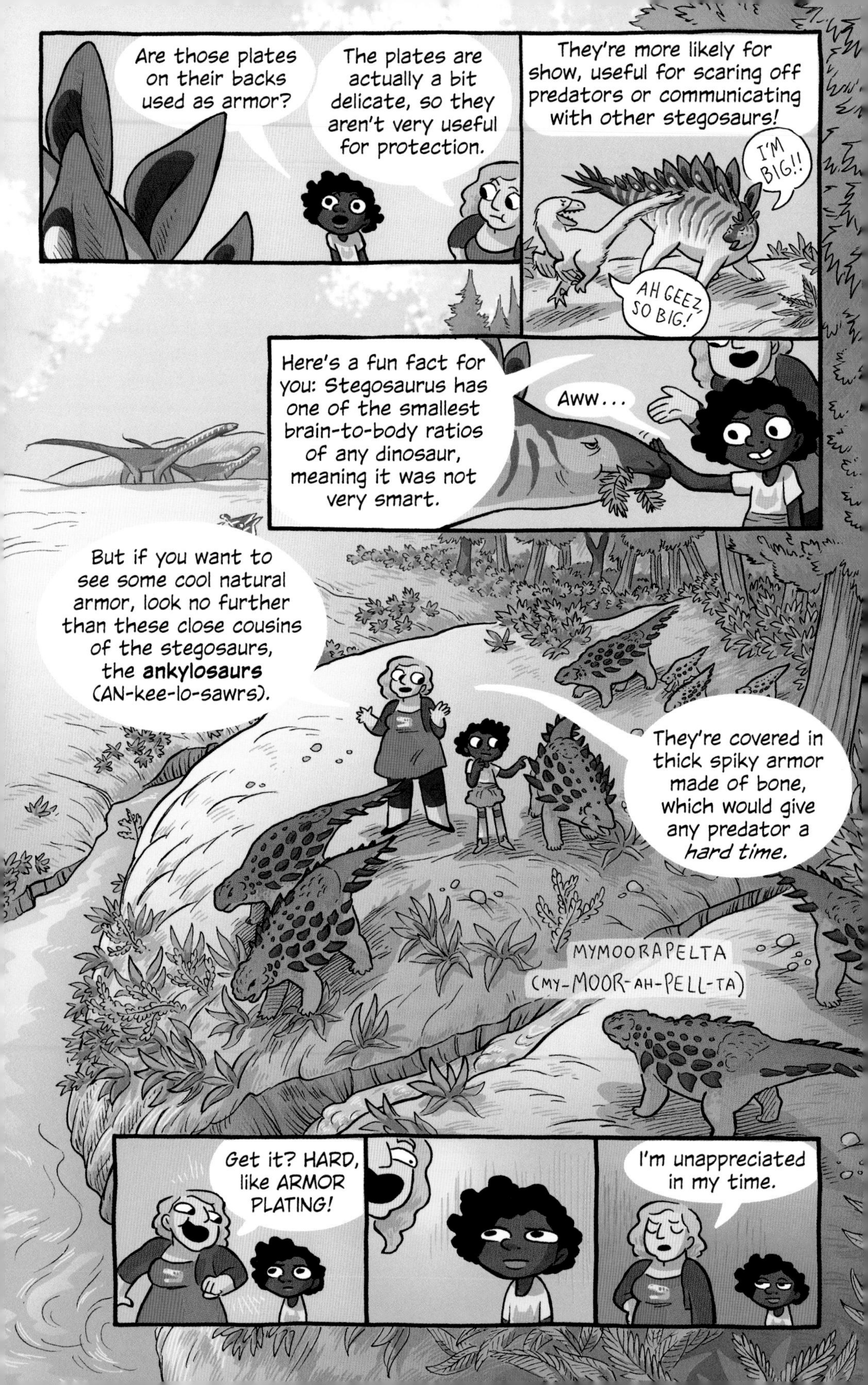
Are those plates on their backs used as armor?
The plates are actually a bit delicate, so they aren't very useful for protection.
They're more likely for show, useful for scaring off predators or communicating with other stegosaurs!
I'M BIG!!
AH GEEZ, SO BIG!
Here's a fun fact for you: Stegosaurus has one of the smallest brain-to-body ratios of any dinosaur, meaning it was not very smart.
Aww...
But if you want to see some cool natural armor, look no further than these close cousins of the stegosaurs, the **ankylosaurs** (AN-kee-lo-sawrs).
They're covered in thick spiky armor made of bone, which would give any predator a *hard time.*
MYMOORAPELTA
(MY-MOOR-AH-PELL-TA)
Get it? HARD, like ARMOR PLATING!
I'm unappreciated in my time.

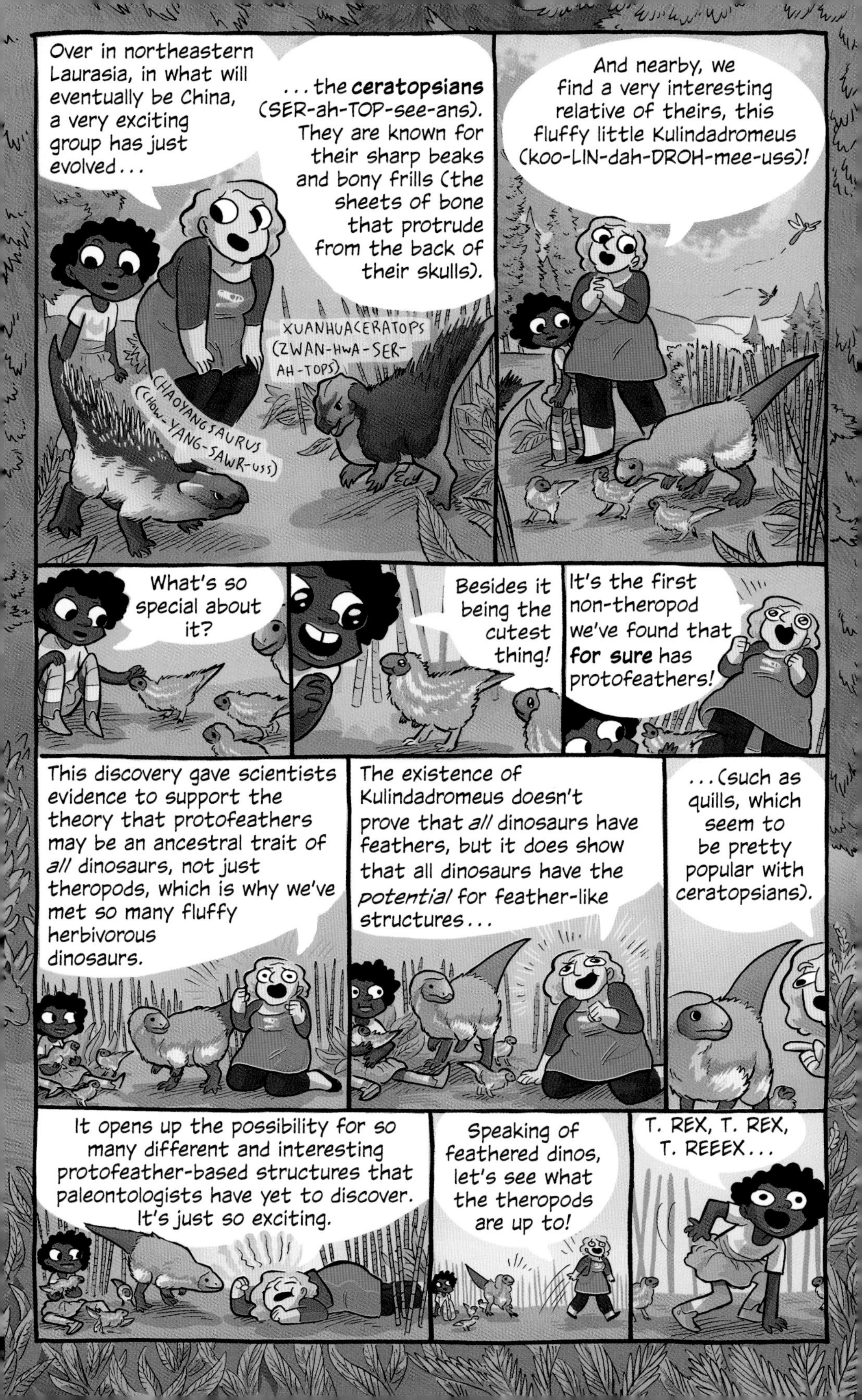

Over in northeastern Laurasia, in what will eventually be China, a very exciting group has just evolved...
...the **ceratopsians** (SER-ah-TOP-see-ans). They are known for their sharp beaks and bony frills (the sheets of bone that protrude from the back of their skulls).
XUANHUACERATOPS (ZWAN-HWA-SER-AH-TOPS)
CHAOYANGSAURUS (CHOW-YANG-SAWR-USS)
And nearby, we find a very interesting relative of theirs, this fluffy little Kulindadromeus (koo-LIN-dah-DROH-mee-uss)!
What's so special about it?
Besides it being the cutest thing!
It's the first non-theropod we've found that **for sure** has protofeathers!
This discovery gave scientists evidence to support the theory that protofeathers may be an ancestral trait of *all* dinosaurs, not just theropods, which is why we've met so many fluffy herbivorous dinosaurs.
The existence of Kulindadromeus doesn't prove that *all* dinosaurs have feathers, but it does show that all dinosaurs have the *potential* for feather-like structures...
...(such as quills, which seem to be pretty popular with ceratopsians).
It opens up the possibility for so many different and interesting protofeather-based structures that paleontologists have yet to discover. It's just so exciting.
Speaking of feathered dinos, let's see what the theropods are up to!
T. REX, T. REX, T. REEEX...

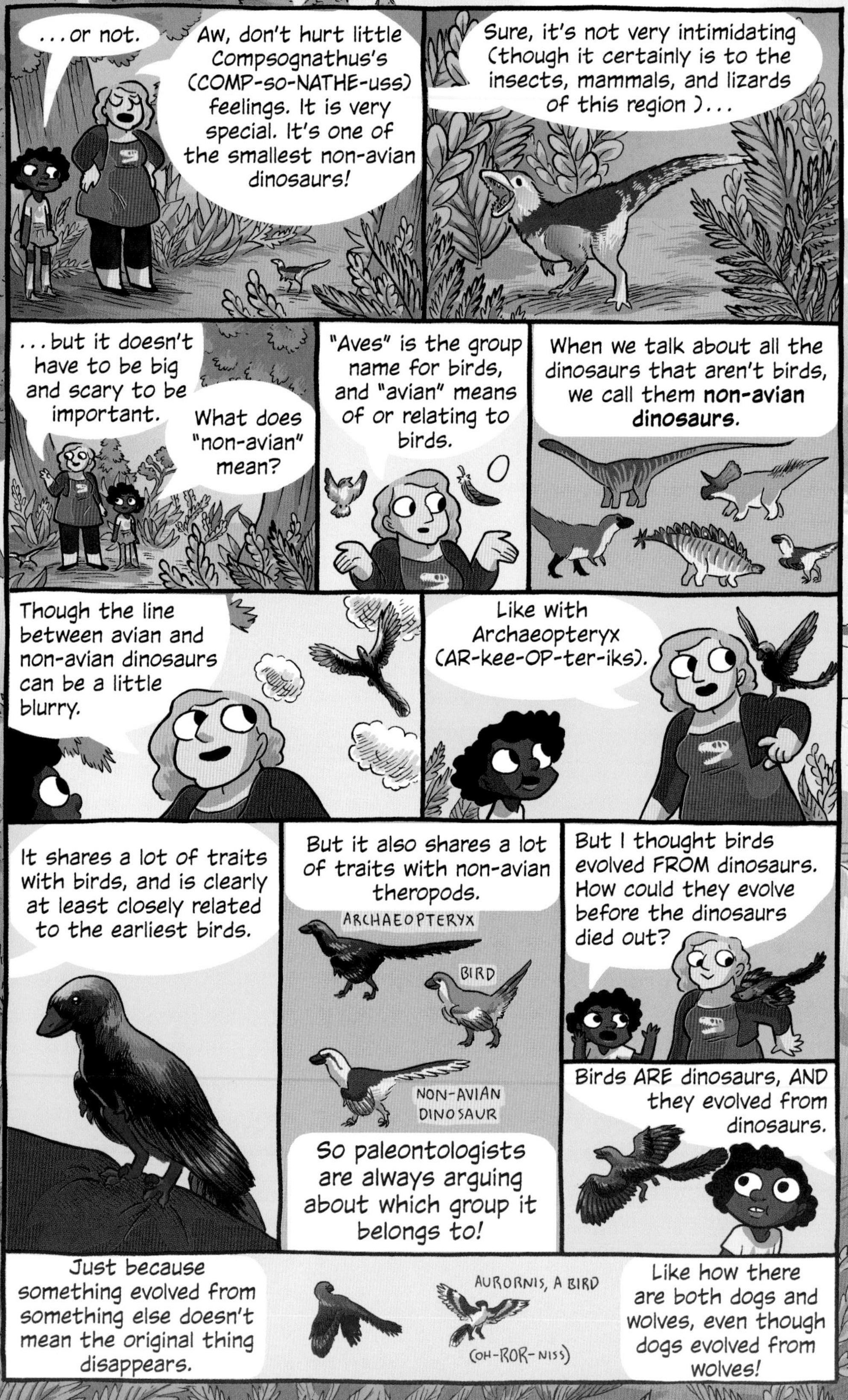
...or not.
Aw, don't hurt little Compsognathus's (COMP-so-NATHE-uss) feelings. It is very special. It's one of the smallest non-avian dinosaurs!
Sure, it's not very intimidating (though it certainly is to the insects, mammals, and lizards of this region)...
...but it doesn't have to be big and scary to be important.
What does "non-avian" mean?
"Aves" is the group name for birds, and "avian" means of or relating to birds.
When we talk about all the dinosaurs that aren't birds, we call them **non-avian dinosaurs**.
Though the line between avian and non-avian dinosaurs can be a little blurry.
Like with Archaeopteryx (AR-kee-OP-ter-iks).
It shares a lot of traits with birds, and is clearly at least closely related to the earliest birds.
But it also shares a lot of traits with non-avian theropods.
ARCHAEOPTERYX
BIRD
NON-AVIAN DINOSAUR
So paleontologists are always arguing about which group it belongs to!
But I thought birds evolved FROM dinosaurs. How could they evolve before the dinosaurs died out?
Birds ARE dinosaurs, AND they evolved from dinosaurs.
Just because something evolved from something else doesn't mean the original thing disappears.
AURORNIS, A BIRD
(OH-ROR-NISS)
Like how there are both dogs and wolves, even though dogs evolved from wolves!

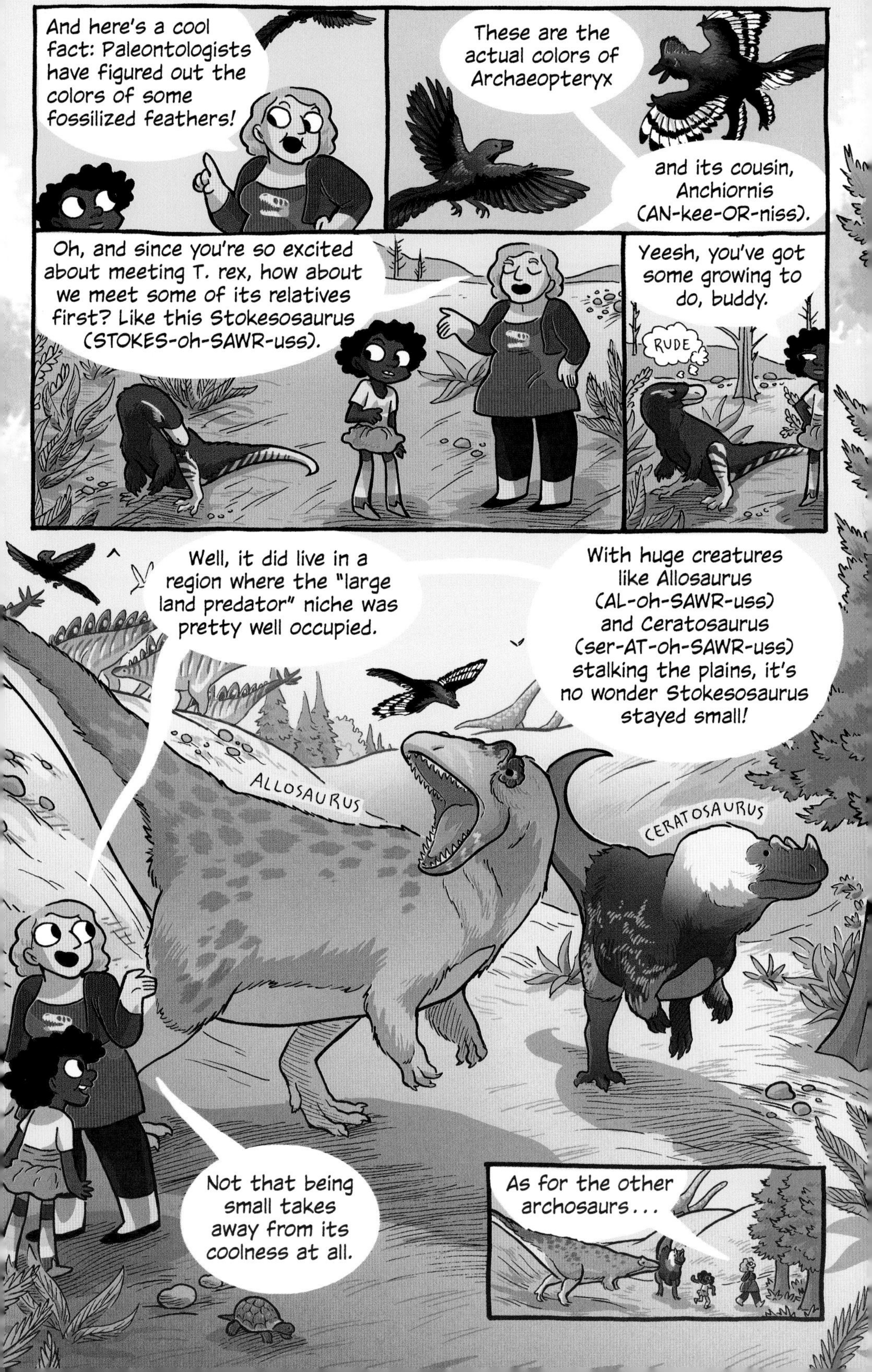
And here's a cool fact: Paleontologists have figured out the colors of some fossilized feathers!
These are the actual colors of Archaeopteryx
and its cousin, Anchiornis (AN-kee-OR-niss).
Oh, and since you're so excited about meeting T. rex, how about we meet some of its relatives first? Like this Stokesosaurus (STOKES-oh-SAWR-uss).
Yeesh, you've got some growing to do, buddy.
RUDE
Well, it did live in a region where the "large land predator" niche was pretty well occupied.
With huge creatures like Allosaurus (AL-oh-SAWR-uss) and Ceratosaurus (ser-AT-oh-SAWR-uss) stalking the plains, it's no wonder Stokesosaurus stayed small!
ALLOSAURUS
CERATOSAURUS
Not that being small takes away from its coolness at all.
As for the other archosaurs . . .

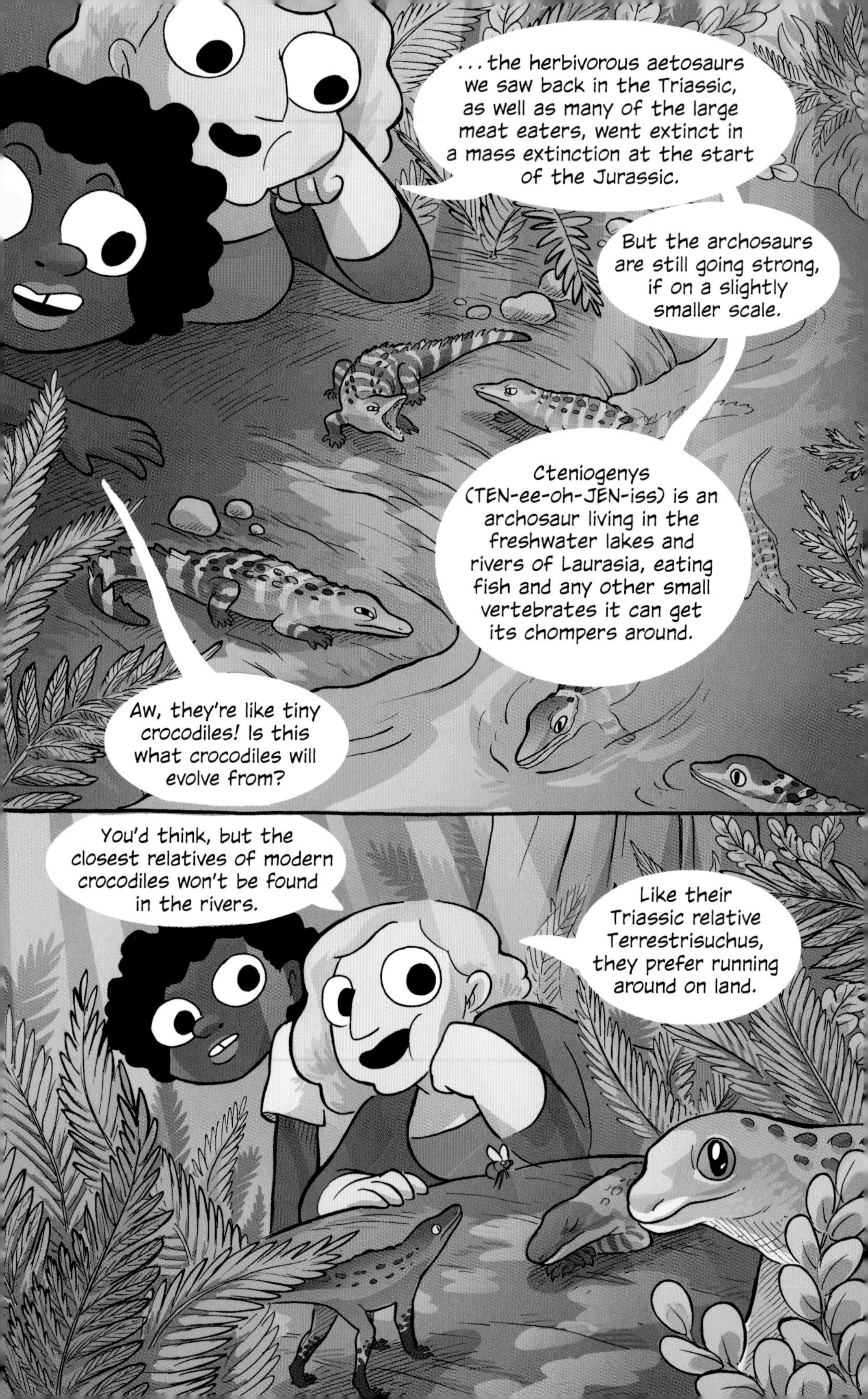
...the herbivorous aetosaurs we saw back in the Triassic, as well as many of the large meat eaters, went extinct in a mass extinction at the start of the Jurassic.
But the archosaurs are still going strong, if on a slightly smaller scale.
Cteniogenys (TEN-ee-oh-JEN-iss) is an archosaur living in the freshwater lakes and rivers of Laurasia, eating fish and any other small vertebrates it can get its chompers around.
Aw, they're like tiny crocodiles! Is this what crocodiles will evolve from?
You'd think, but the closest relatives of modern crocodiles won't be found in the rivers.
Like their Triassic relative Terrestrisuchus, they prefer running around on land.

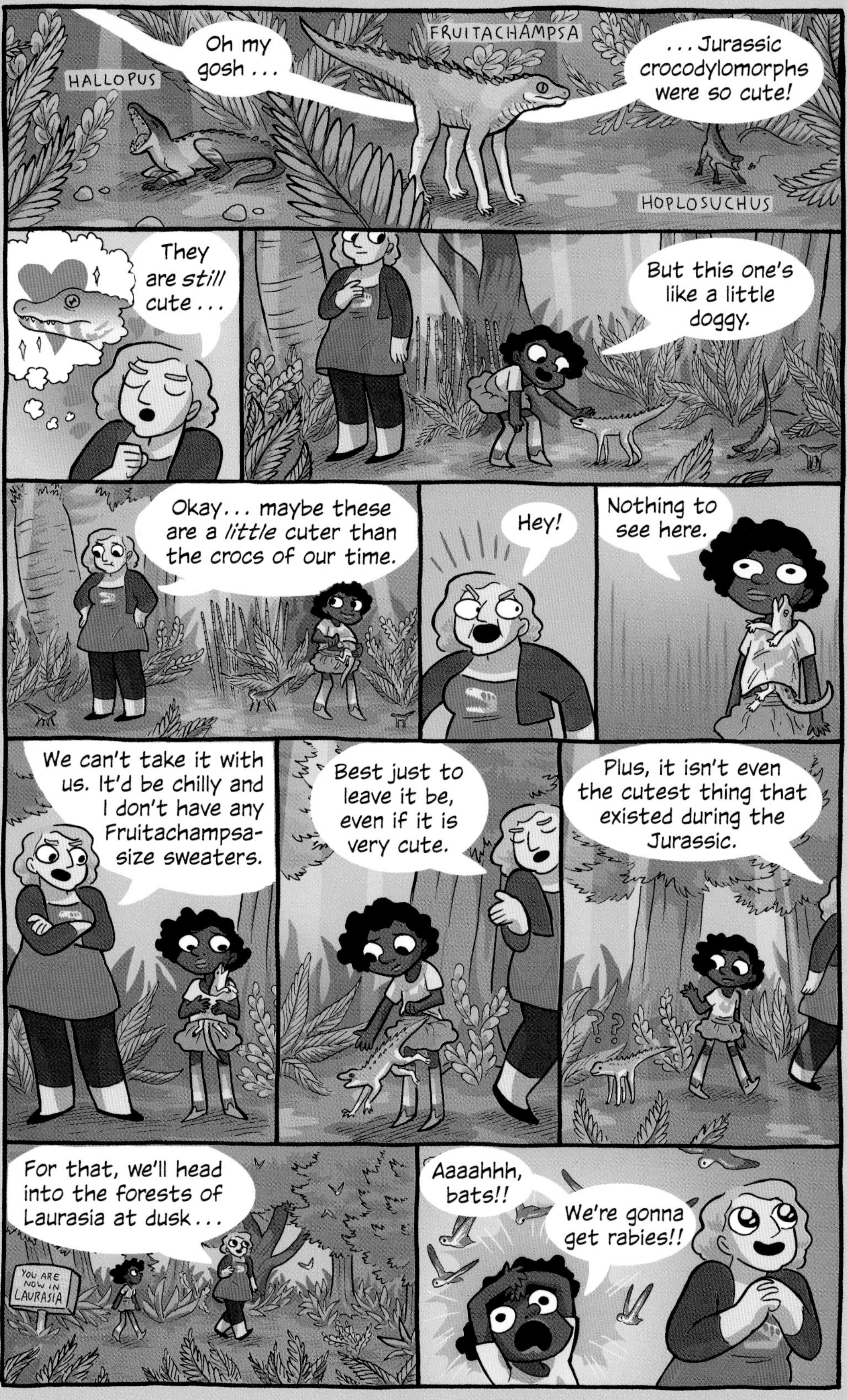
Oh my gosh . . .
FRUITACHAMPSA
HALLOPUS
. . . Jurassic crocodylomorphs were so cute!
HOPLOSUCHUS
They are *still* cute . . .
But this one's like a little doggy.
Okay . . . maybe these are a *little* cuter than the crocs of our time.
Hey!
Nothing to see here.
We can't take it with us. It'd be chilly and I don't have any Fruitachampsa-size sweaters.
Best just to leave it be, even if it is very cute.
Plus, it isn't even the cutest thing that existed during the Jurassic.
For that, we'll head into the forests of Laurasia at dusk . . .
YOU ARE NOW IN LAURASIA
Aaaahhh, bats!!
We're gonna get rabies!!

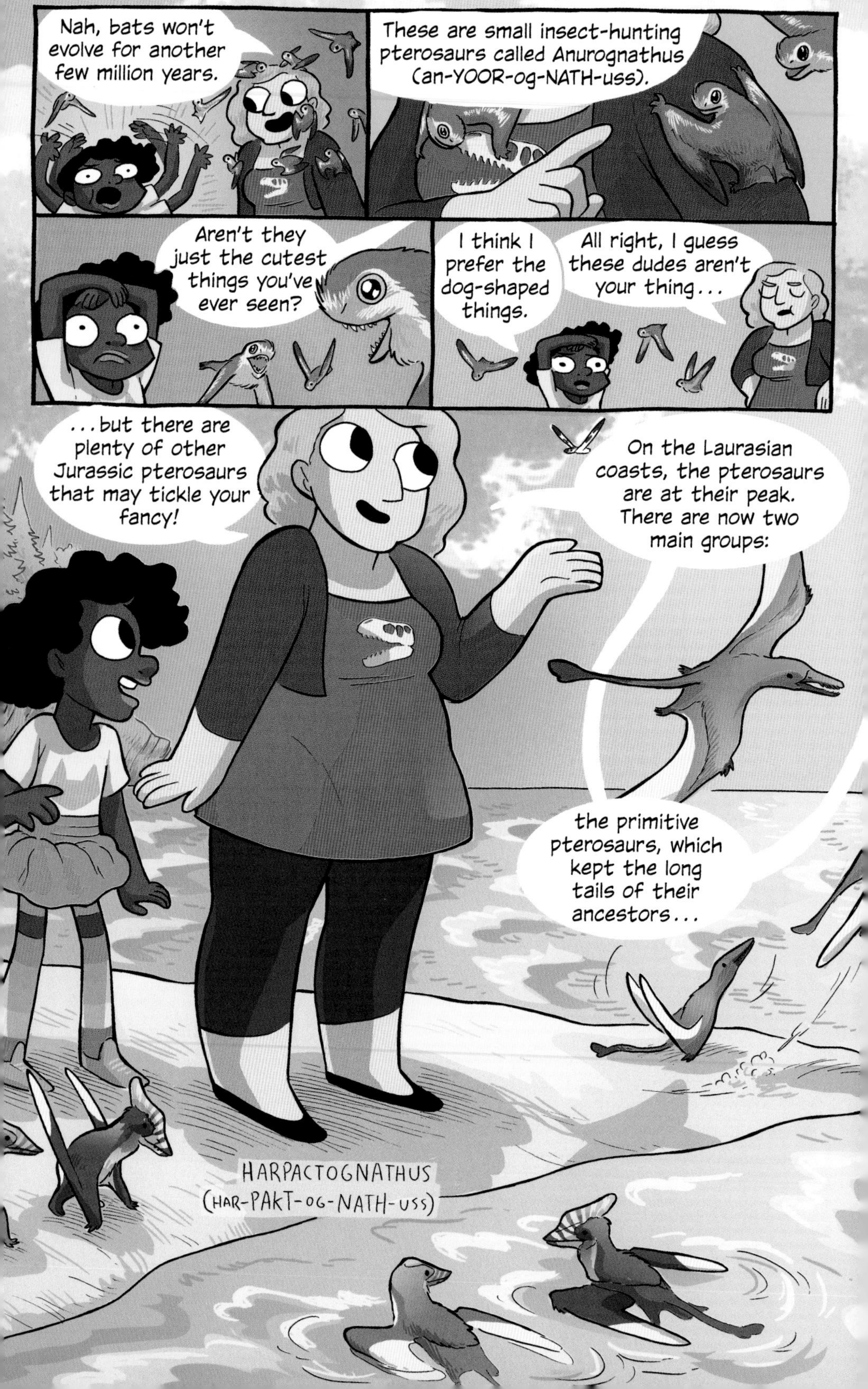

Nah, bats won't evolve for another few million years.
These are small insect-hunting pterosaurs called Anurognathus (an-YOOR-og-NATH-uss).
Aren't they just the cutest things you've ever seen?
I think I prefer the dog-shaped things.
All right, I guess these dudes aren't your thing...
...but there are plenty of other Jurassic pterosaurs that may tickle your fancy!
On the Laurasian coasts, the pterosaurs are at their peak. There are now two main groups:
the primitive pterosaurs, which kept the long tails of their ancestors...
HARPACTOGNATHUS (HAR-PAKT-OG-NATH-USS)

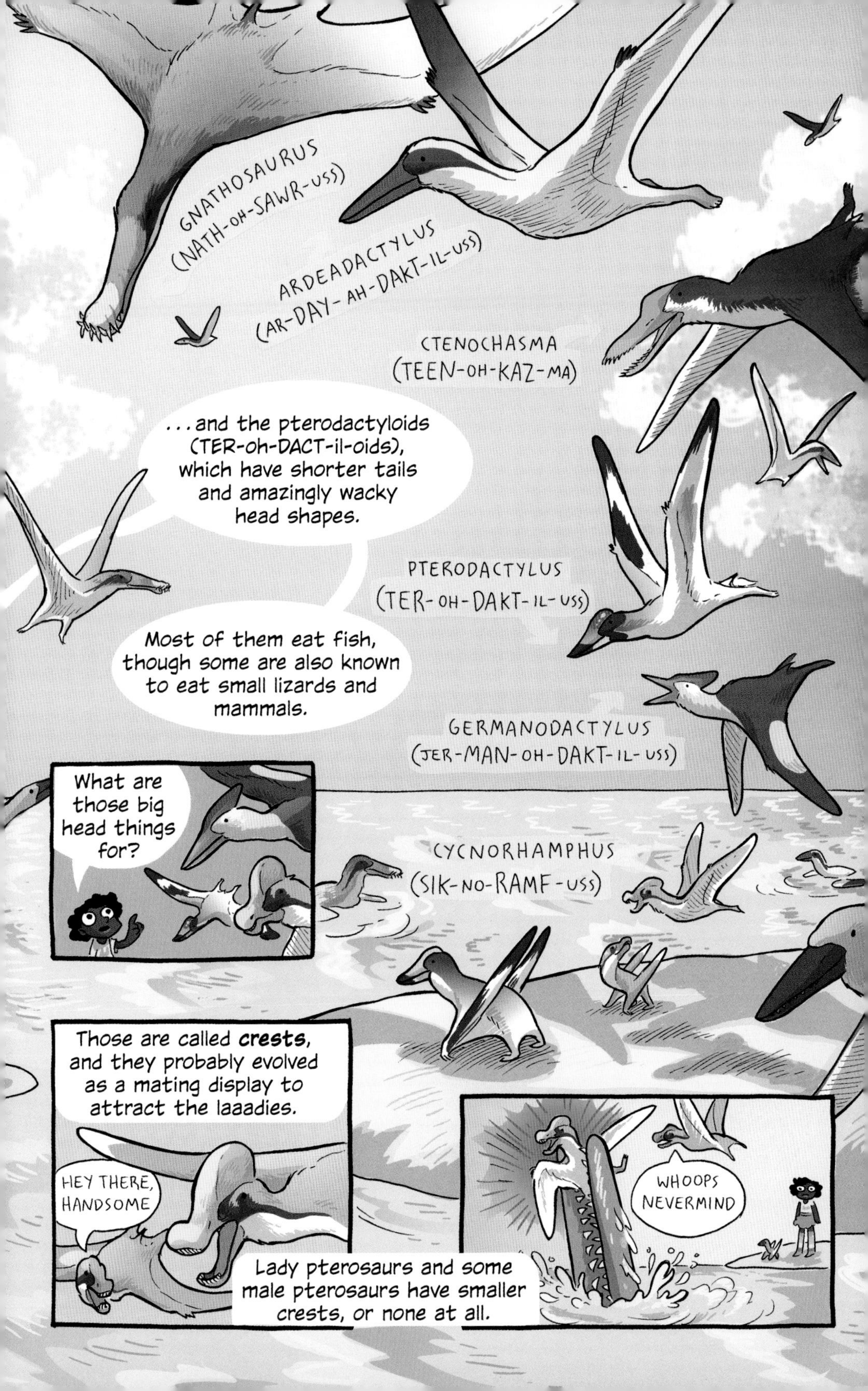
GNATHOSAURUS
(NATH-OH-SAWR-USS)
ARDEADACTYLUS
(AR-DAY-AH-DAKT-IL-USS)
CTENOCHASMA
(TEEN-OH-KAZ-MA)
...and the pterodactyloids (TER-oh-DACT-il-oids), which have shorter tails and amazingly wacky head shapes.
PTERODACTYLUS
(TER-OH-DAKT-IL-USS)
Most of them eat fish, though some are also known to eat small lizards and mammals.
GERMANODACTYLUS
(JER-MAN-OH-DAKT-IL-USS)
What are those big head things for?
CYCNORHAMPHUS
(SIK-NO-RAMF-USS)
Those are called **crests**, and they probably evolved as a mating display to attract the laaadies.
HEY THERE, HANDSOME
WHOOPS NEVERMIND
Lady pterosaurs and some male pterosaurs have smaller crests, or none at all.

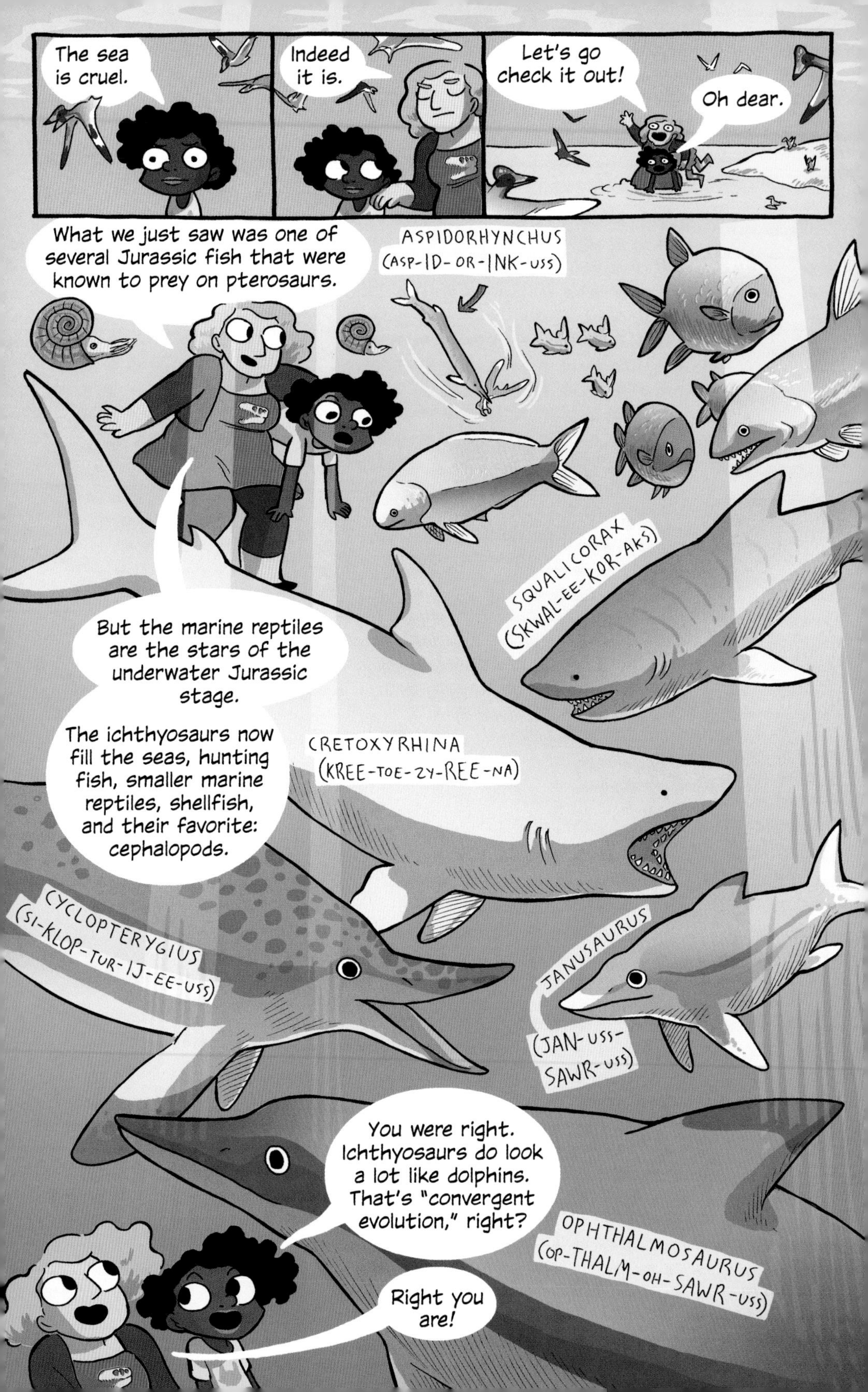
The sea is cruel.
Indeed it is.
Let's go check it out!
Oh dear.
What we just saw was one of several Jurassic fish that were known to prey on pterosaurs.
ASPIDORHYNCHUS (ASP-ID-OR-INK-USS)
SQUALICORAX (SKWAL-EE-KOR-AKS)
But the marine reptiles are the stars of the underwater Jurassic stage.
The ichthyosaurs now fill the seas, hunting fish, smaller marine reptiles, shellfish, and their favorite: cephalopods.
CRETOXYRHINA (KREE-TOE-ZY-REE-NA)
CYCLOPTERYGIUS (SI-KLOP-TUR-IJ-EE-USS)
JANUSAURUS (JAN-USS-SAWR-USS)
You were right. Ichthyosaurs do look a lot like dolphins. That's "convergent evolution," right?
OPHTHALMOSAURUS (OP-THALM-OH-SAWR-USS)
Right you are!

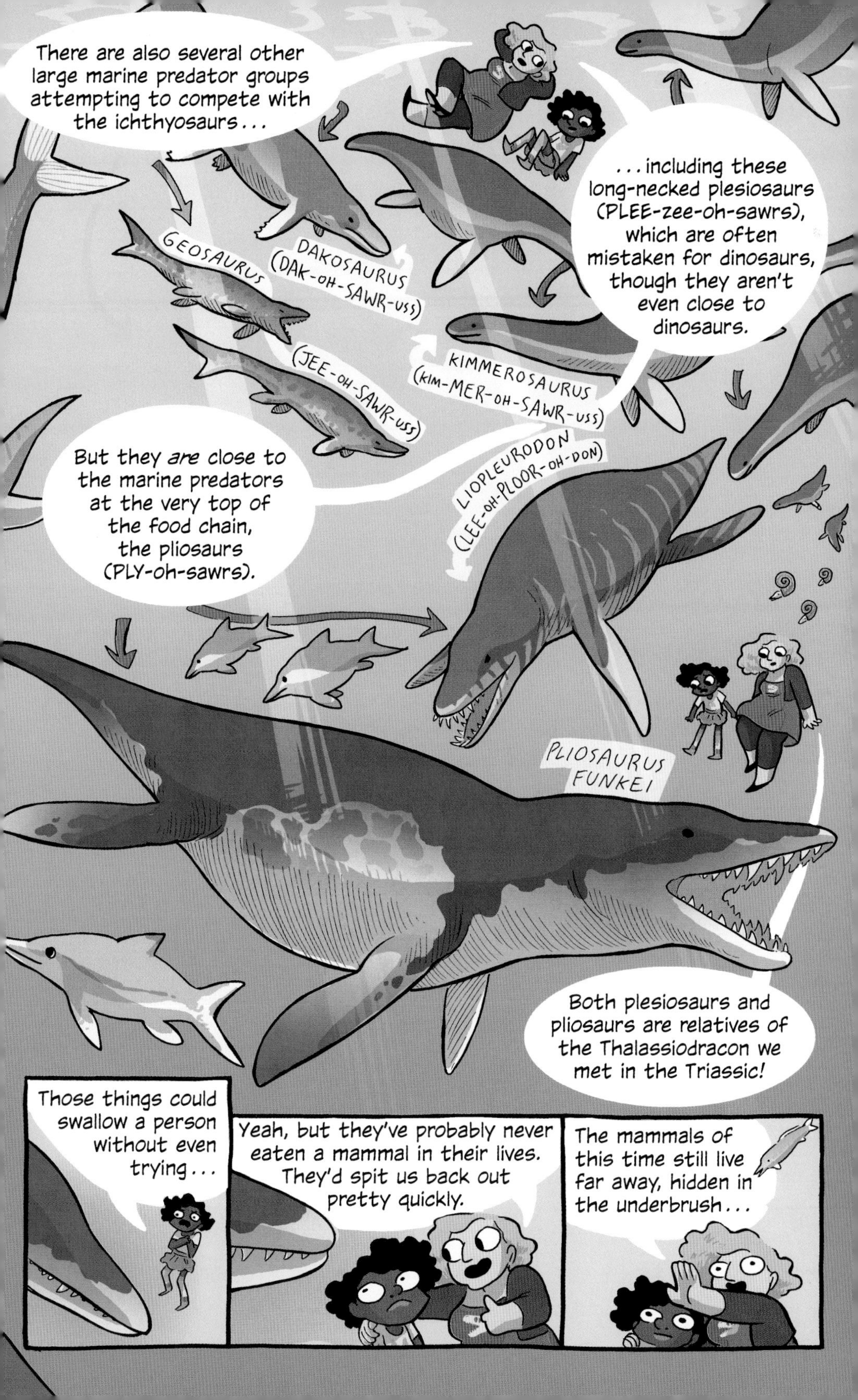
There are also several other large marine predator groups attempting to compete with the ichthyosaurs...
...including these long-necked plesiosaurs (PLEE-zee-oh-sawrs), which are often mistaken for dinosaurs, though they aren't even close to dinosaurs.
GEOSAURUS
(JEE-OH-SAWR-USS)
DAKOSAURUS
(DAK-OH-SAWR-USS)
KIMMEROSAURUS
(KIM-MER-OH-SAWR-USS)
But they are close to the marine predators at the very top of the food chain, the pliosaurs (PLY-oh-sawrs).
LIOPLEURODON
(LEE-OH-PLOOR-OH-DON)
PLIOSAURUS FUNKEI
Both plesiosaurs and pliosaurs are relatives of the Thalassiodracon we met in the Triassic!
Those things could swallow a person without even trying...
Yeah, but they've probably never eaten a mammal in their lives. They'd spit us back out pretty quickly.
The mammals of this time still live far away, hidden in the underbrush...

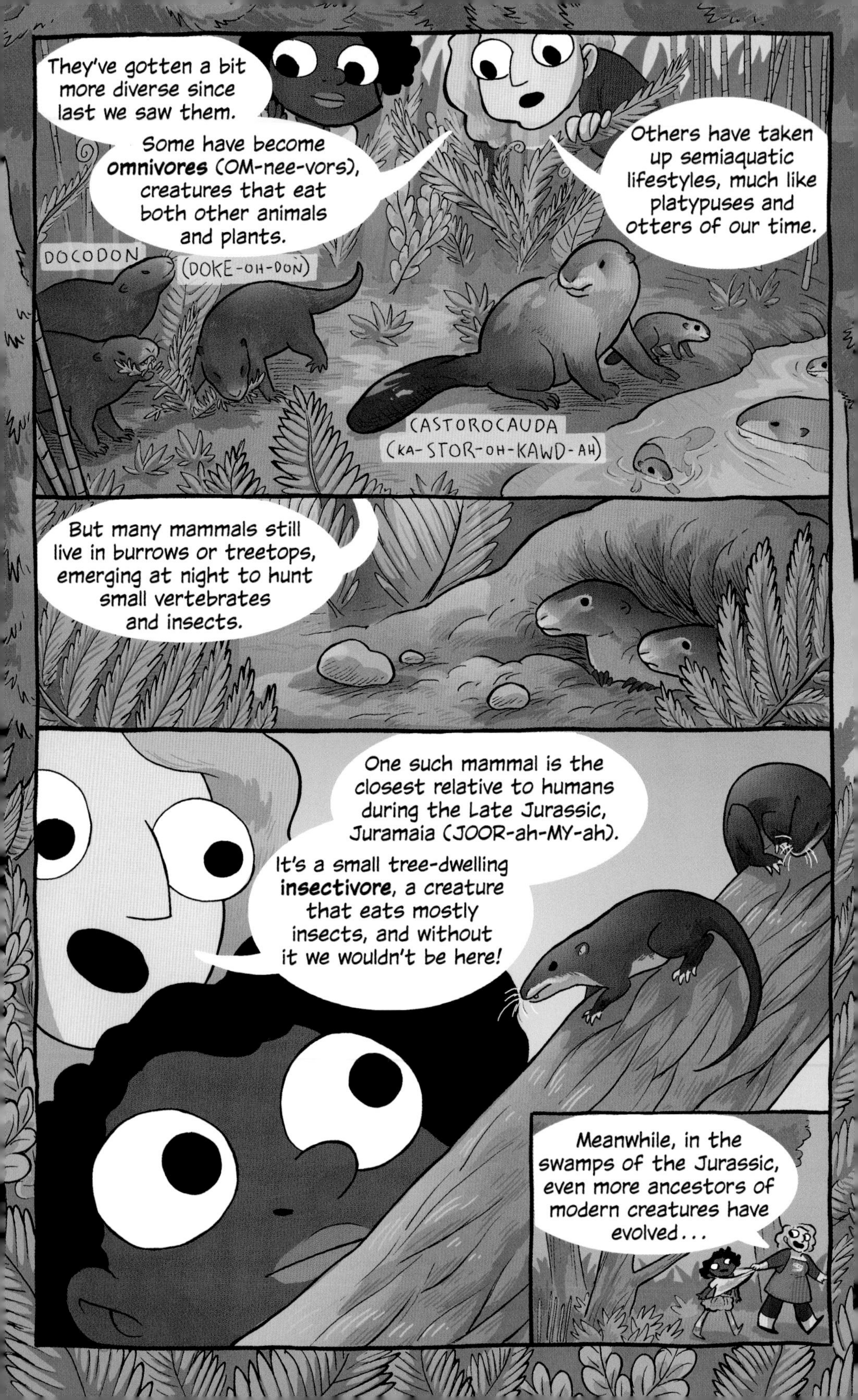

They've gotten a bit more diverse since last we saw them.
Some have become **omnivores** (OM-nee-vors), creatures that eat both other animals and plants.
Others have taken up semiaquatic lifestyles, much like platypuses and otters of our time.
DOCODON
(DOKE-OH-DON)
CASTOROCAUDA
(KA-STOR-OH-KAWD-AH)
But many mammals still live in burrows or treetops, emerging at night to hunt small vertebrates and insects.
One such mammal is the closest relative to humans during the Late Jurassic, Juramaia (JOOR-ah-MY-ah).
It's a small tree-dwelling **insectivore**, a creature that eats mostly insects, and without it we wouldn't be here!
Meanwhile, in the swamps of the Jurassic, even more ancestors of modern creatures have evolved . . .

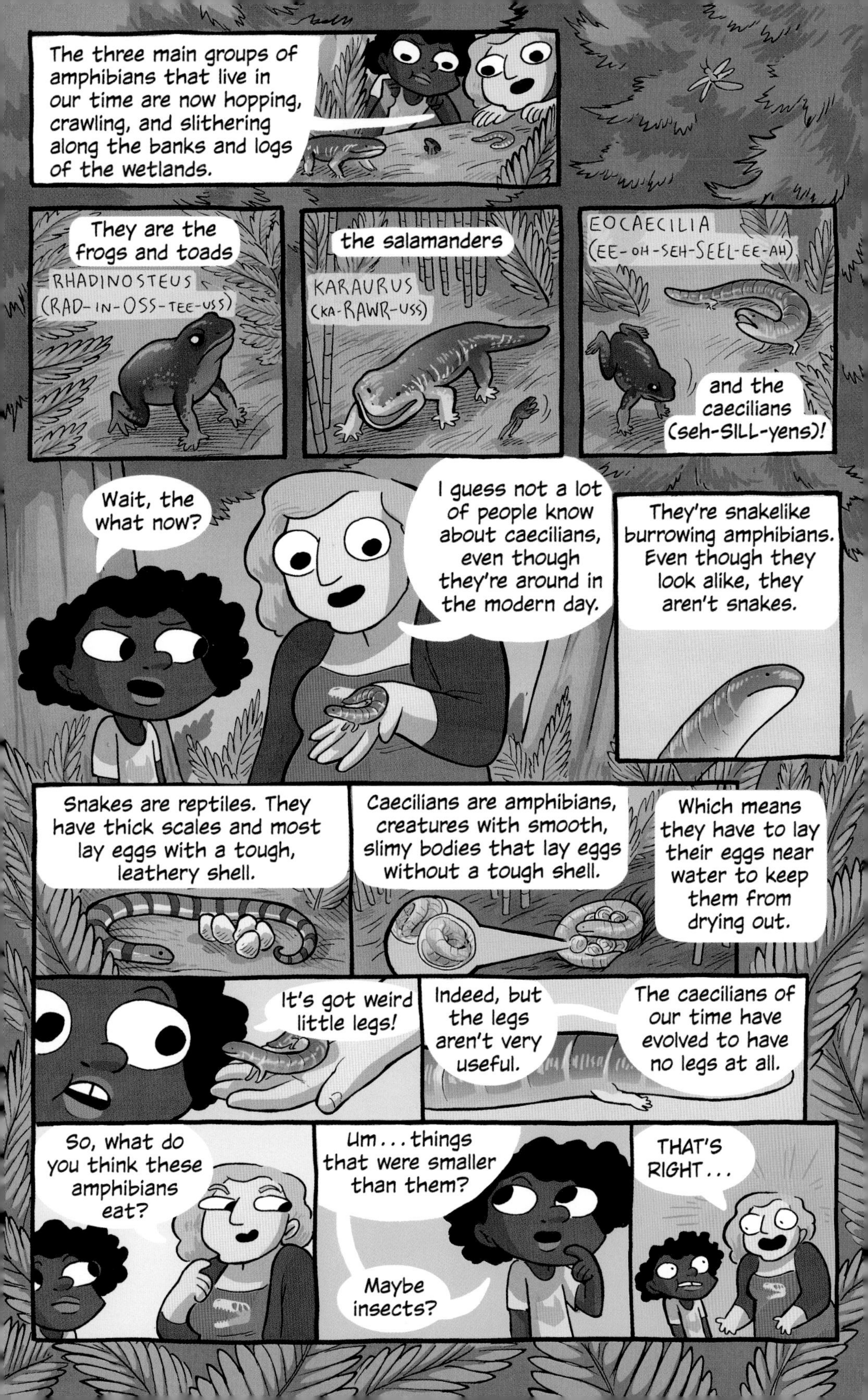
The three main groups of amphibians that live in our time are now hopping, crawling, and slithering along the banks and logs of the wetlands.
They are the frogs and toads
RHADINOSTEUS (RAD-IN-OSS-TEE-USS)
the salamanders
KARAURUS (KA-RAWR-USS)
EOCAECILIA (EE-OH-SEH-SEEL-EE-AH)
and the caecilians (seh-SILL-yens)!
Wait, the what now?
I guess not a lot of people know about caecilians, even though they're around in the modern day.
They're snakelike burrowing amphibians. Even though they look alike, they aren't snakes.
Snakes are reptiles. They have thick scales and most lay eggs with a tough, leathery shell.
Caecilians are amphibians, creatures with smooth, slimy bodies that lay eggs without a tough shell.
Which means they have to lay their eggs near water to keep them from drying out.
It's got weird little legs!
Indeed, but the legs aren't very useful.
The caecilians of our time have evolved to have no legs at all.
So, what do you think these amphibians eat?
Um . . . things that were smaller than them?
Maybe insects?
THAT'S RIGHT . . .

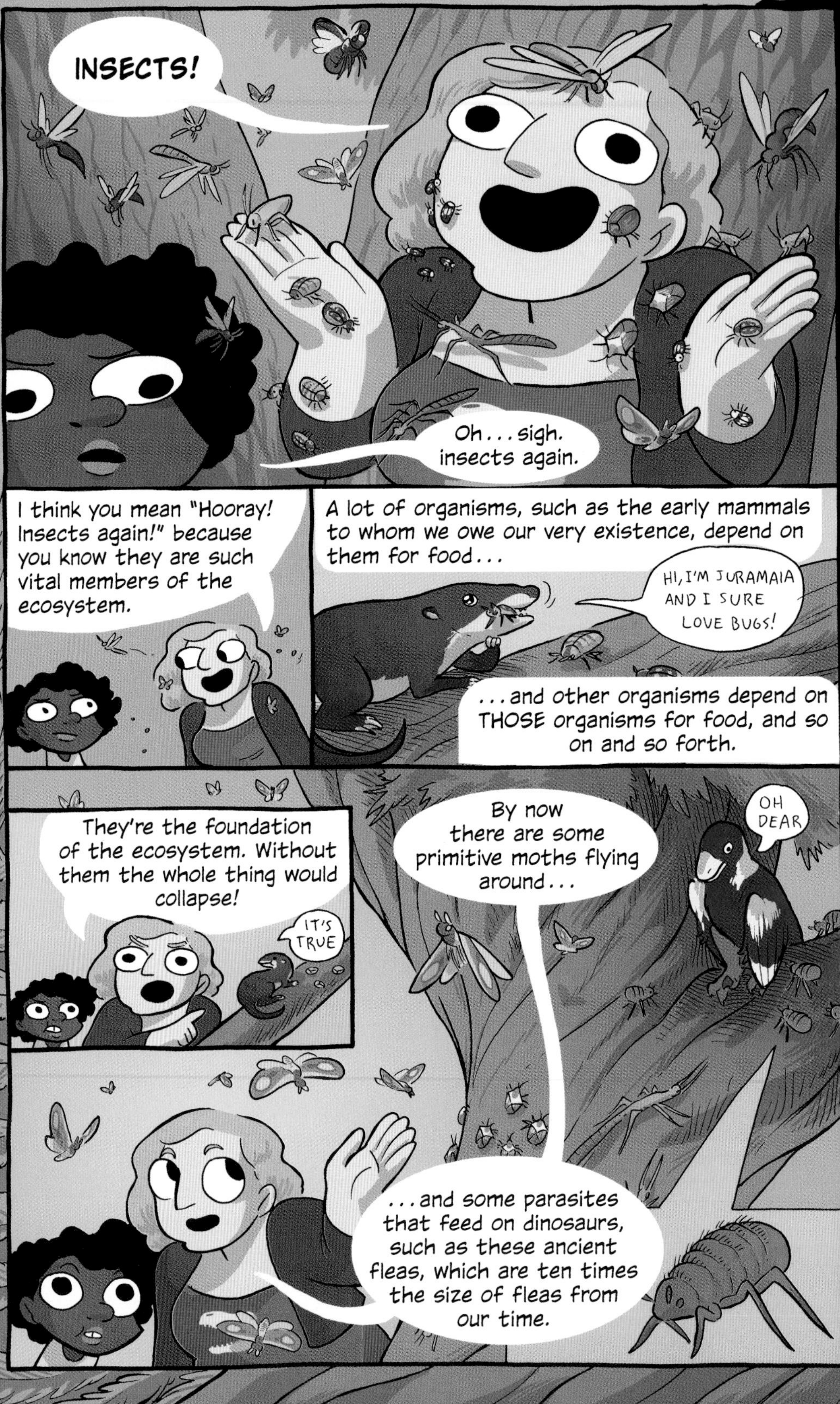
INSECTS!
Oh... sigh. insects again.
I think you mean "Hooray! Insects again!" because you know they are such vital members of the ecosystem.
A lot of organisms, such as the early mammals to whom we owe our very existence, depend on them for food...
HI, I'M JURAMAIA AND I SURE LOVE BUGS!
...and other organisms depend on THOSE organisms for food, and so on and so forth.
They're the foundation of the ecosystem. Without them the whole thing would collapse!
IT'S TRUE
By now there are some primitive moths flying around...
OH DEAR
...and some parasites that feed on dinosaurs, such as these ancient fleas, which are ten times the size of fleas from our time.

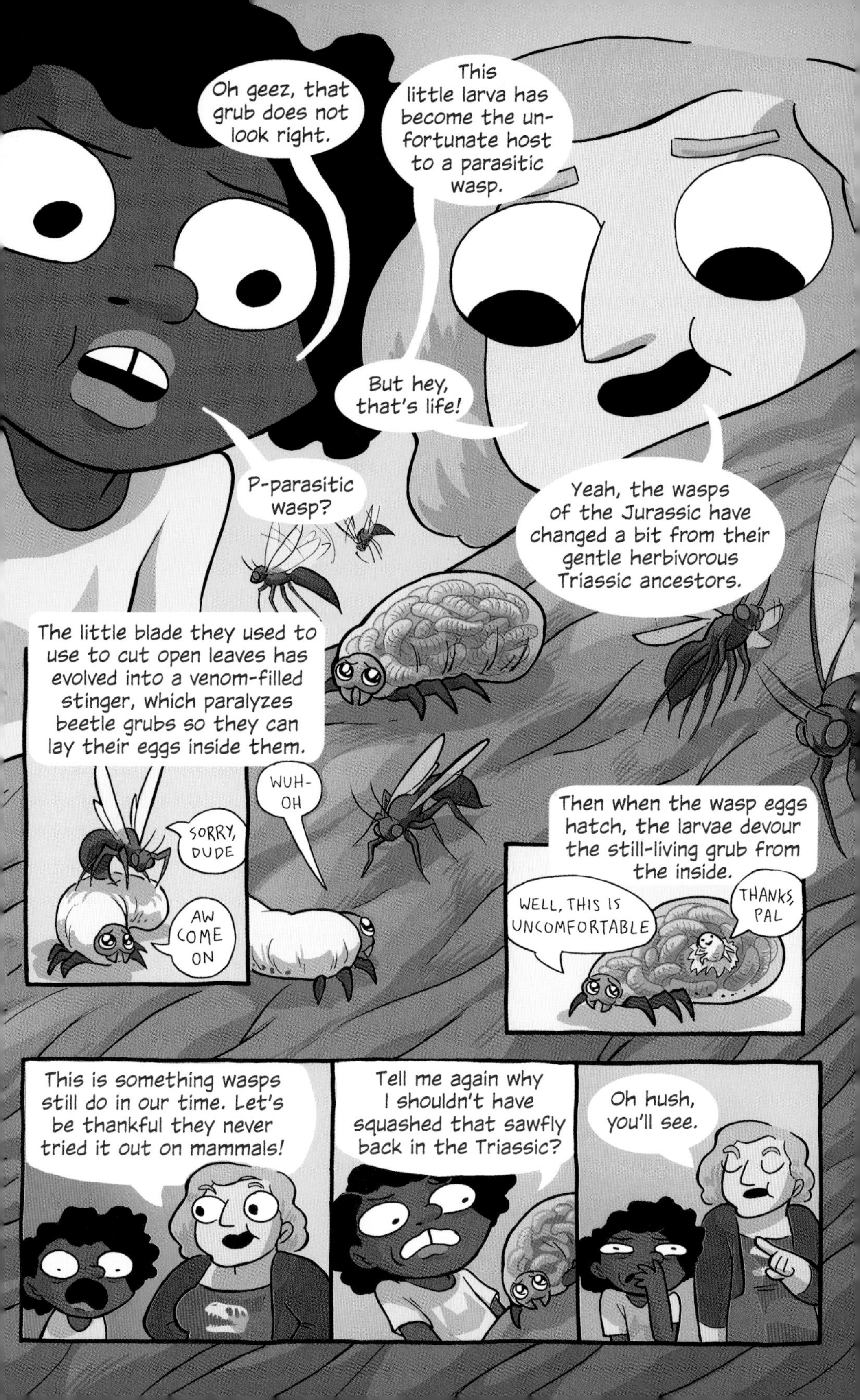
Oh geez, that grub does not look right.
This little larva has become the unfortunate host to a parasitic wasp.
But hey, that's life!
P-parasitic wasp?
Yeah, the wasps of the Jurassic have changed a bit from their gentle herbivorous Triassic ancestors.
The little blade they used to use to cut open leaves has evolved into a venom-filled stinger, which paralyzes beetle grubs so they can lay their eggs inside them.
SORRY, DUDE
WUH-OH
AW COME ON
Then when the wasp eggs hatch, the larvae devour the still-living grub from the inside.
WELL, THIS IS UNCOMFORTABLE
THANKS, PAL
This is something wasps still do in our time. Let's be thankful they never tried it out on mammals!
Tell me again why I shouldn't have squashed that sawfly back in the Triassic?
Oh hush, you'll see.

I know what you're probably wondering...

When am I gonna see a T. rex?

Oh...no, I figured you'd be wondering "How did feathers evolve to be so great for flying if they started out as just a bunch of protofeather fluff?"

Now that you mention it, I guess that is a little mysterious.

Good, because I'm gonna tell you about it right now!

Protofeathers, as you've seen, are single-stranded and hairlike.

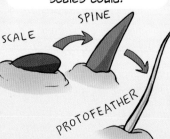

They're mutated scales that helped keep dinosaurs at the right temperature much better than regular scales could.

SPINE
SCALE
PROTOFEATHER

Over the generations, protofeathers kept mutating and getting better and better at keeping dinosaurs and their eggs well insulated.

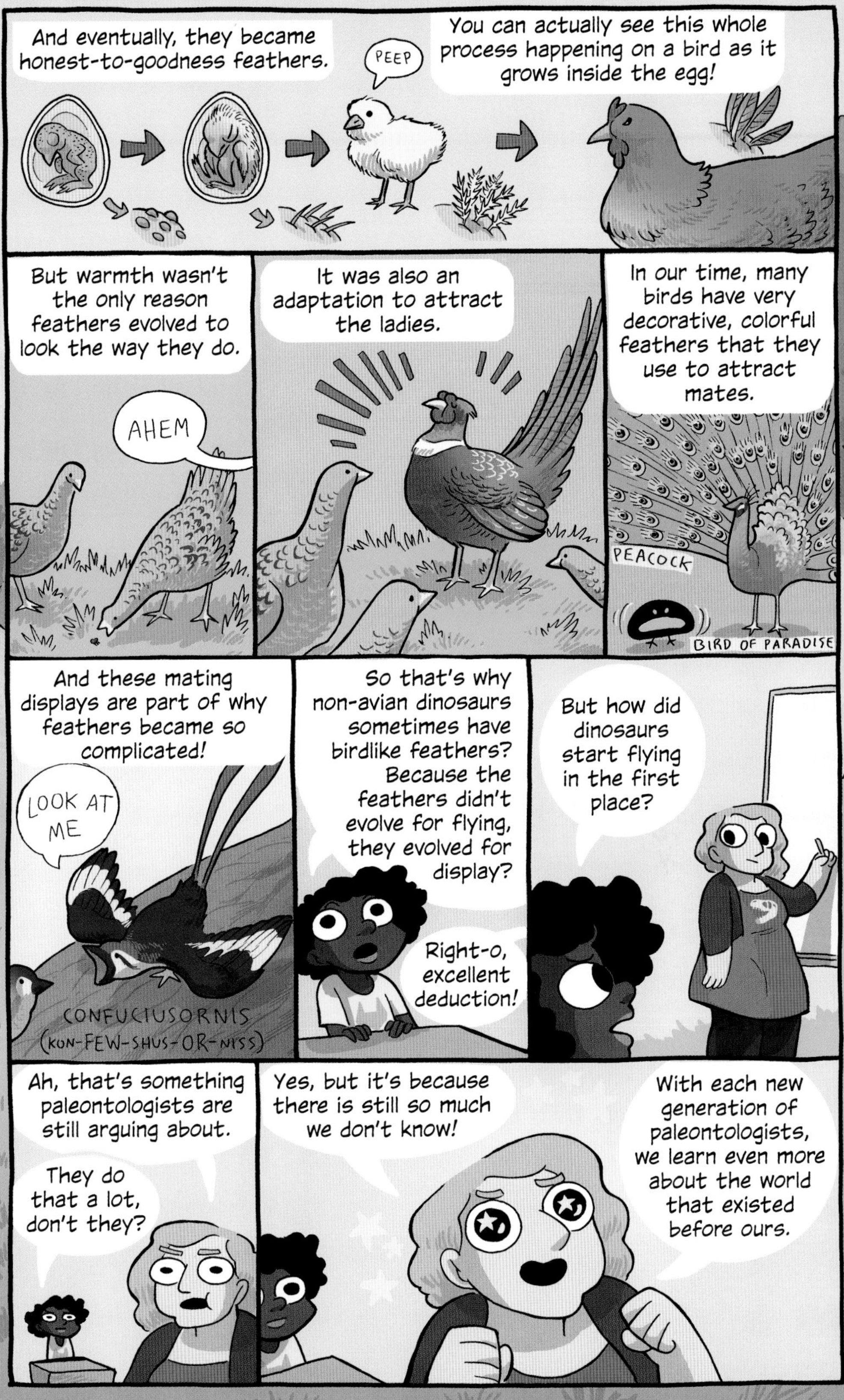
And eventually, they became honest-to-goodness feathers.
PEEP
You can actually see this whole process happening on a bird as it grows inside the egg!
But warmth wasn't the only reason feathers evolved to look the way they do.
AHEM
It was also an adaptation to attract the ladies.
In our time, many birds have very decorative, colorful feathers that they use to attract mates.
PEACOCK
BIRD OF PARADISE
And these mating displays are part of why feathers became so complicated!
LOOK AT ME
CONFUCIUSORNIS
(KON-FEW-SHUS-OR-NISS)
So that's why non-avian dinosaurs sometimes have birdlike feathers? Because the feathers didn't evolve for flying, they evolved for display?
Right-o, excellent deduction!
But how did dinosaurs start flying in the first place?
Ah, that's something paleontologists are still arguing about.
They do that a lot, don't they?
Yes, but it's because there is still so much we don't know!
With each new generation of paleontologists, we learn even more about the world that existed before ours.

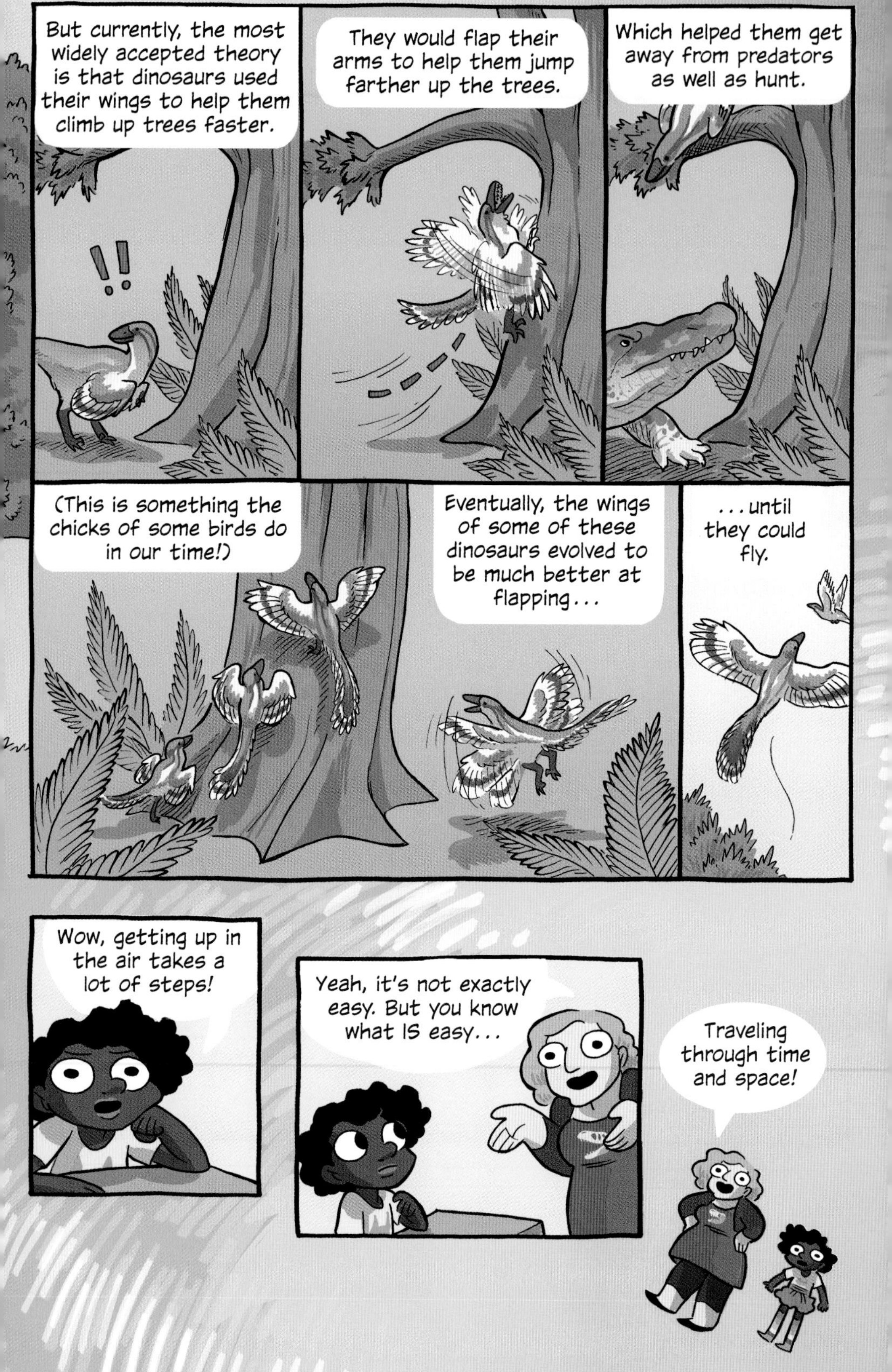

But currently, the most widely accepted theory is that dinosaurs used their wings to help them climb up trees faster.
!!
They would flap their arms to help them jump farther up the trees.
Which helped them get away from predators as well as hunt.
(This is something the chicks of some birds do in our time!)
Eventually, the wings of some of these dinosaurs evolved to be much better at flapping...
...until they could fly.
Wow, getting up in the air takes a lot of steps!
Yeah, it's not exactly easy. But you know what IS easy...
Traveling through time and space!

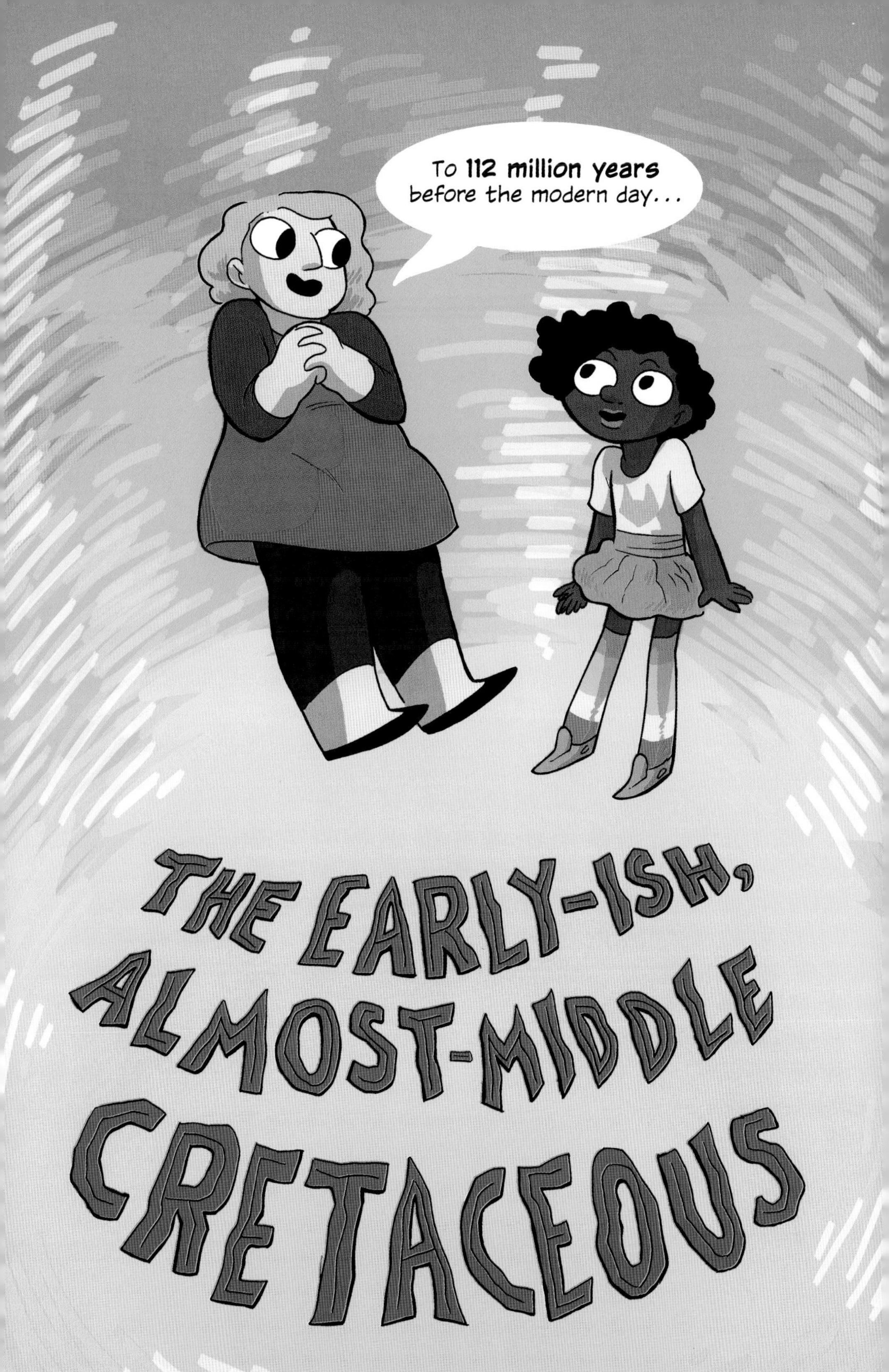
To **112 million years** before the modern day...
THE EARLY-ISH, ALMOST-MIDDLE CRETACEOUS

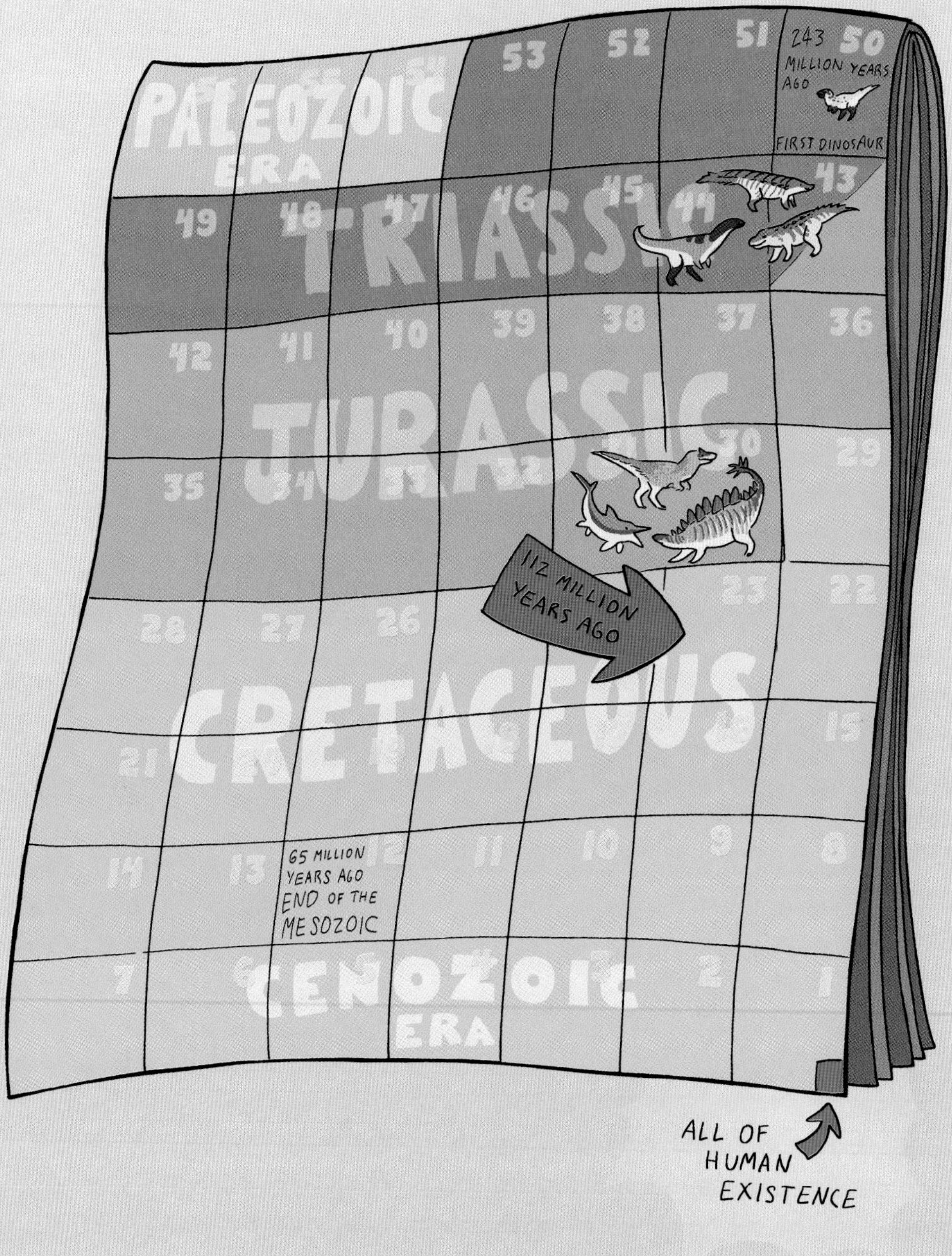
243 MILLION YEARS AGO
FIRST DINOSAUR
PALEOZOIC ERA
TRIASSIC
JURASSIC
112 MILLION YEARS AGO
CRETACEOUS
65 MILLION YEARS AGO END OF THE MESOZOIC
CENOZOIC ERA
ALL OF HUMAN EXISTENCE

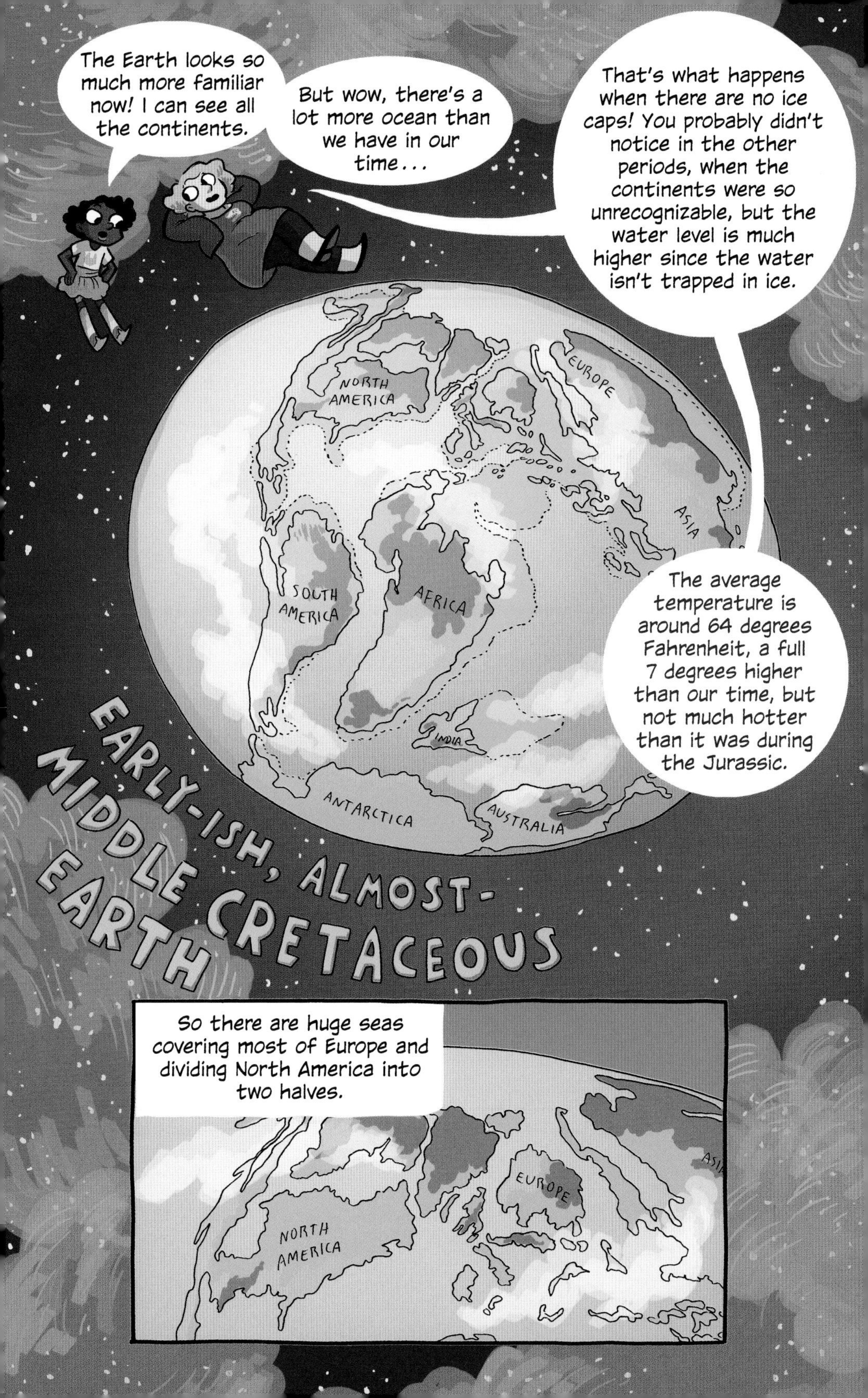
The Earth looks so much more familiar now! I can see all the continents.
But wow, there's a lot more ocean than we have in our time...
That's what happens when there are no ice caps! You probably didn't notice in the other periods, when the continents were so unrecognizable, but the water level is much higher since the water isn't trapped in ice.
NORTH AMERICA
EUROPE
ASIA
SOUTH AMERICA
AFRICA
INDIA
ANTARCTICA
AUSTRALIA
The average temperature is around 64 degrees Fahrenheit, a full 7 degrees higher than our time, but not much hotter than it was during the Jurassic.
EARLY-ISH, ALMOST-MIDDLE CRETACEOUS EARTH
So there are huge seas covering most of Europe and dividing North America into two halves.
EUROPE
NORTH AMERICA

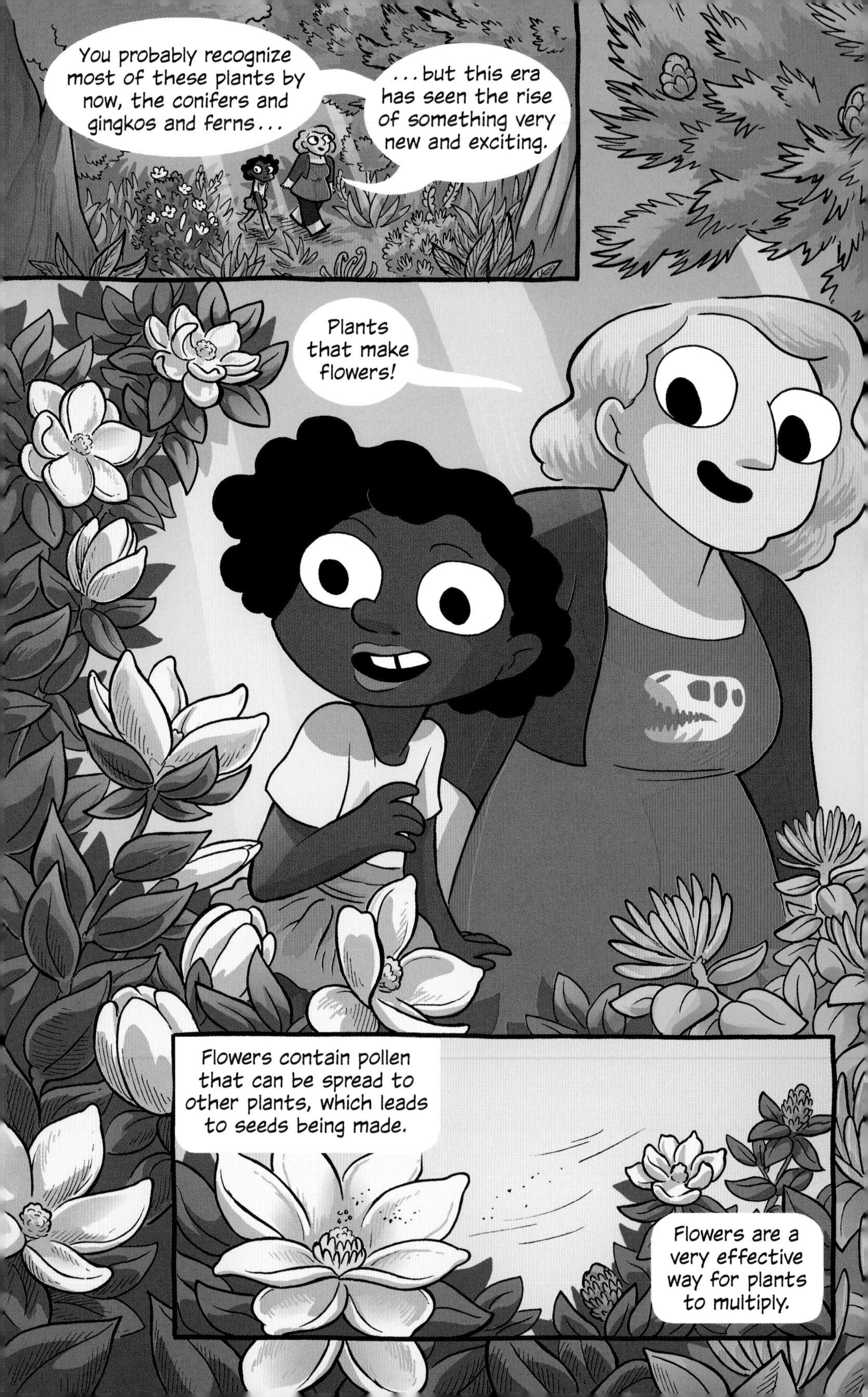
You probably recognize most of these plants by now, the conifers and gingkos and ferns...
...but this era has seen the rise of something very new and exciting.
Plants that make flowers!
Flowers contain pollen that can be spread to other plants, which leads to seeds being made.
Flowers are a very effective way for plants to multiply.

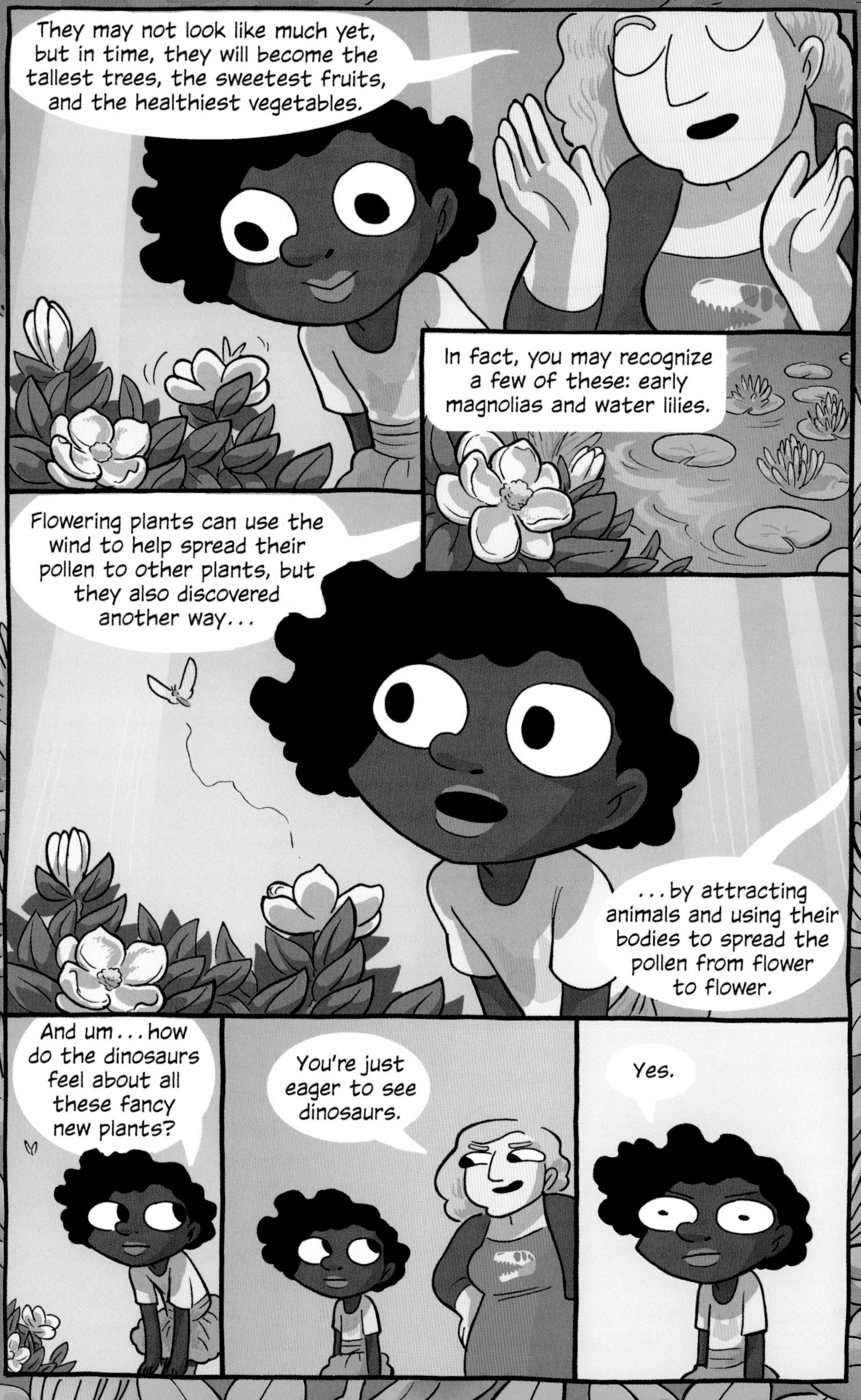

They may not look like much yet, but in time, they will become the tallest trees, the sweetest fruits, and the healthiest vegetables.
In fact, you may recognize a few of these: early magnolias and water lilies.
Flowering plants can use the wind to help spread their pollen to other plants, but they also discovered another way...
...by attracting animals and using their bodies to spread the pollen from flower to flower.
And um...how do the dinosaurs feel about all these fancy new plants?
You're just eager to see dinosaurs.
Yes.

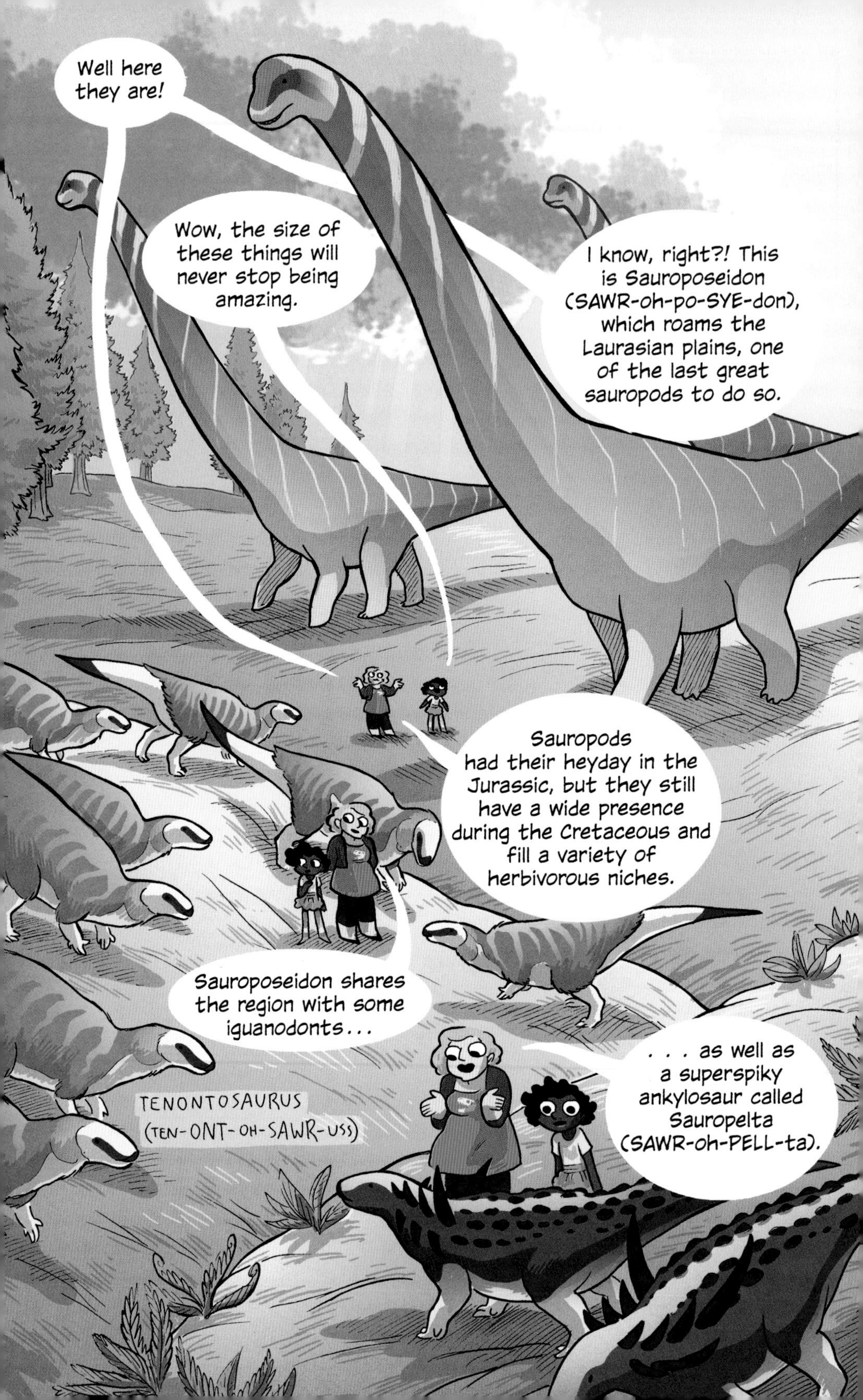
Well here they are!
Wow, the size of these things will never stop being amazing.
I know, right?! This is Sauroposeidon (SAWR-oh-po-SYE-don), which roams the Laurasian plains, one of the last great sauropods to do so.
Sauropods had their heyday in the Jurassic, but they still have a wide presence during the Cretaceous and fill a variety of herbivorous niches.
Sauroposeidon shares the region with some iguanodonts . . .
TENONTOSAURUS (TEN-ONT-OH-SAWR-USS)
. . . as well as a superspiky ankylosaur called Sauropelta (SAWR-oh-PELL-ta).

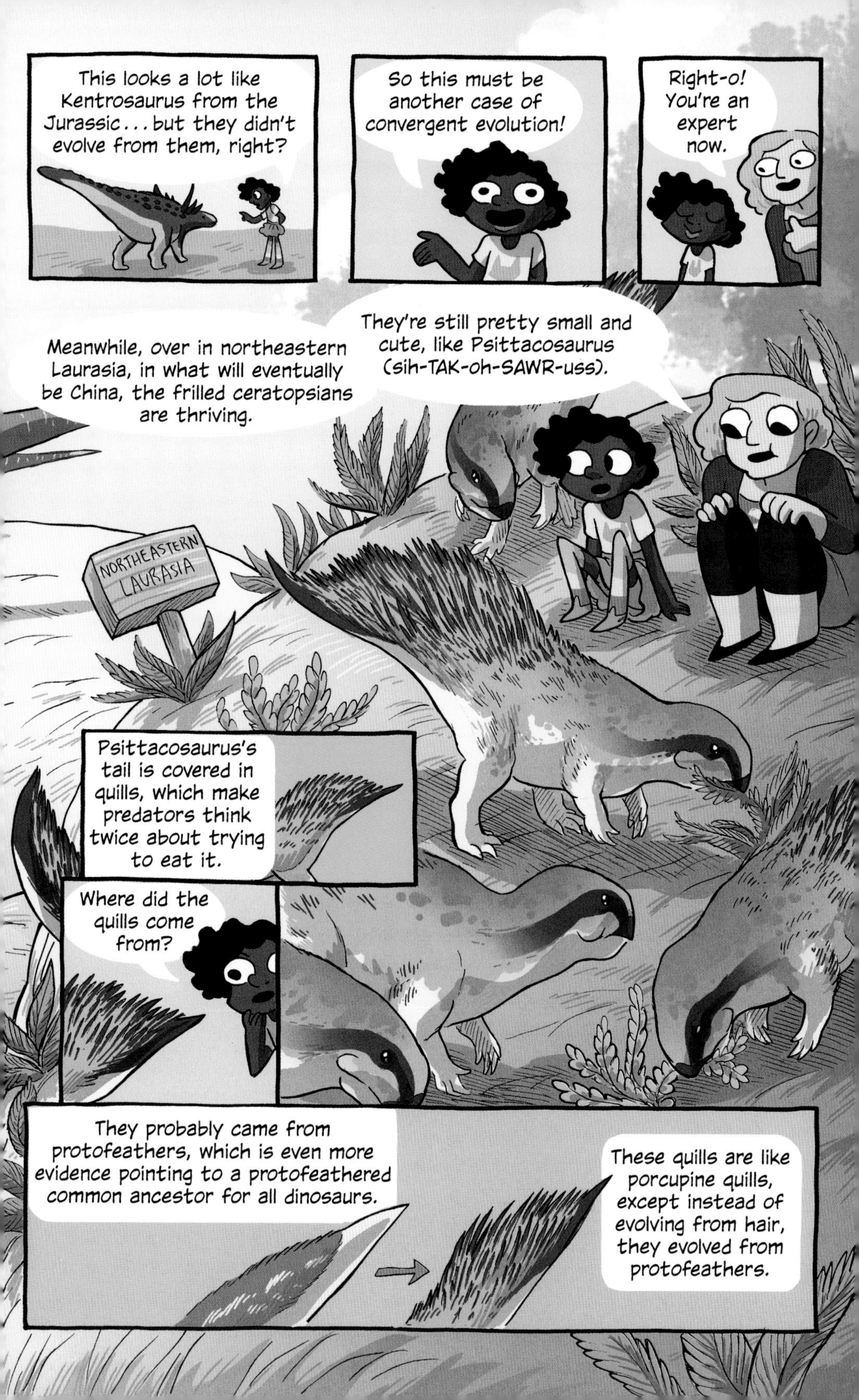
This looks a lot like Kentrosaurus from the Jurassic . . . but they didn't evolve from them, right?
So this must be another case of convergent evolution!
Right-o! You're an expert now.
Meanwhile, over in northeastern Laurasia, in what will eventually be China, the frilled ceratopsians are thriving.
They're still pretty small and cute, like Psittacosaurus (sih-TAK-oh-SAWR-uss).
NORTHEASTERN LAURASIA
Psittacosaurus's tail is covered in quills, which make predators think twice about trying to eat it.
Where did the quills come from?
They probably came from protofeathers, which is even more evidence pointing to a protofeathered common ancestor for all dinosaurs.
These quills are like porcupine quills, except instead of evolving from hair, they evolved from protofeathers.

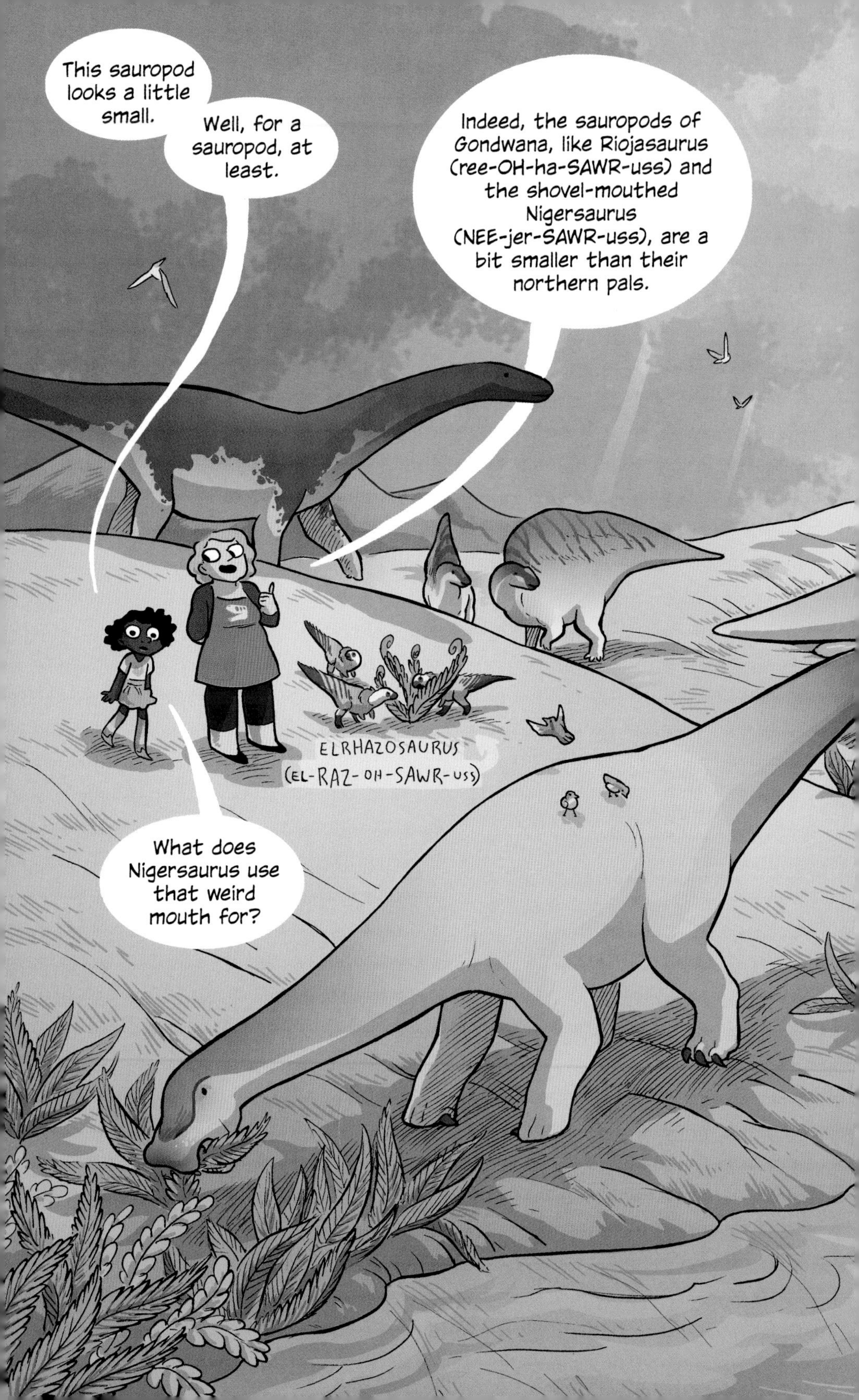
This sauropod looks a little small.
Well, for a sauropod, at least.
Indeed, the sauropods of Gondwana, like Riojasaurus (ree-OH-ha-SAWR-uss) and the shovel-mouthed Nigersaurus (NEE-jer-SAWR-uss), are a bit smaller than their northern pals.
ELRHAZOSAURUS (EL-RAZ-OH-SAWR-USS)
What does Nigersaurus use that weird mouth for?

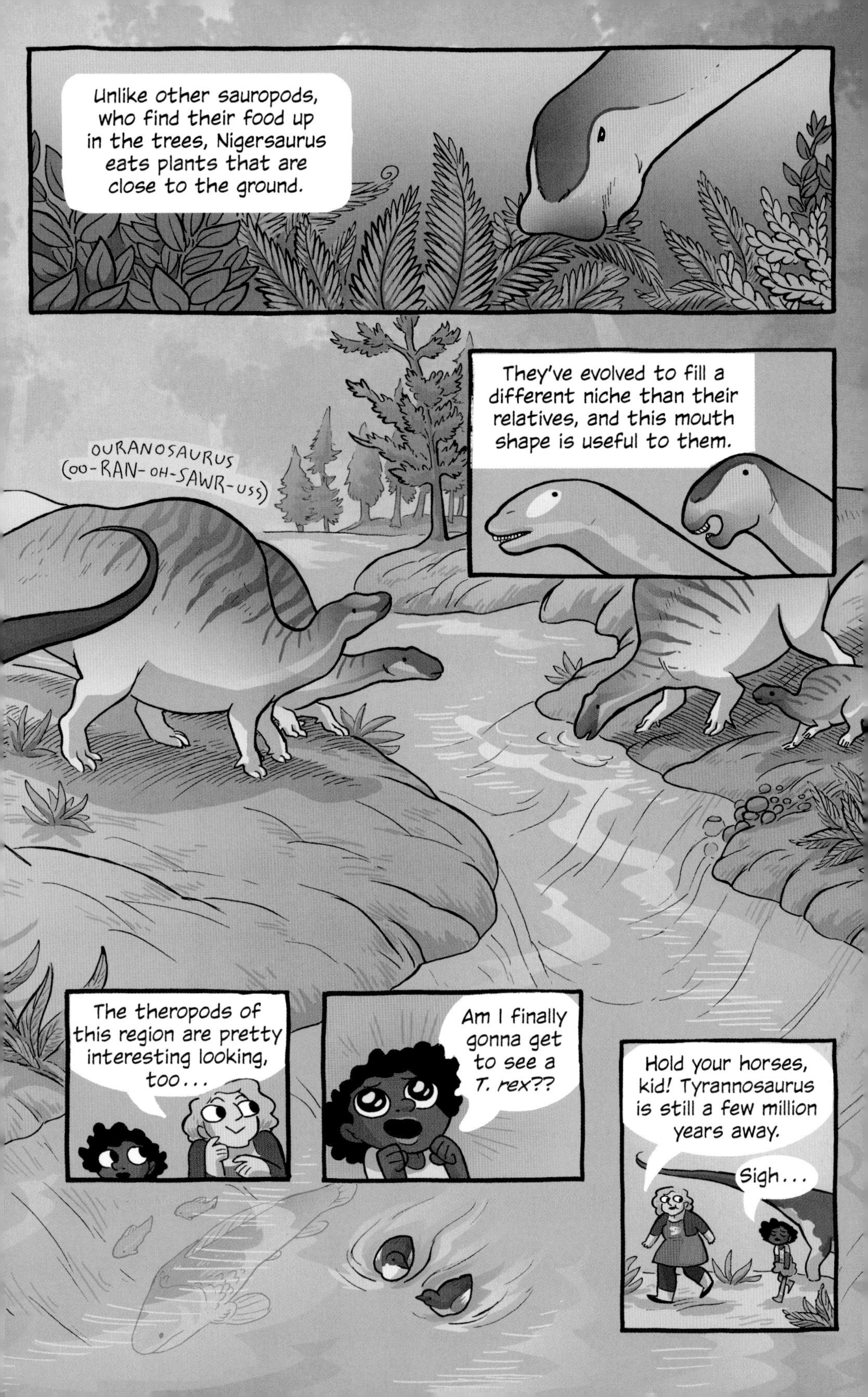
Unlike other sauropods, who find their food up in the trees, Nigersaurus eats plants that are close to the ground.
They've evolved to fill a different niche than their relatives, and this mouth shape is useful to them.
OURANOSAURUS (OO-RAN-OH-SAWR-USS)
The theropods of this region are pretty interesting looking, too...
Am I finally gonna get to see a *T. rex*??
Hold your horses, kid! Tyrannosaurus is still a few million years away.
Sigh...

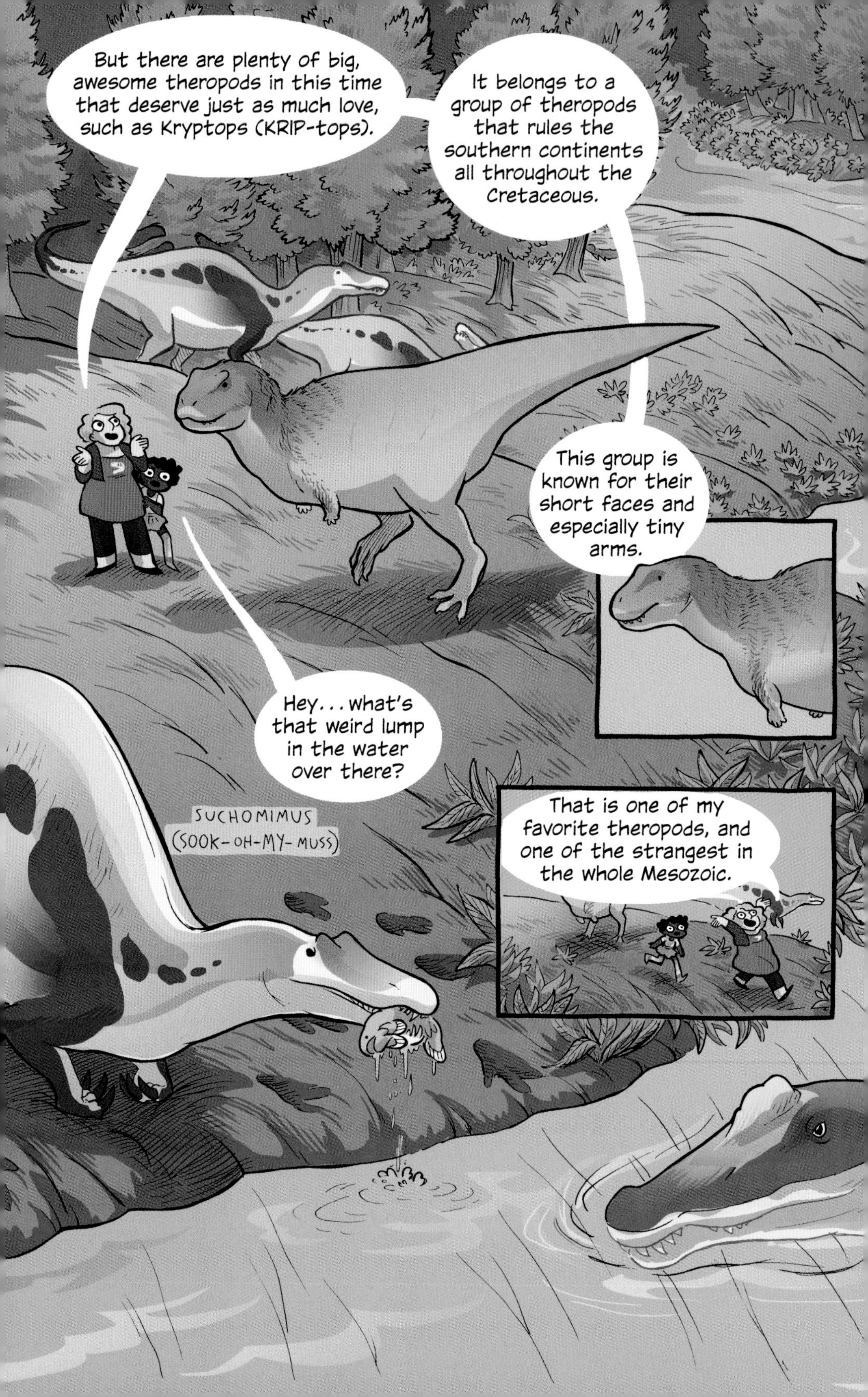
But there are plenty of big, awesome theropods in this time that deserve just as much love, such as Kryptops (KRIP-tops).
It belongs to a group of theropods that rules the southern continents all throughout the Cretaceous.
This group is known for their short faces and especially tiny arms.
Hey. . . what's that weird lump in the water over there?
SUCHOMIMUS (SOOK-OH-MY-MUSS)
That is one of my favorite theropods, and one of the strangest in the whole Mesozoic.

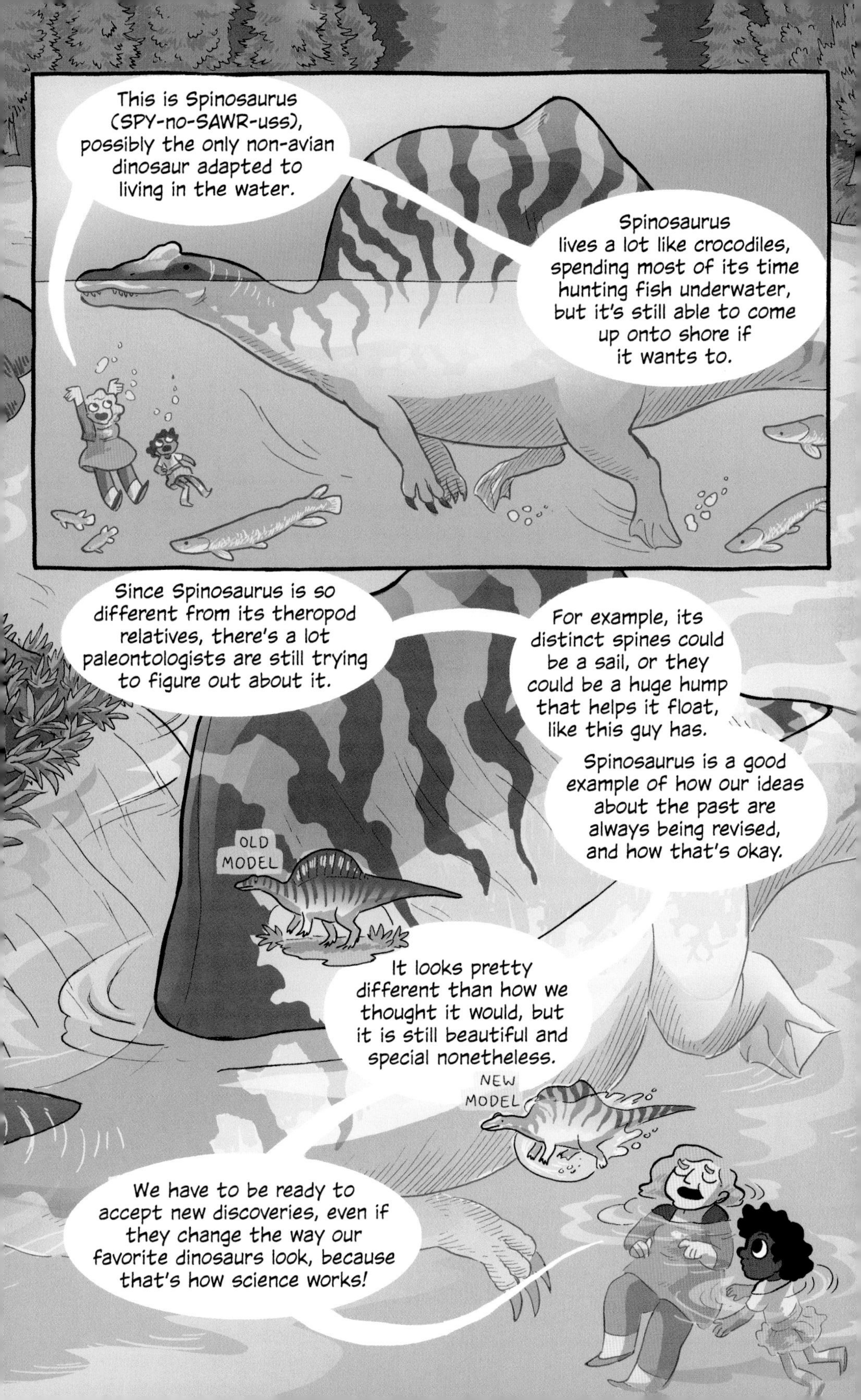
This is Spinosaurus (SPY-no-SAWR-uss), possibly the only non-avian dinosaur adapted to living in the water.
Spinosaurus lives a lot like crocodiles, spending most of its time hunting fish underwater, but it's still able to come up onto shore if it wants to.
Since Spinosaurus is so different from its theropod relatives, there's a lot paleontologists are still trying to figure out about it.
For example, its distinct spines could be a sail, or they could be a huge hump that helps it float, like this guy has.
Spinosaurus is a good example of how our ideas about the past are always being revised, and how that's okay.
OLD MODEL
It looks pretty different than how we thought it would, but it is still beautiful and special nonetheless.
NEW MODEL
We have to be ready to accept new discoveries, even if they change the way our favorite dinosaurs look, because that's how science works!

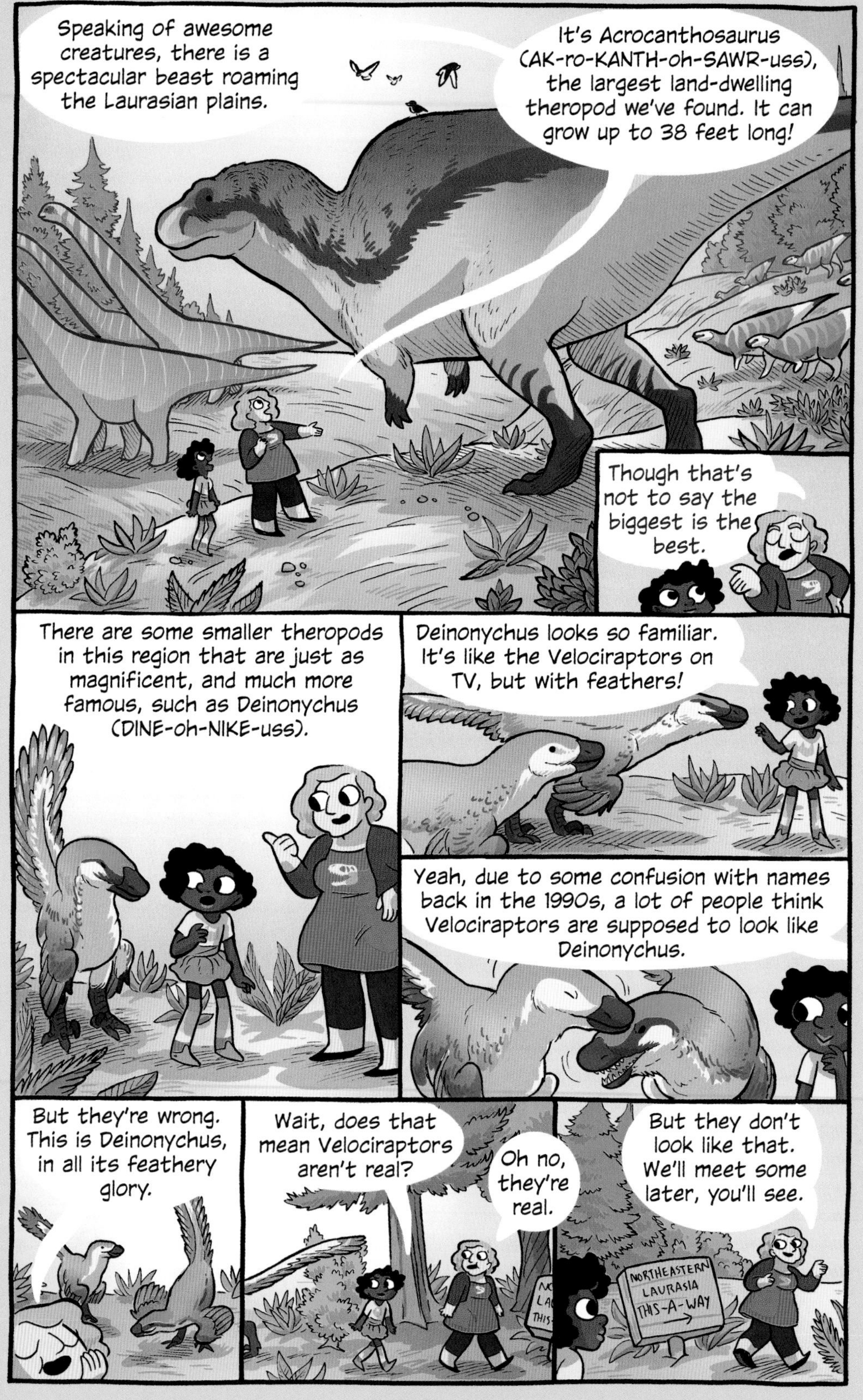
Speaking of awesome creatures, there is a spectacular beast roaming the Laurasian plains.
It's Acrocanthosaurus (AK-ro-KANTH-oh-SAWR-uss), the largest land-dwelling theropod we've found. It can grow up to 38 feet long!
Though that's not to say the biggest is the best.
There are some smaller theropods in this region that are just as magnificent, and much more famous, such as Deinonychus (DINE-oh-NIKE-uss).
Deinonychus looks so familiar. It's like the Velociraptors on TV, but with feathers!
Yeah, due to some confusion with names back in the 1990s, a lot of people think Velociraptors are supposed to look like Deinonychus.
But they're wrong. This is Deinonychus, in all its feathery glory.
Wait, does that mean Velociraptors aren't real?
Oh no, they're real.
But they don't look like that. We'll meet some later, you'll see.
NORTHEASTERN LAURASIA THIS-A-WAY

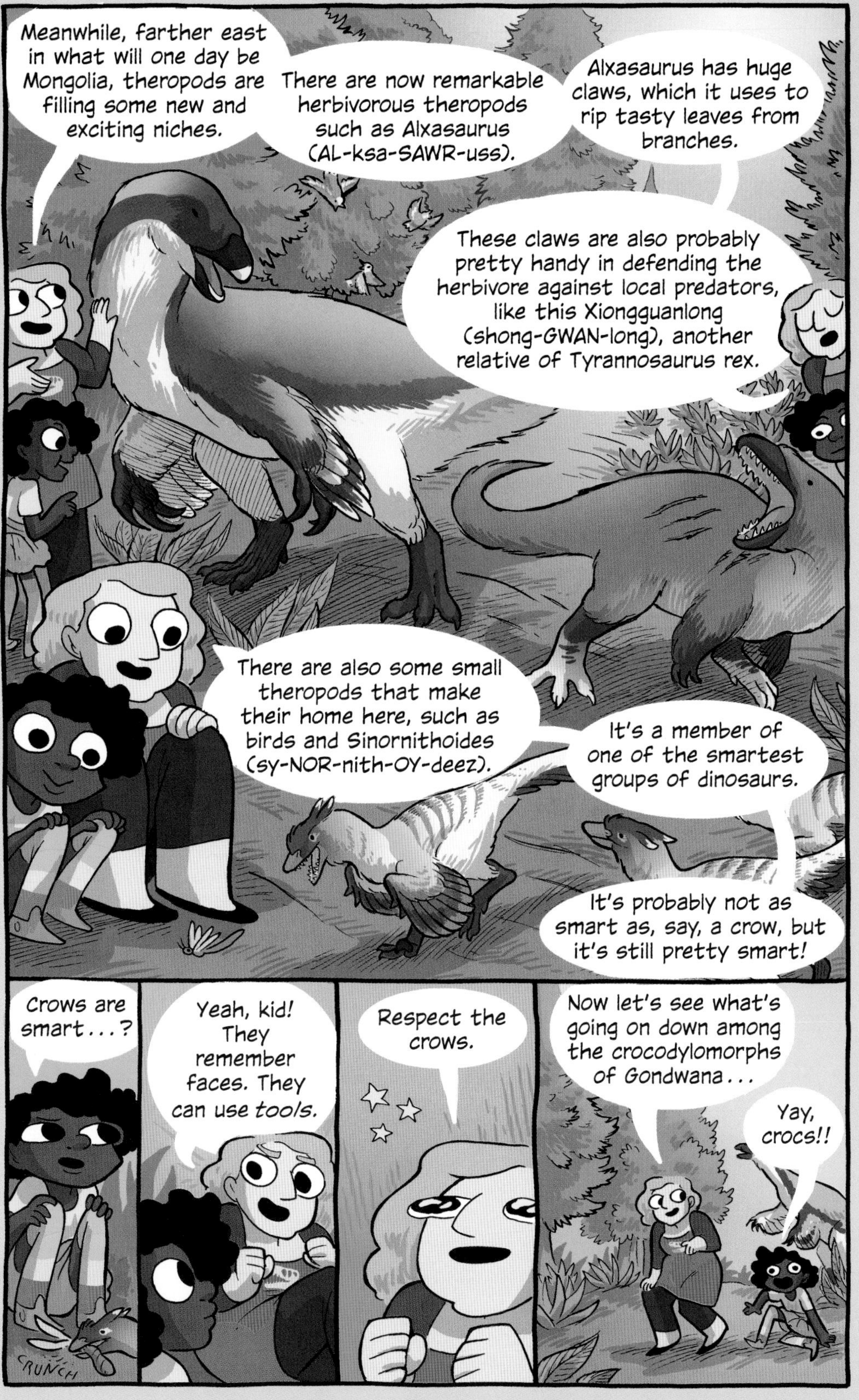
Meanwhile, farther east in what will one day be Mongolia, theropods are filling some new and exciting niches.
There are now remarkable herbivorous theropods such as Alxasaurus (AL-ksa-SAWR-uss).
Alxasaurus has huge claws, which it uses to rip tasty leaves from branches.
These claws are also probably pretty handy in defending the herbivore against local predators, like this Xiongguanlong (shong-GWAN-long), another relative of Tyrannosaurus rex.
There are also some small theropods that make their home here, such as birds and Sinornithoides (sy-NOR-nith-OY-deez).
It's a member of one of the smartest groups of dinosaurs.
It's probably not as smart as, say, a crow, but it's still pretty smart!
Crows are smart . . . ?
CRUNCH
Yeah, kid! They remember faces. They can use *tools*.
Respect the crows.
Now let's see what's going on down among the crocodylomorphs of Gondwana . . .
Yay, crocs!!

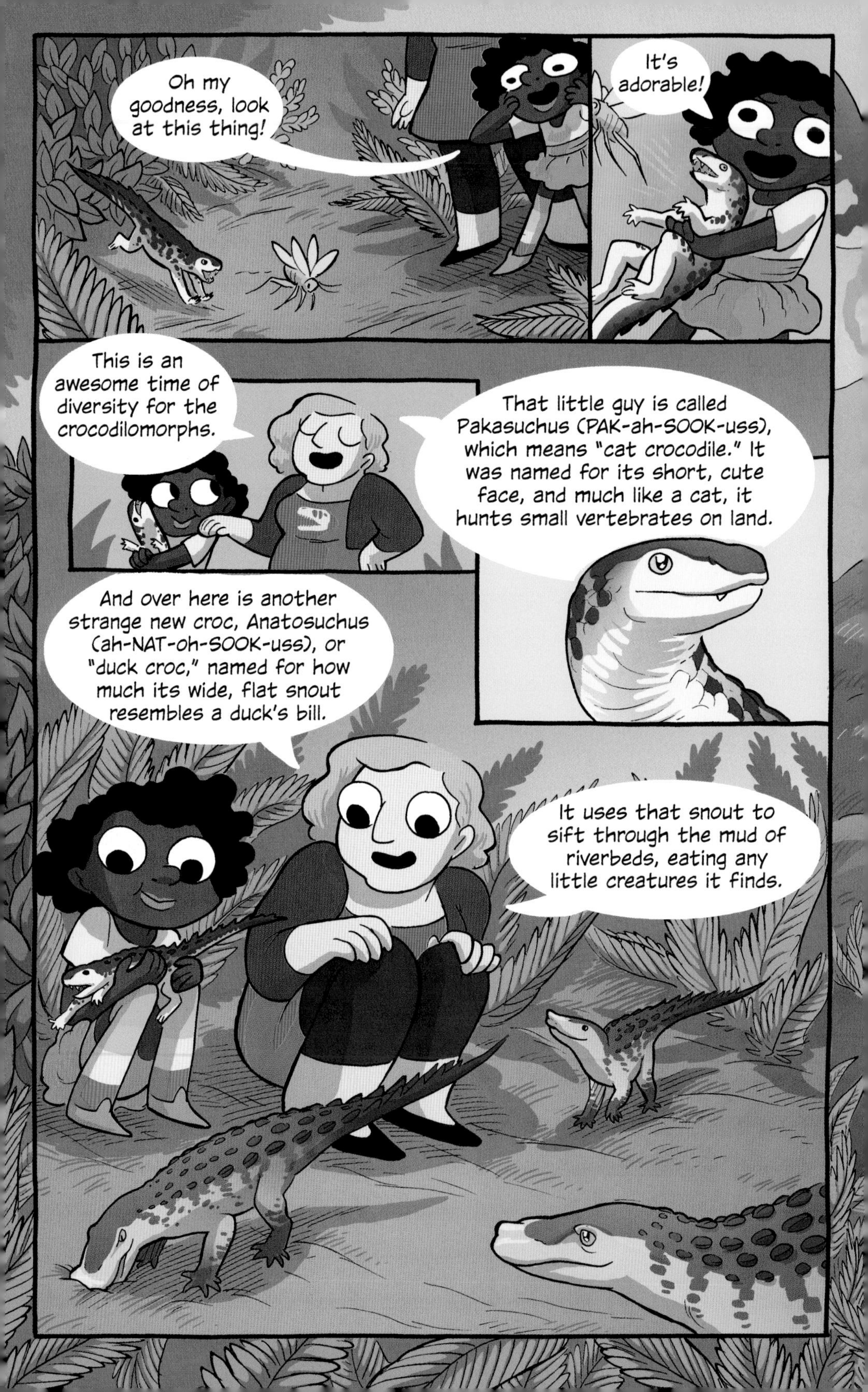
Oh my goodness, look at this thing!
It's adorable!
This is an awesome time of diversity for the crocodilomorphs.
That little guy is called Pakasuchus (PAK-ah-SOOK-uss), which means "cat crocodile." It was named for its short, cute face, and much like a cat, it hunts small vertebrates on land.
And over here is another strange new croc, Anatosuchus (ah-NAT-oh-SOOK-uss), or "duck croc," named for how much its wide, flat snout resembles a duck's bill.
It uses that snout to sift through the mud of riverbeds, eating any little creatures it finds.

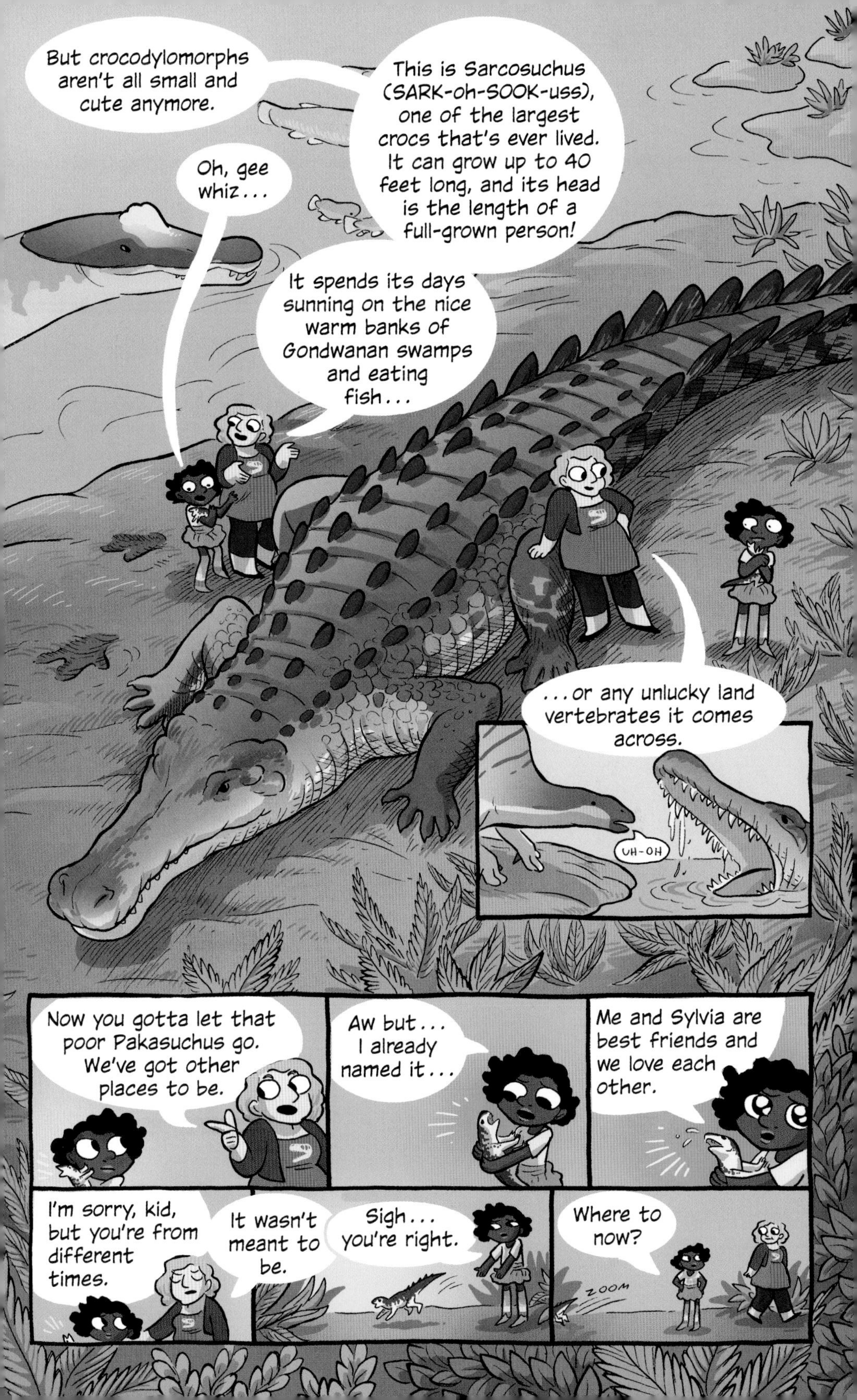
But crocodylomorphs aren't all small and cute anymore.
This is Sarcosuchus (SARK-oh-SOOK-uss), one of the largest crocs that's ever lived. It can grow up to 40 feet long, and its head is the length of a full-grown person!
Oh, gee whiz...
It spends its days sunning on the nice warm banks of Gondwanan swamps and eating fish...
...or any unlucky land vertebrates it comes across.
UH-OH
Now you gotta let that poor Pakasuchus go. We've got other places to be.
Aw but... I already named it...
Me and Sylvia are best friends and we love each other.
I'm sorry, kid, but you're from different times.
It wasn't meant to be.
Sigh... you're right.
ZOOM
Where to now?

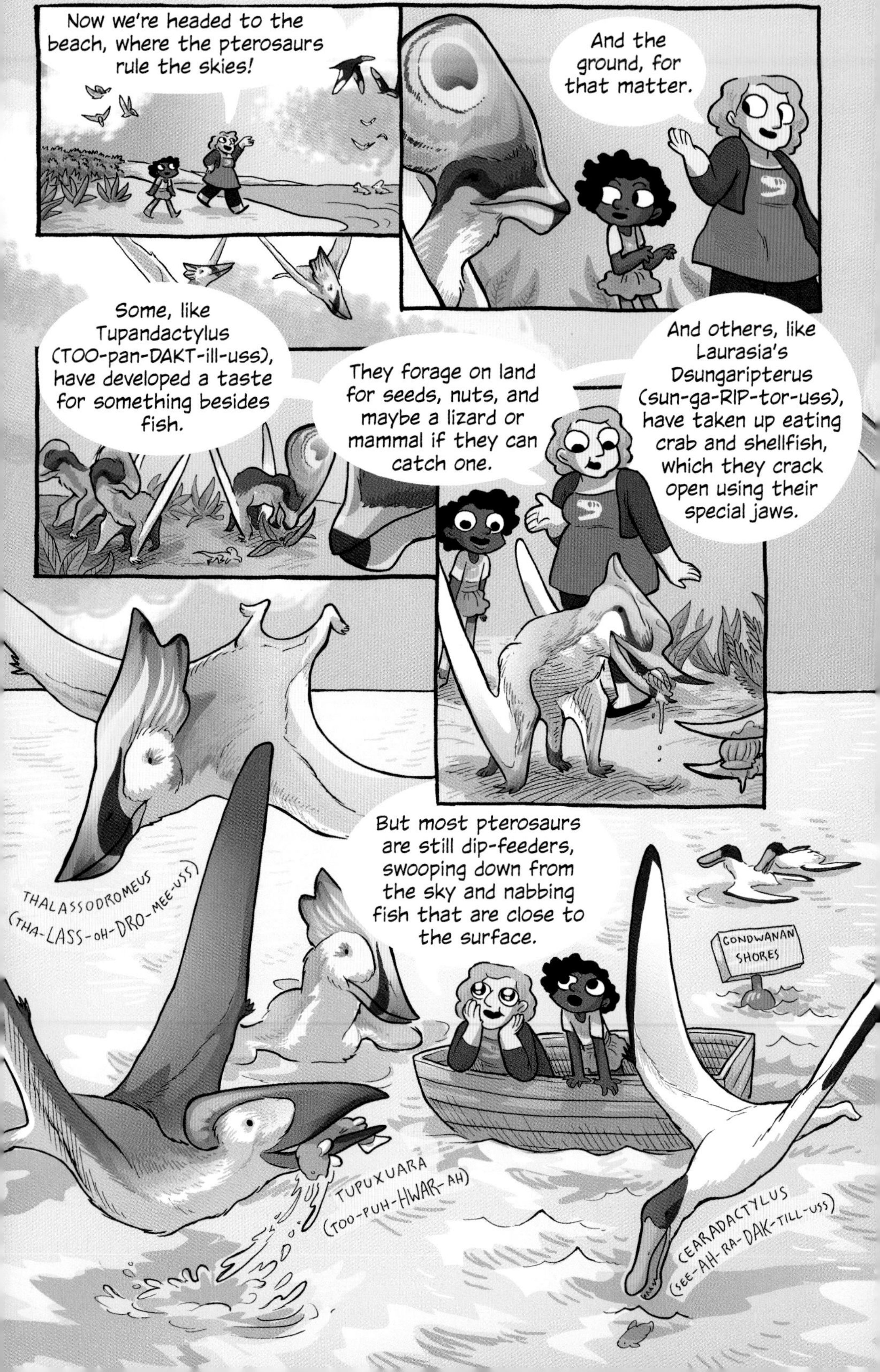
Now we're headed to the beach, where the pterosaurs rule the skies!
And the ground, for that matter.
Some, like Tupandactylus (TOO-pan-DAKT-ill-uss), have developed a taste for something besides fish.
They forage on land for seeds, nuts, and maybe a lizard or mammal if they can catch one.
And others, like Laurasia's Dsungaripterus (sun-ga-RIP-tor-uss), have taken up eating crab and shellfish, which they crack open using their special jaws.
But most pterosaurs are still dip-feeders, swooping down from the sky and nabbing fish that are close to the surface.
THALASSODROMEUS (THA-LASS-OH-DRO-MEE-USS)
GONDWANAN SHORES
TUPUXUARA (TOO-PUH-HWAR-AH)
CEARADACTYLUS (SEE-AH-RA-DAK-TILL-USS)

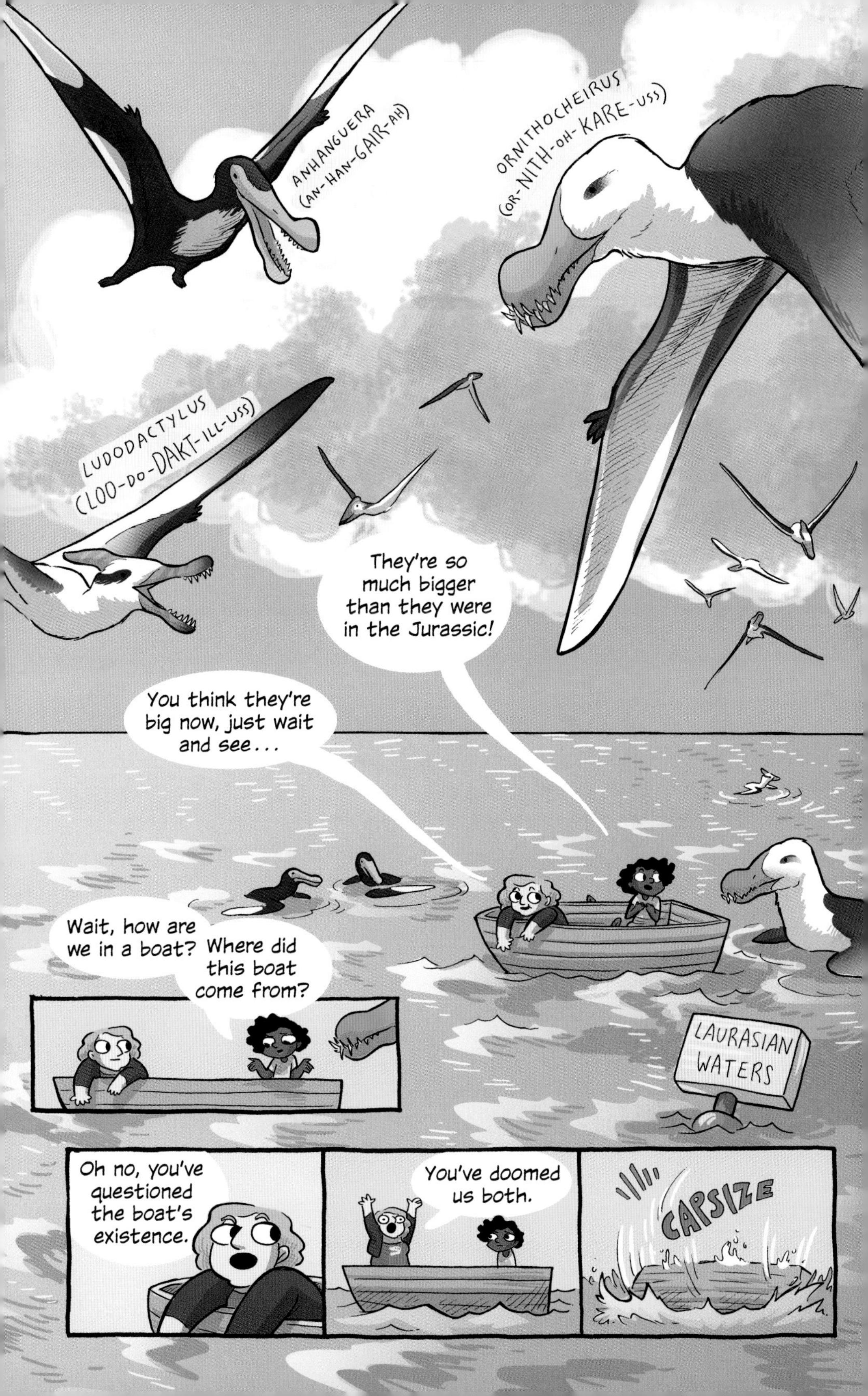
ANHANGUERA
(AN-HAN-GAIR-AH)
ORNITHOCHEIRUS
(OR-NITH-OH-KARE-USS)
LUDODACTYLUS
(LOO-DO-DAKT-ILL-USS)
They're so much bigger than they were in the Jurassic!
You think they're big now, just wait and see...
Wait, how are we in a boat?
Where did this boat come from?
LAURASIAN WATERS
Oh no, you've questioned the boat's existence.
You've doomed us both.
CAPSIZE

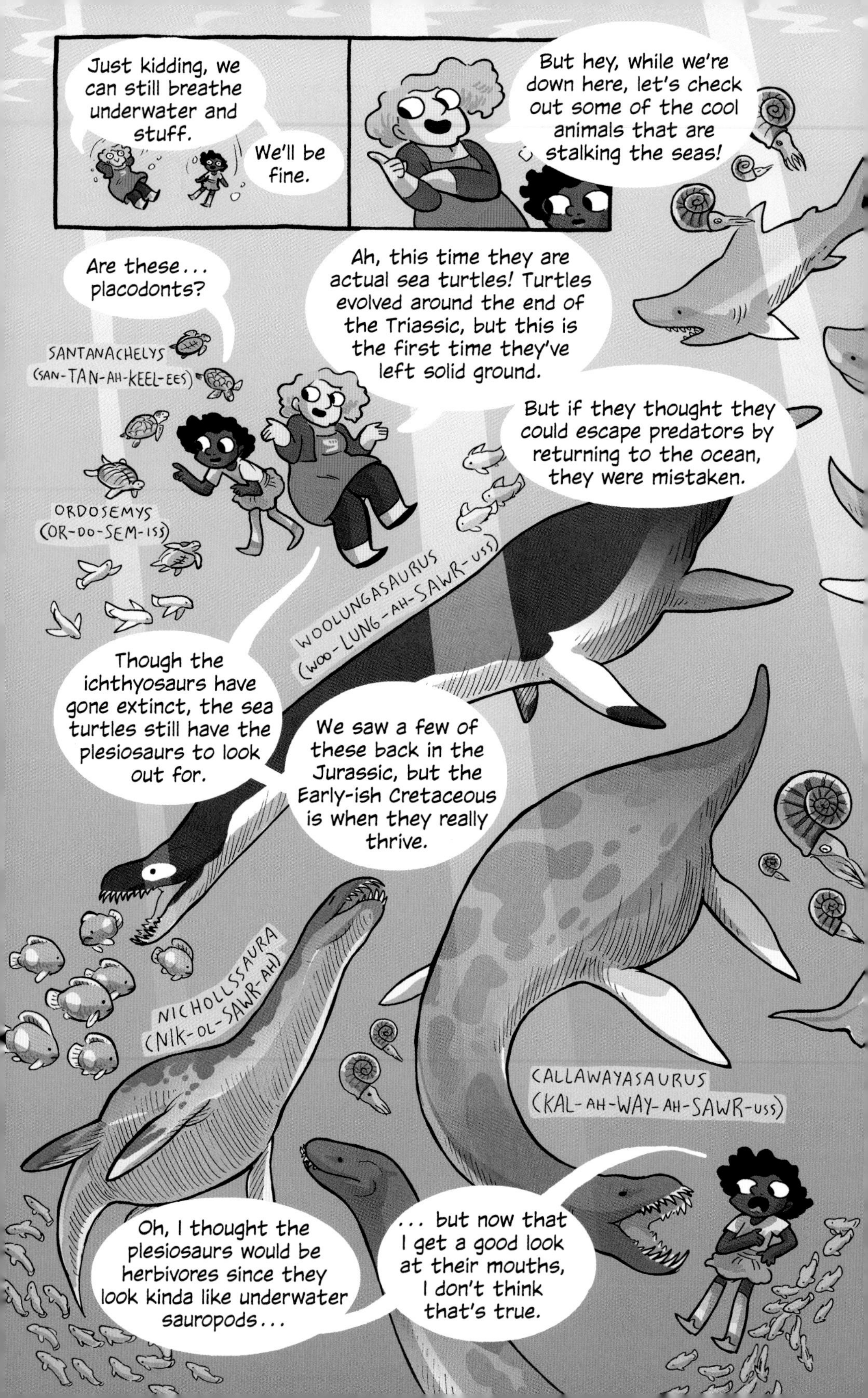

Just kidding, we can still breathe underwater and stuff.
We'll be fine.
But hey, while we're down here, let's check out some of the cool animals that are stalking the seas!
Are these... placodonts?
Ah, this time they are actual sea turtles! Turtles evolved around the end of the Triassic, but this is the first time they've left solid ground.
But if they thought they could escape predators by returning to the ocean, they were mistaken.
SANTANACHELYS (SAN-TAN-AH-KEEL-EES)
ORDOSEMYS (OR-DO-SEM-ISS)
WOOLUNGASAURUS (WOO-LUNG-AH-SAWR-USS)
Though the ichthyosaurs have gone extinct, the sea turtles still have the plesiosaurs to look out for.
We saw a few of these back in the Jurassic, but the Early-ish Cretaceous is when they really thrive.
NICHOLLSSAURA (NIK-OL-SAWR-AH)
CALLAWAYASAURUS (KAL-AH-WAY-AH-SAWR-USS)
Oh, I thought the plesiosaurs would be herbivores since they look kinda like underwater sauropods...
... but now that I get a good look at their mouths, I don't think that's true.

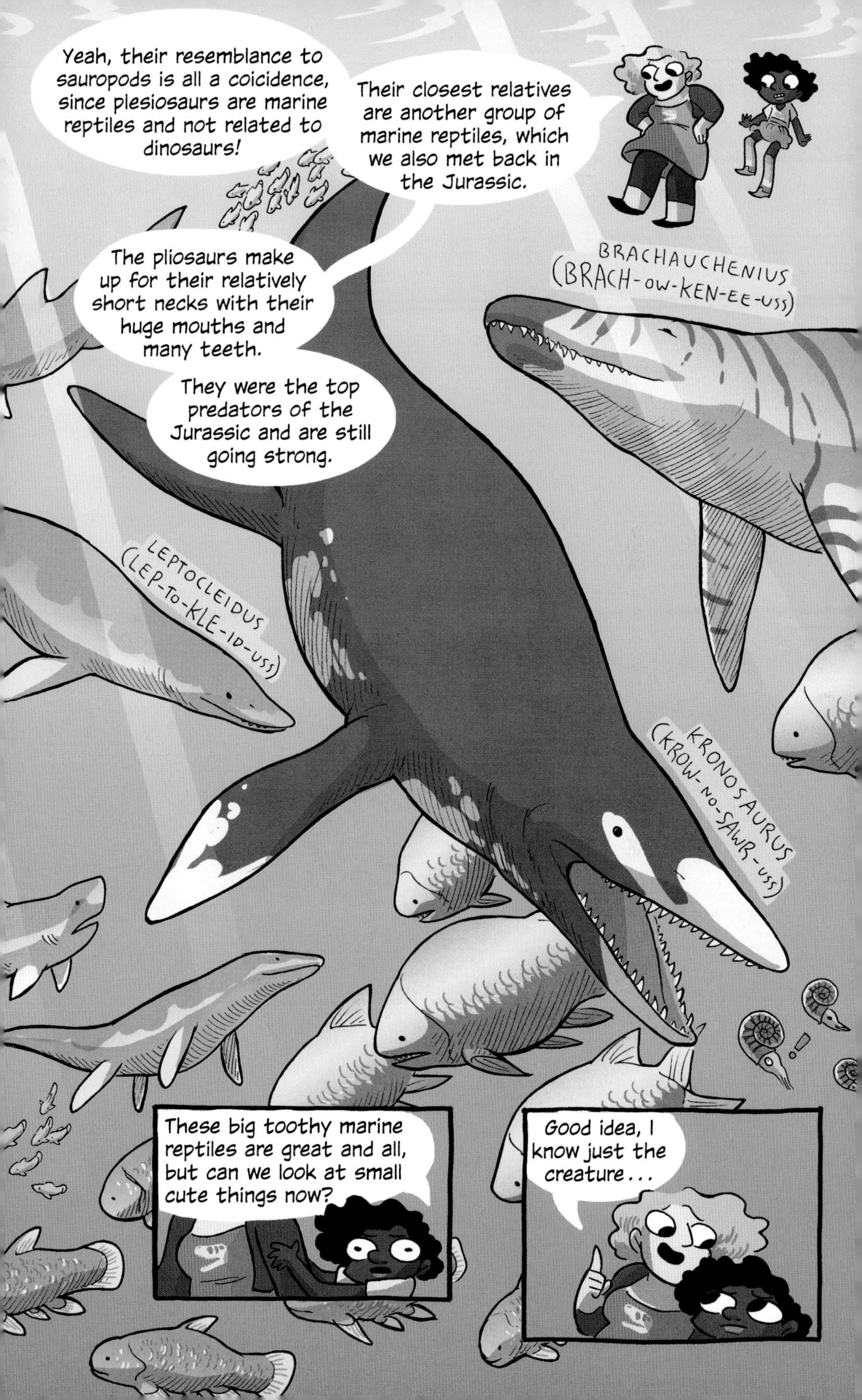
Yeah, their resemblance to sauropods is all a coicidence, since plesiosaurs are marine reptiles and not related to dinosaurs!
Their closest relatives are another group of marine reptiles, which we also met back in the Jurassic.
The pliosaurs make up for their relatively short necks with their huge mouths and many teeth.
They were the top predators of the Jurassic and are still going strong.
BRACHAUCHENIUS (BRACH-OW-KEN-EE-USS)
LEPTOCLEIDUS (LEP-TO-KLE-ID-USS)
KRONOSAURUS (KROW-NO-SAWR-USS)
These big toothy marine reptiles are great and all, but can we look at small cute things now?
Good idea, I know just the creature...

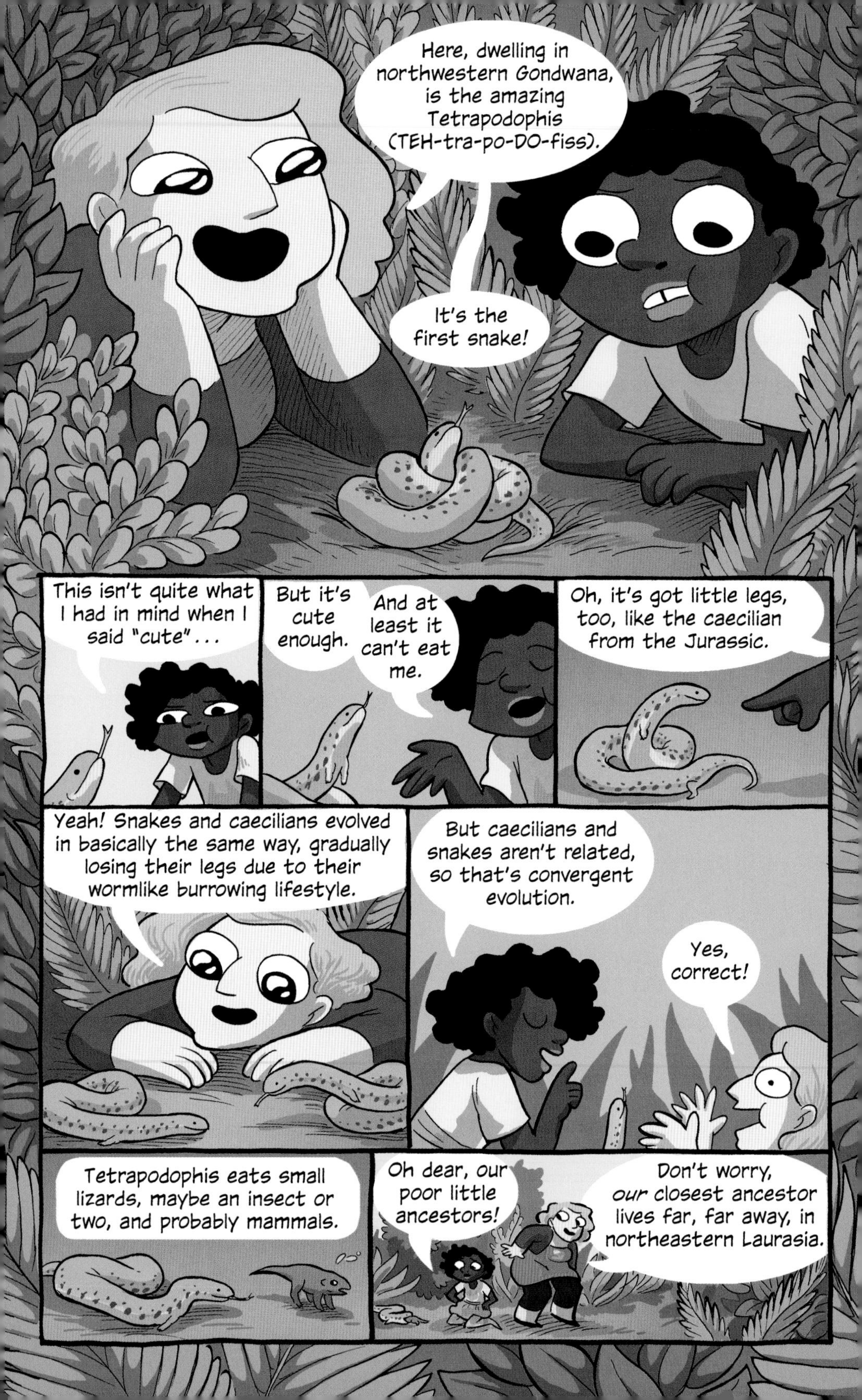
Here, dwelling in northwestern Gondwana, is the amazing Tetrapodophis (TEH-tra-po-DO-fiss).
It's the first snake!
This isn't quite what I had in mind when I said "cute"...
But it's cute enough.
And at least it can't eat me.
Oh, it's got little legs, too, like the caecilian from the Jurassic.
Yeah! Snakes and caecilians evolved in basically the same way, gradually losing their legs due to their wormlike burrowing lifestyle.
But caecilians and snakes aren't related, so that's convergent evolution.
Yes, correct!
Tetrapodophis eats small lizards, maybe an insect or two, and probably mammals.
Oh dear, our poor little ancestors!
Don't worry, *our* closest ancestor lives far, far away, in northeastern Laurasia.

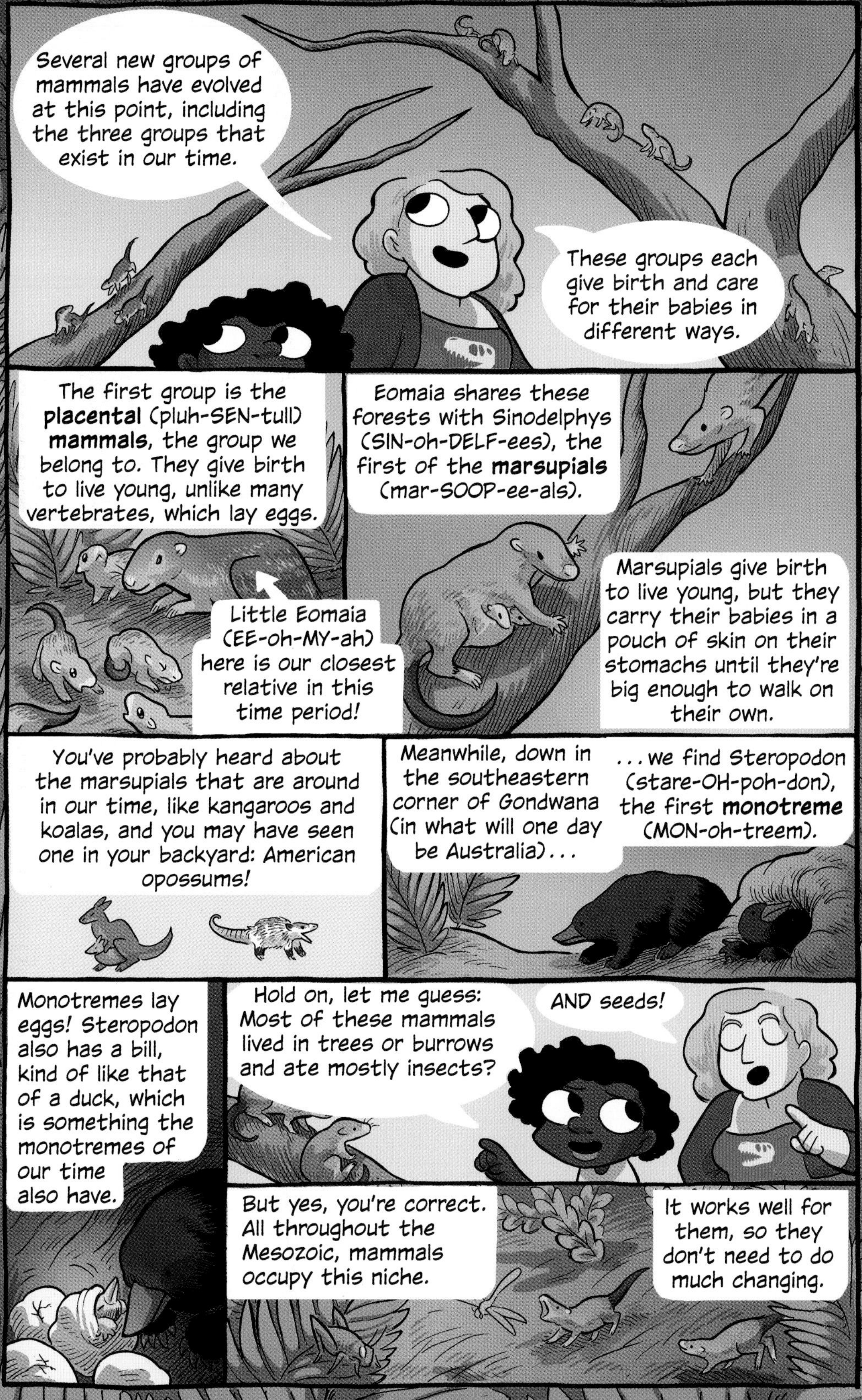
Several new groups of mammals have evolved at this point, including the three groups that exist in our time.
These groups each give birth and care for their babies in different ways.
The first group is the **placental** (pluh-SEN-tull) **mammals**, the group we belong to. They give birth to live young, unlike many vertebrates, which lay eggs.
Little Eomaia (EE-oh-MY-ah) here is our closest relative in this time period!
Eomaia shares these forests with Sinodelphys (SIN-oh-DELF-ees), the first of the **marsupials** (mar-SOOP-ee-als).
Marsupials give birth to live young, but they carry their babies in a pouch of skin on their stomachs until they're big enough to walk on their own.
You've probably heard about the marsupials that are around in our time, like kangaroos and koalas, and you may have seen one in your backyard: American opossums!
Meanwhile, down in the southeastern corner of Gondwana (in what will one day be Australia)...
...we find Steropodon (stare-OH-poh-don), the first **monotreme** (MON-oh-treem).
Monotremes lay eggs! Steropodon also has a bill, kind of like that of a duck, which is something the monotremes of our time also have.
Hold on, let me guess: Most of these mammals lived in trees or burrows and ate mostly insects?
AND seeds!
But yes, you're correct. All throughout the Mesozoic, mammals occupy this niche.
It works well for them, so they don't need to do much changing.

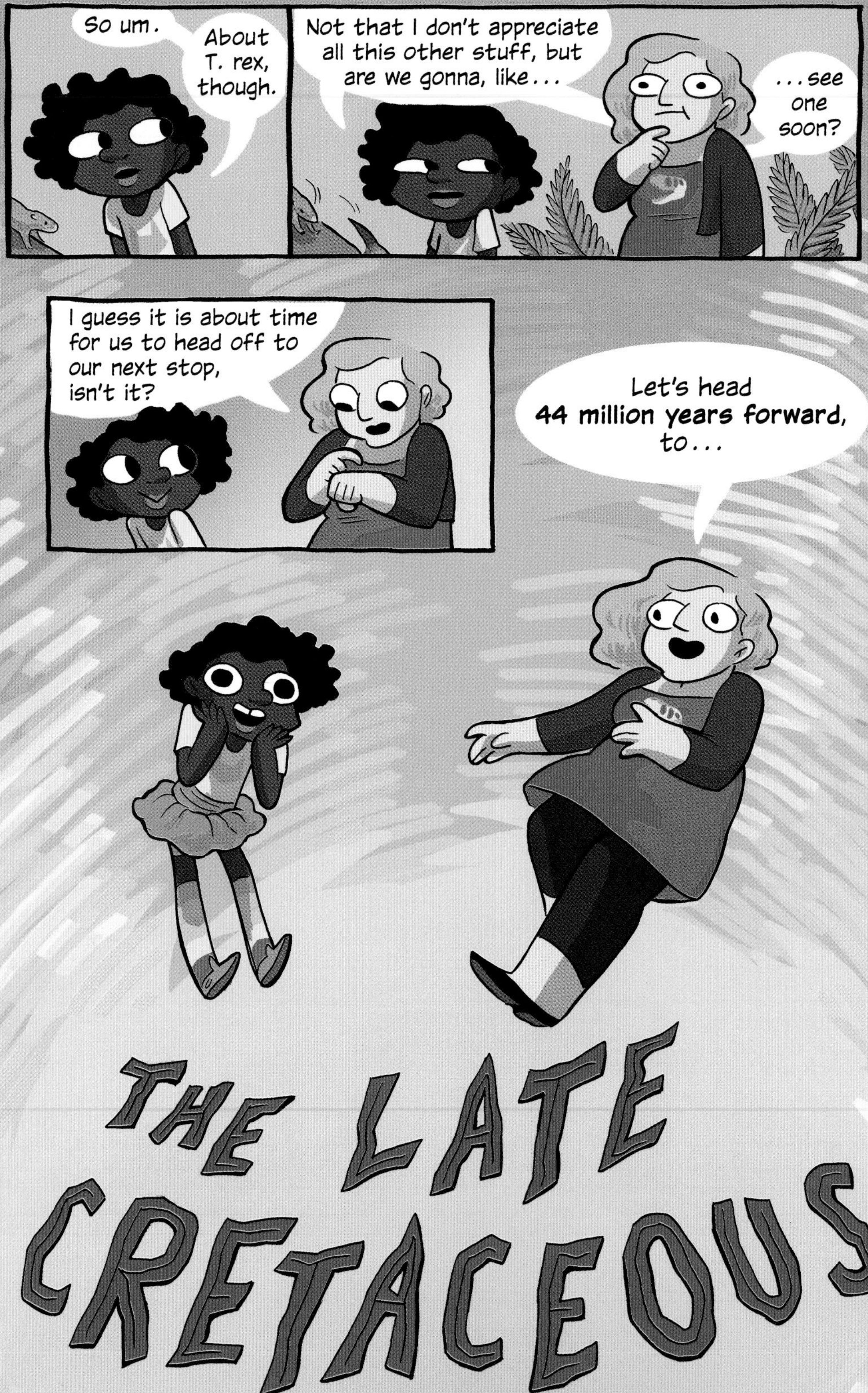
So um.
About T. rex, though.
Not that I don't appreciate all this other stuff, but are we gonna, like...
...see one soon?
I guess it is about time for us to head off to our next stop, isn't it?
Let's head **44 million years forward,** to...
THE LATE CRETACEOUS

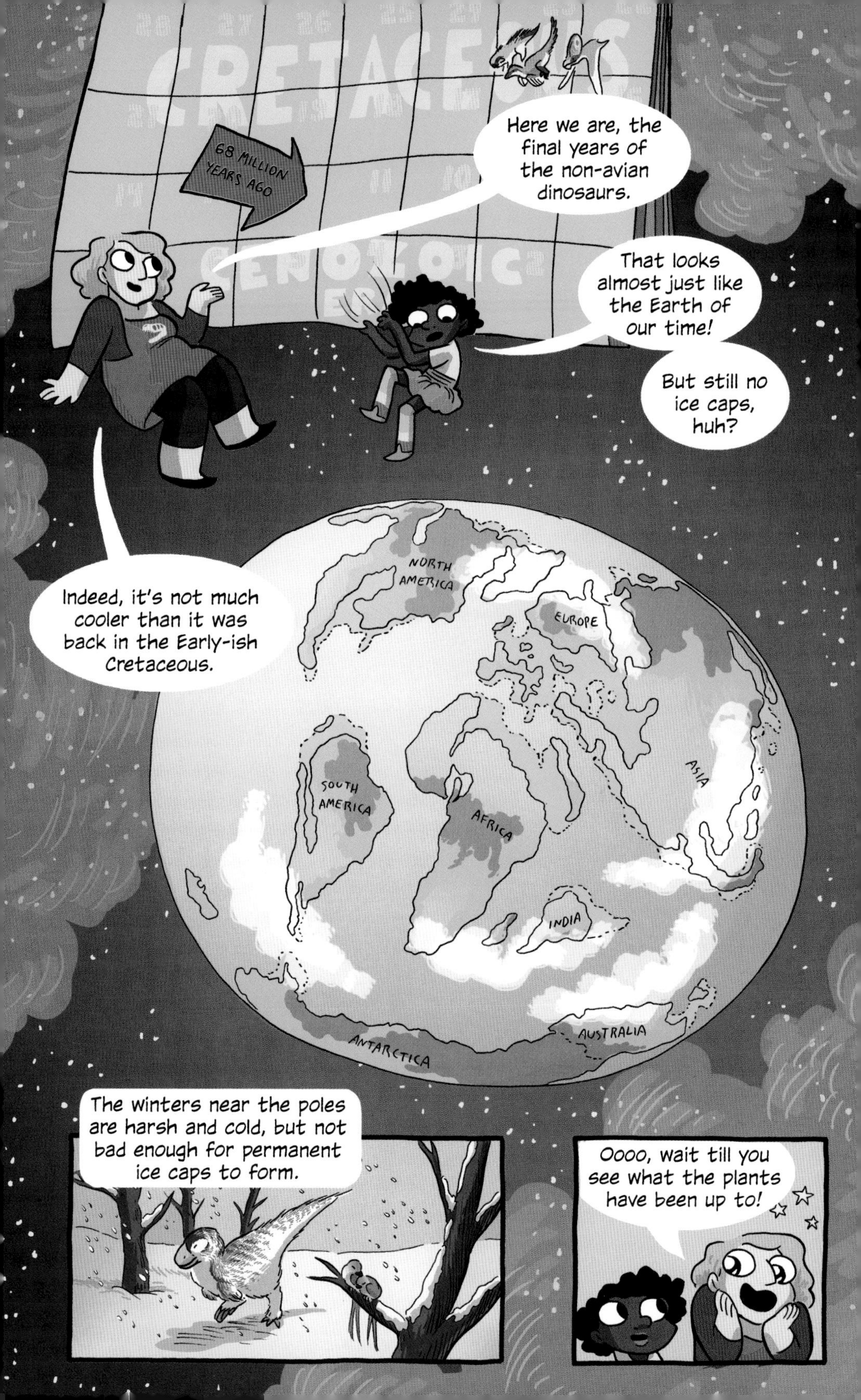

68 MILLION YEARS AGO
Here we are, the final years of the non-avian dinosaurs.
That looks almost just like the Earth of our time!
But still no ice caps, huh?
Indeed, it's not much cooler than it was back in the Early-ish Cretaceous.
NORTH AMERICA
EUROPE
ASIA
SOUTH AMERICA
AFRICA
INDIA
AUSTRALIA
ANTARCTICA
The winters near the poles are harsh and cold, but not bad enough for permanent ice caps to form.
Oooo, wait till you see what the plants have been up to!

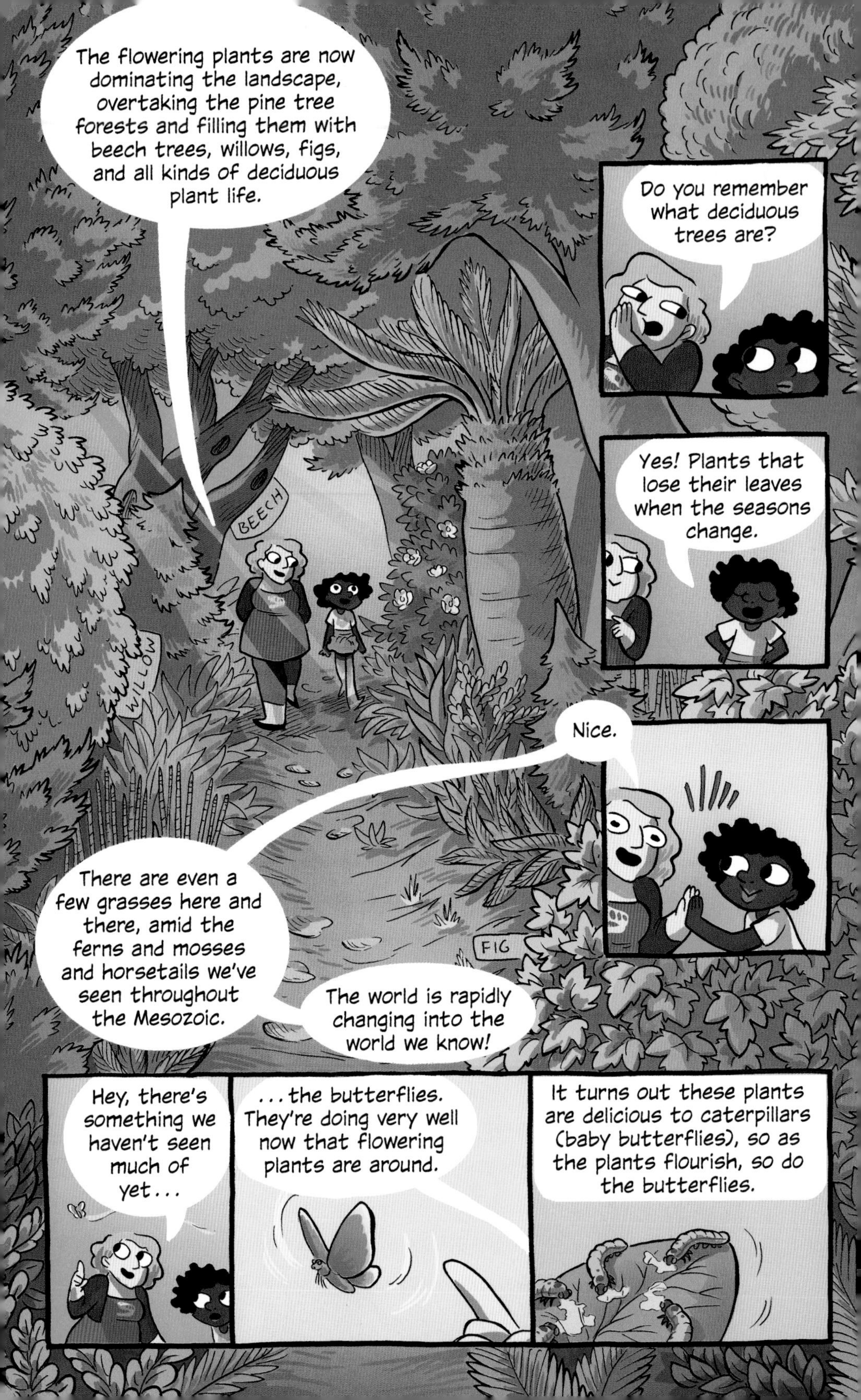
The flowering plants are now dominating the landscape, overtaking the pine tree forests and filling them with beech trees, willows, figs, and all kinds of deciduous plant life.
BEECH
WILLOW
Do you remember what deciduous trees are?
Yes! Plants that lose their leaves when the seasons change.
Nice.
There are even a few grasses here and there, amid the ferns and mosses and horsetails we've seen throughout the Mesozoic.
FIG
The world is rapidly changing into the world we know!
Hey, there's something we haven't seen much of yet...
...the butterflies. They're doing very well now that flowering plants are around.
It turns out these plants are delicious to caterpillars (baby butterflies), so as the plants flourish, so do the butterflies.

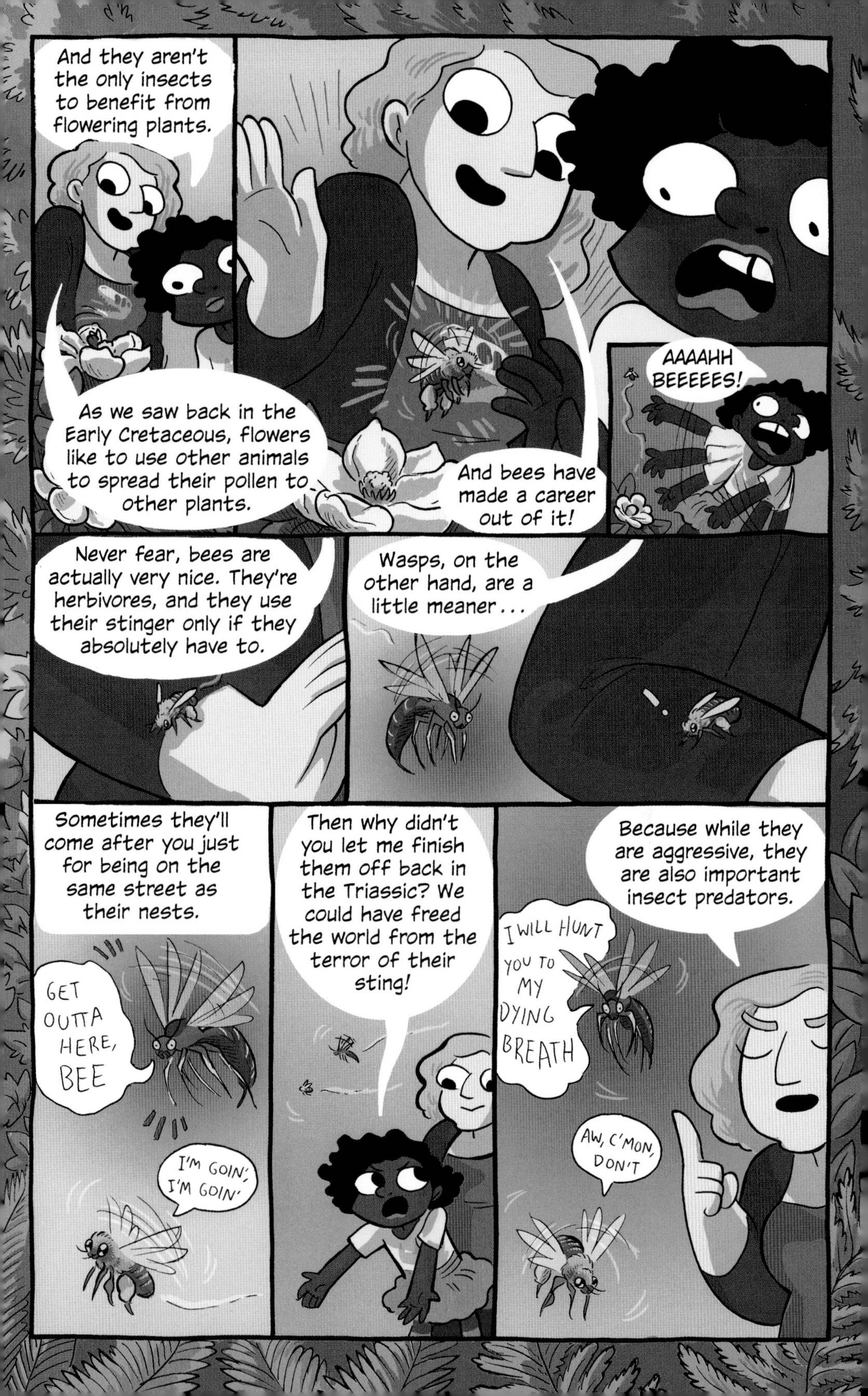
And they aren't the only insects to benefit from flowering plants.
As we saw back in the Early Cretaceous, flowers like to use other animals to spread their pollen to other plants.
And bees have made a career out of it!
AAAAHH BEEEEES!
Never fear, bees are actually very nice. They're herbivores, and they use their stinger only if they absolutely have to.
Wasps, on the other hand, are a little meaner . . .
Sometimes they'll come after you just for being on the same street as their nests.
GET OUTTA HERE, BEE
I'M GOIN', I'M GOIN'
Then why didn't you let me finish them off back in the Triassic? We could have freed the world from the terror of their sting!
Because while they are aggressive, they are also important insect predators.
I WILL HUNT YOU TO MY DYING BREATH
AW, C'MON, DON'T

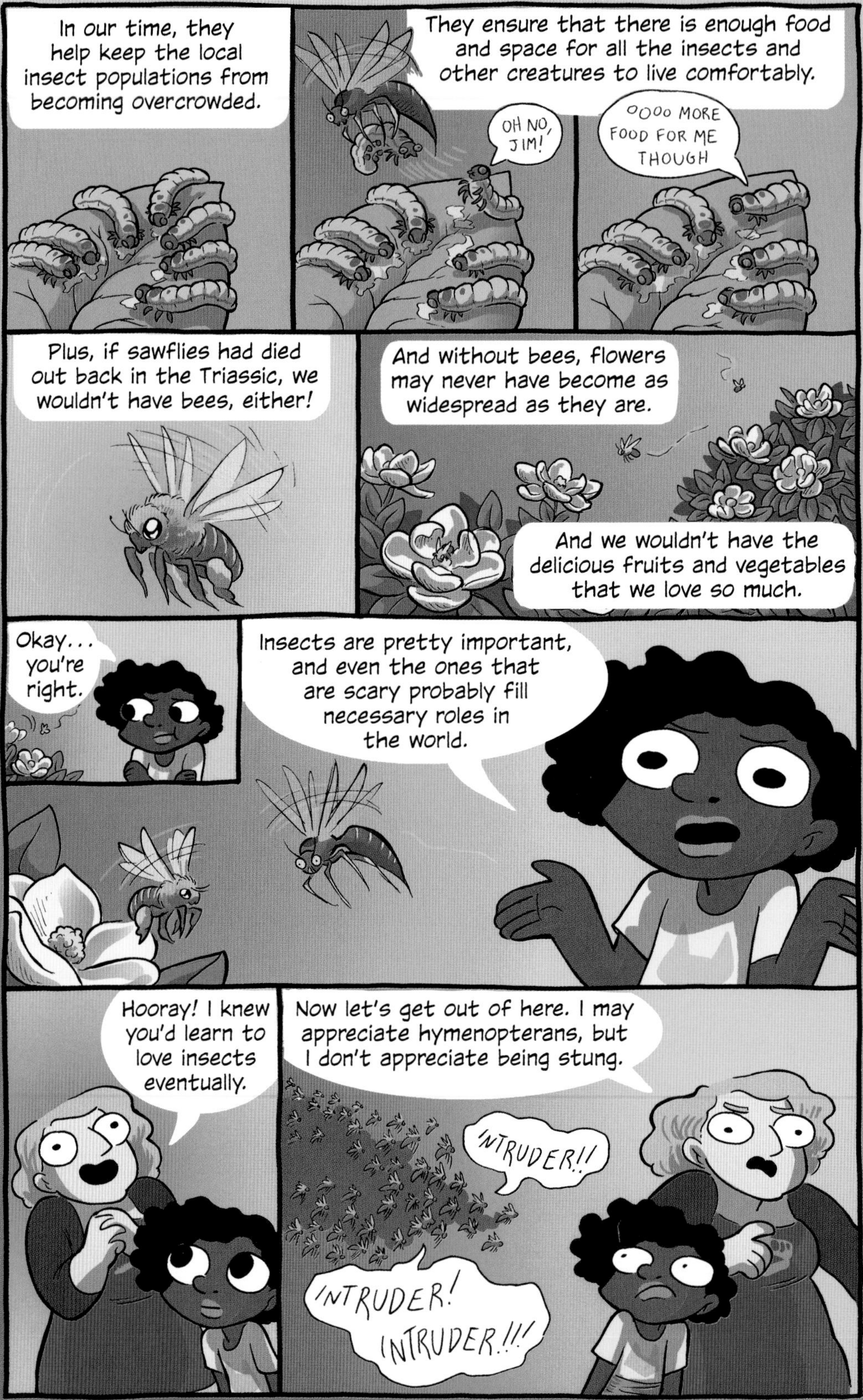
In our time, they help keep the local insect populations from becoming overcrowded.
They ensure that there is enough food and space for all the insects and other creatures to live comfortably.
OH NO, JIM!
OOOO MORE FOOD FOR ME THOUGH
Plus, if sawflies had died out back in the Triassic, we wouldn't have bees, either!
And without bees, flowers may never have become as widespread as they are.
And we wouldn't have the delicious fruits and vegetables that we love so much.
Okay... you're right.
Insects are pretty important, and even the ones that are scary probably fill necessary roles in the world.
Hooray! I knew you'd learn to love insects eventually.
Now let's get out of here. I may appreciate hymenopterans, but I don't appreciate being stung.
INTRUDER!!
INTRUDER! INTRUDER!!!

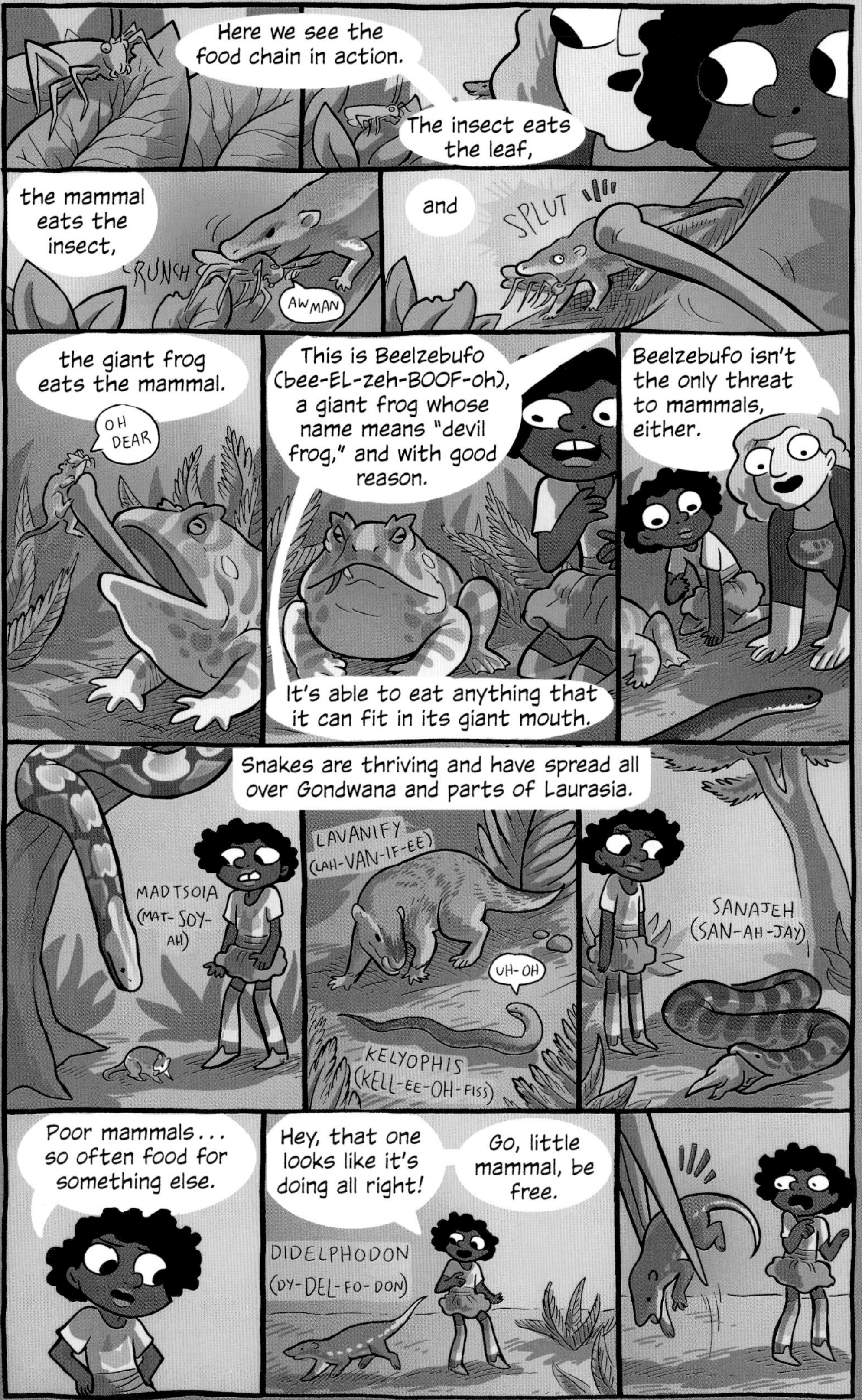

Here we see the food chain in action.
The insect eats the leaf,
the mammal eats the insect,
CRUNCH
AW MAN
and
SPLUT
the giant frog eats the mammal.
OH DEAR
This is Beelzebufo (bee-EL-zeh-BOOF-oh), a giant frog whose name means "devil frog," and with good reason.
It's able to eat anything that it can fit in its giant mouth.
Beelzebufo isn't the only threat to mammals, either.
Snakes are thriving and have spread all over Gondwana and parts of Laurasia.
MADTSOIA (MAT-SOY-AH)
LAVANIFY (LAH-VAN-IF-EE)
UH-OH
KELYOPHIS (KELL-EE-OH-FISS)
SANAJEH (SAN-AH-JAY)
Poor mammals... so often food for something else.
Hey, that one looks like it's doing all right!
Go, little mammal, be free.
DIDELPHODON (DY-DEL-FO-DON)

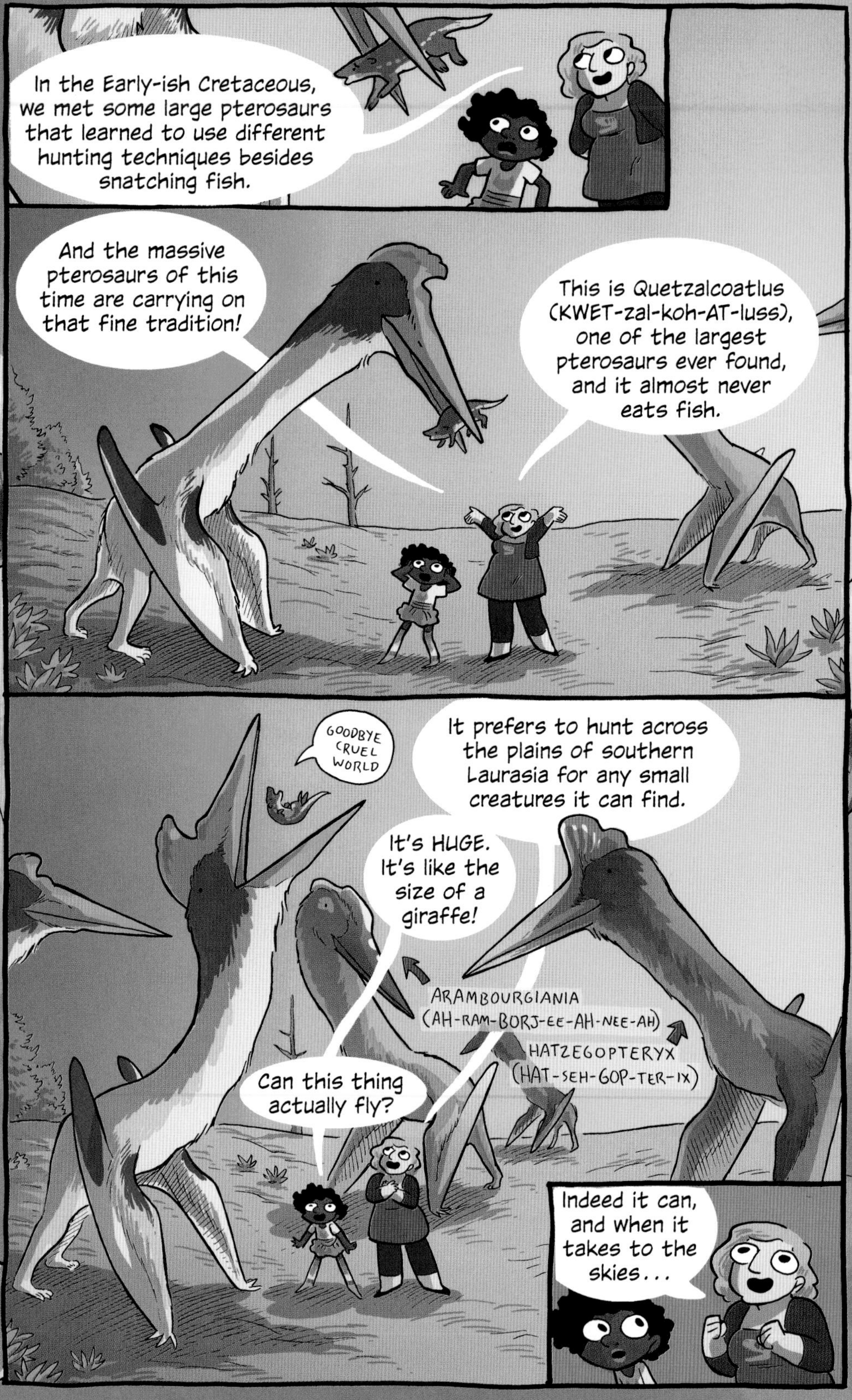
In the Early-ish Cretaceous, we met some large pterosaurs that learned to use different hunting techniques besides snatching fish.
And the massive pterosaurs of this time are carrying on that fine tradition!
This is Quetzalcoatlus (KWET-zal-koh-AT-luss), one of the largest pterosaurs ever found, and it almost never eats fish.
GOODBYE CRUEL WORLD
It prefers to hunt across the plains of southern Laurasia for any small creatures it can find.
It's HUGE. It's like the size of a giraffe!
ARAMBOURGIANIA (AH-RAM-BORJ-EE-AH-NEE-AH)
HATZEGOPTERYX (HAT-SEH-GOP-TER-IX)
Can this thing actually fly?
Indeed it can, and when it takes to the skies...

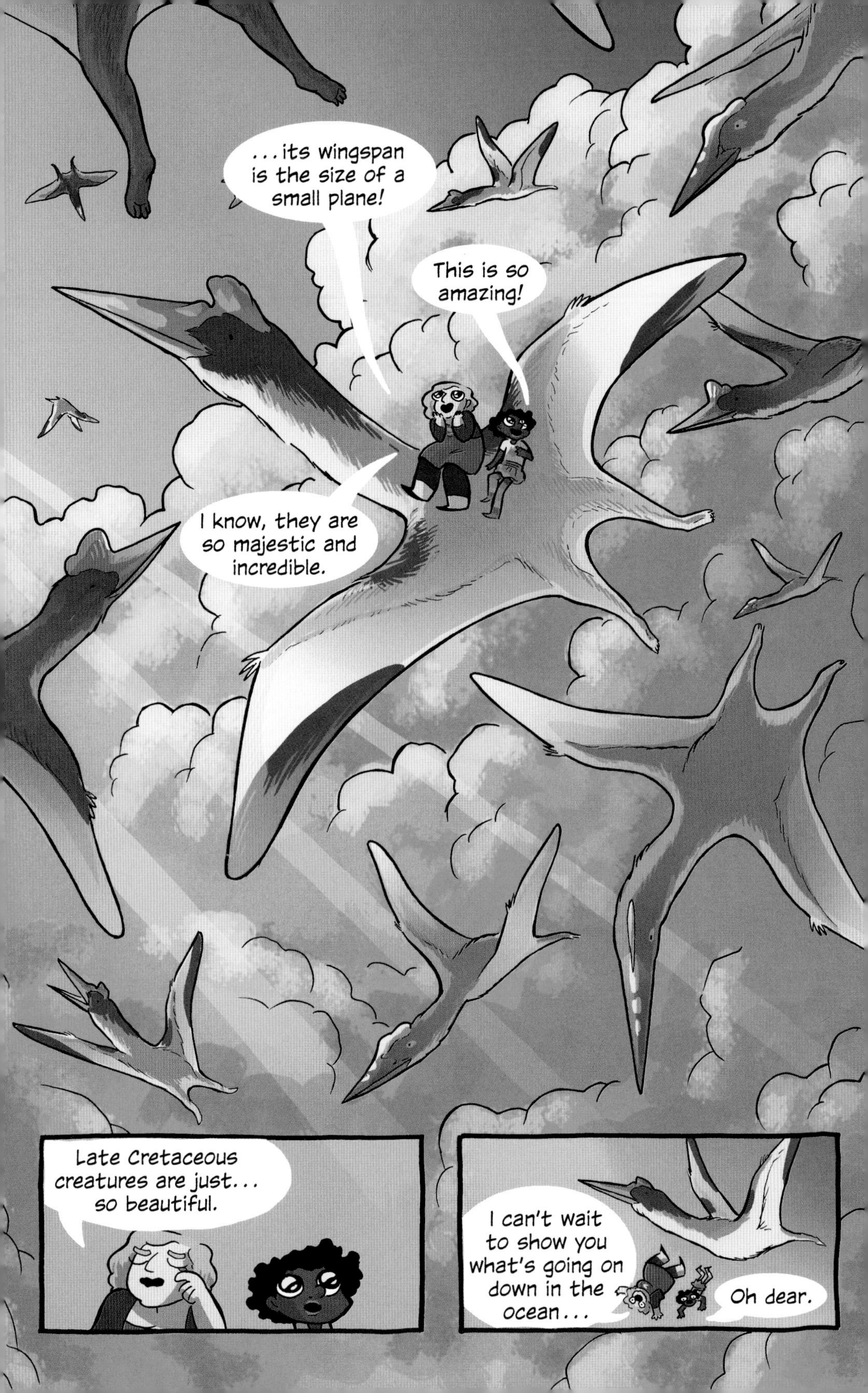
...its wingspan is the size of a small plane!
This is so amazing!
I know, they are so majestic and incredible.
Late Cretaceous creatures are just... so beautiful.
I can't wait to show you what's going on down in the ocean...
Oh dear.

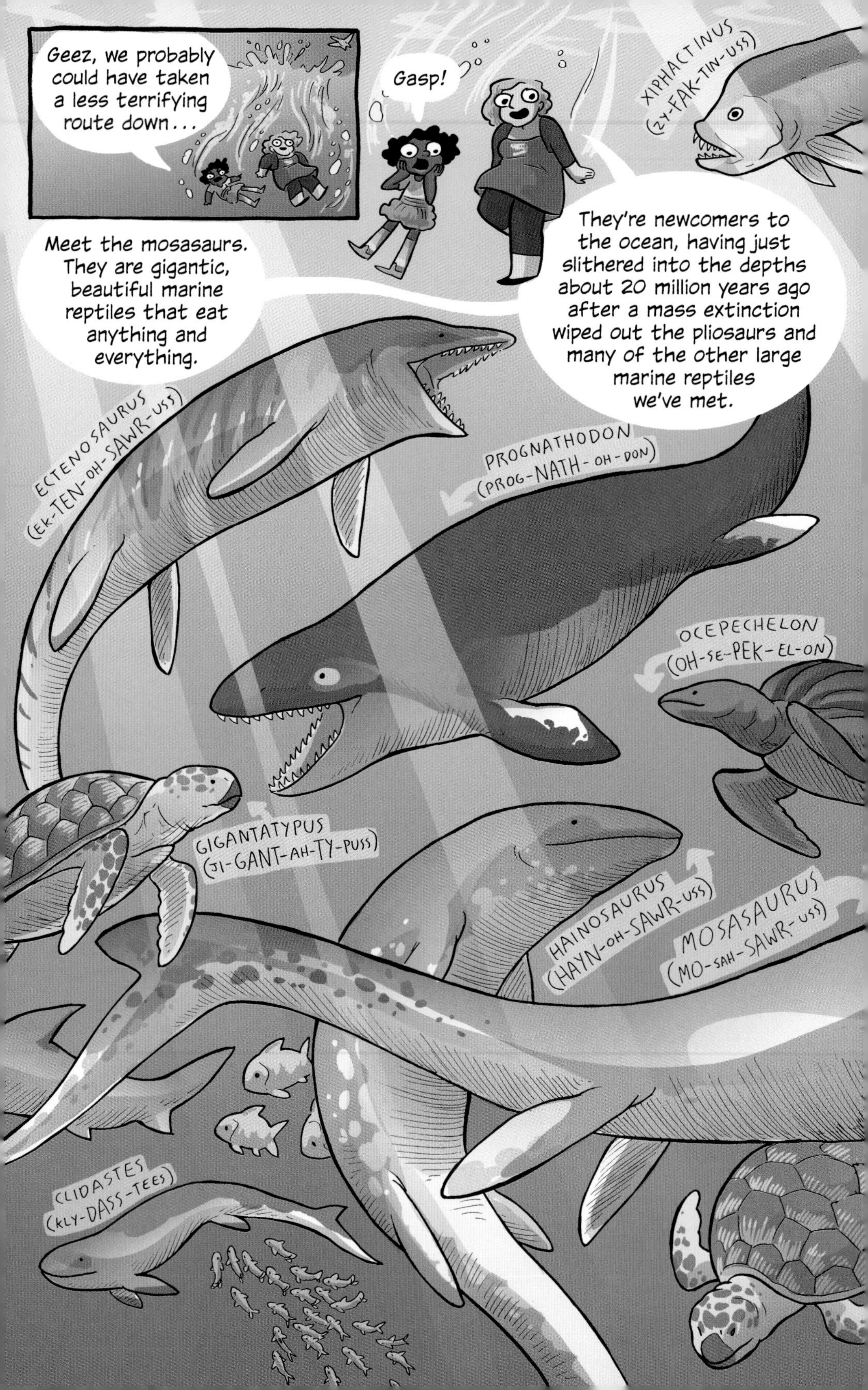

Geez, we probably could have taken a less terrifying route down...
Gasp!
XIPHACTINUS (ZY-FAK-TIN-USS)
They're newcomers to the ocean, having just slithered into the depths about 20 million years ago after a mass extinction wiped out the pliosaurs and many of the other large marine reptiles we've met.
Meet the mosasaurs. They are gigantic, beautiful marine reptiles that eat anything and everything.
ECTENOSAURUS (EK-TEN-OH-SAWR-USS)
PROGNATHODON (PROG-NATH-OH-DON)
OCEPECHELON (OH-SE-PEK-EL-ON)
GIGANTATYPUS (JI-GANT-AH-TY-PUSS)
HAINOSAURUS (HAYN-OH-SAWR-USS)
MOSASAURUS (MO-SAH-SAWR-USS)
CLIDASTES (KLY-DASS-TEES)

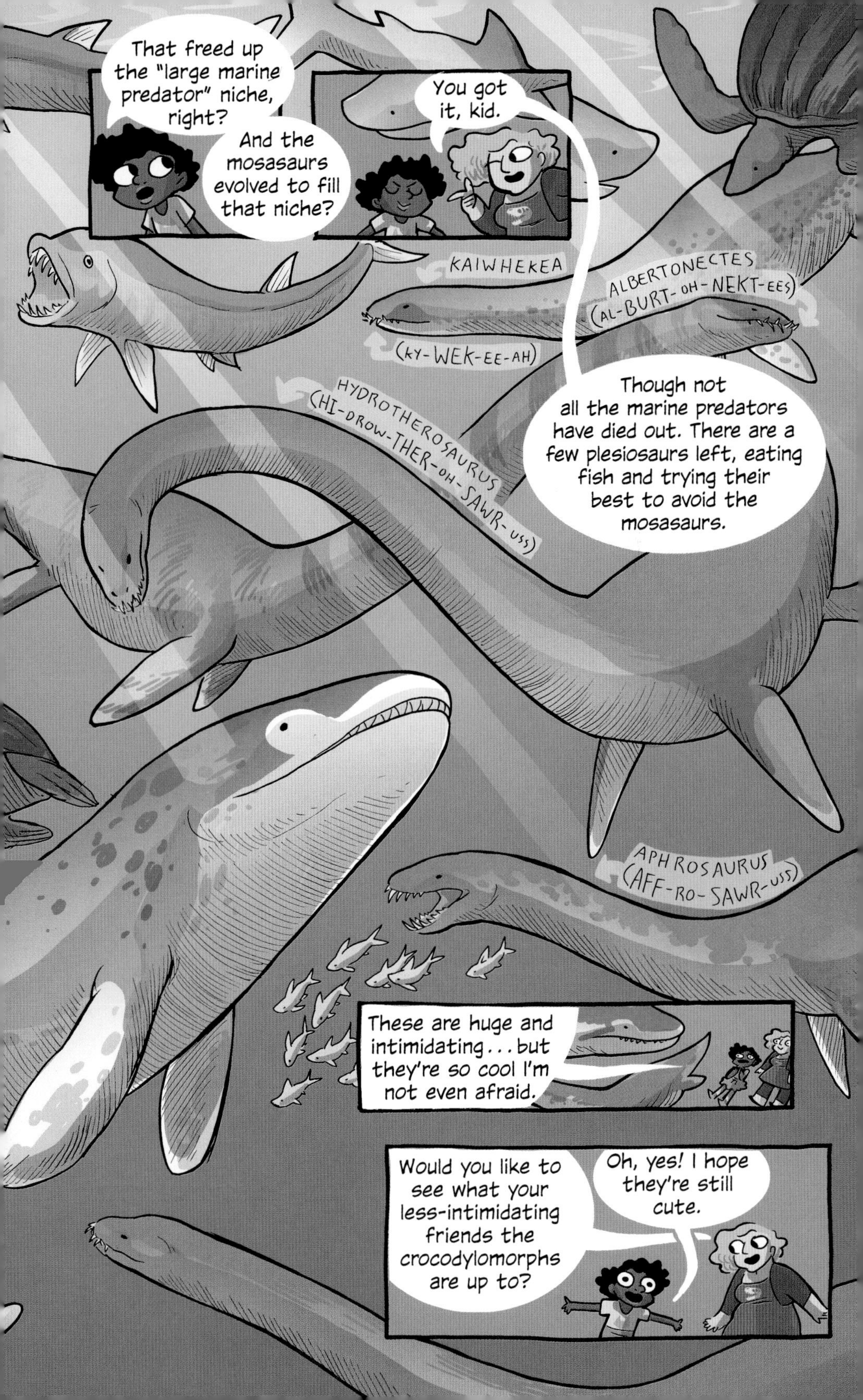

That freed up the "large marine predator" niche, right?
And the mosasaurs evolved to fill that niche?
You got it, kid.
KAIWHEKEA
(KY-WEK-EE-AH)
ALBERTONECTES
(AL-BURT-OH-NEKT-EES)
HYDROTHEROSAURUS
(HI-DROW-THER-OH-SAWR-USS)
Though not all the marine predators have died out. There are a few plesiosaurs left, eating fish and trying their best to avoid the mosasaurs.
APHROSAURUS
(AFF-RO-SAWR-USS)
These are huge and intimidating . . . but they're so cool I'm not even afraid.
Would you like to see what your less-intimidating friends the crocodylomorphs are up to?
Oh, yes! I hope they're still cute.

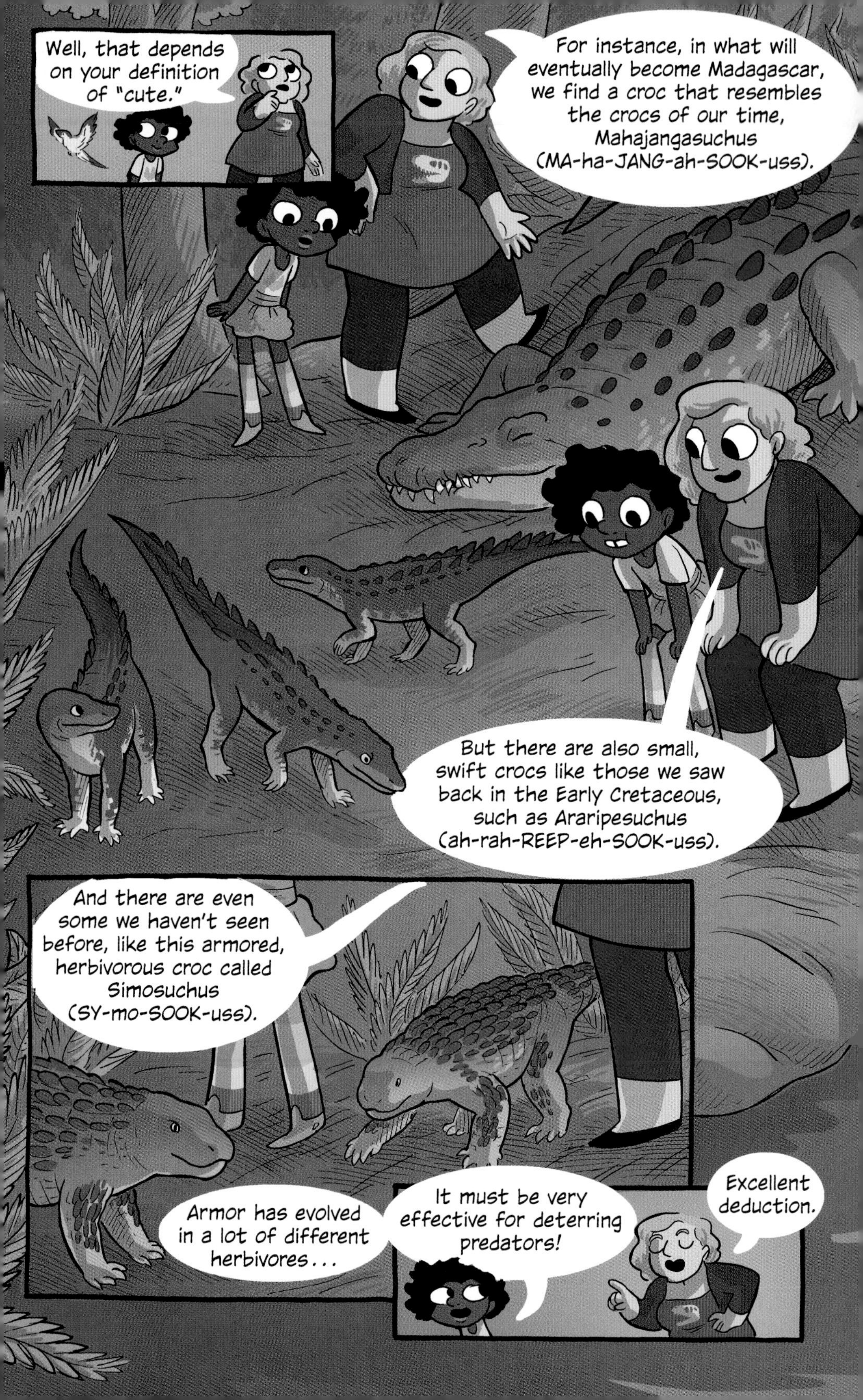
Well, that depends on your definition of "cute."
For instance, in what will eventually become Madagascar, we find a croc that resembles the crocs of our time, Mahajangasuchus (MA-ha-JANG-ah-SOOK-uss).
But there are also small, swift crocs like those we saw back in the Early Cretaceous, such as Araripesuchus (ah-rah-REEP-eh-SOOK-uss).
And there are even some we haven't seen before, like this armored, herbivorous croc called Simosuchus (SY-mo-SOOK-uss).
Armor has evolved in a lot of different herbivores...
It must be very effective for deterring predators!
Excellent deduction.

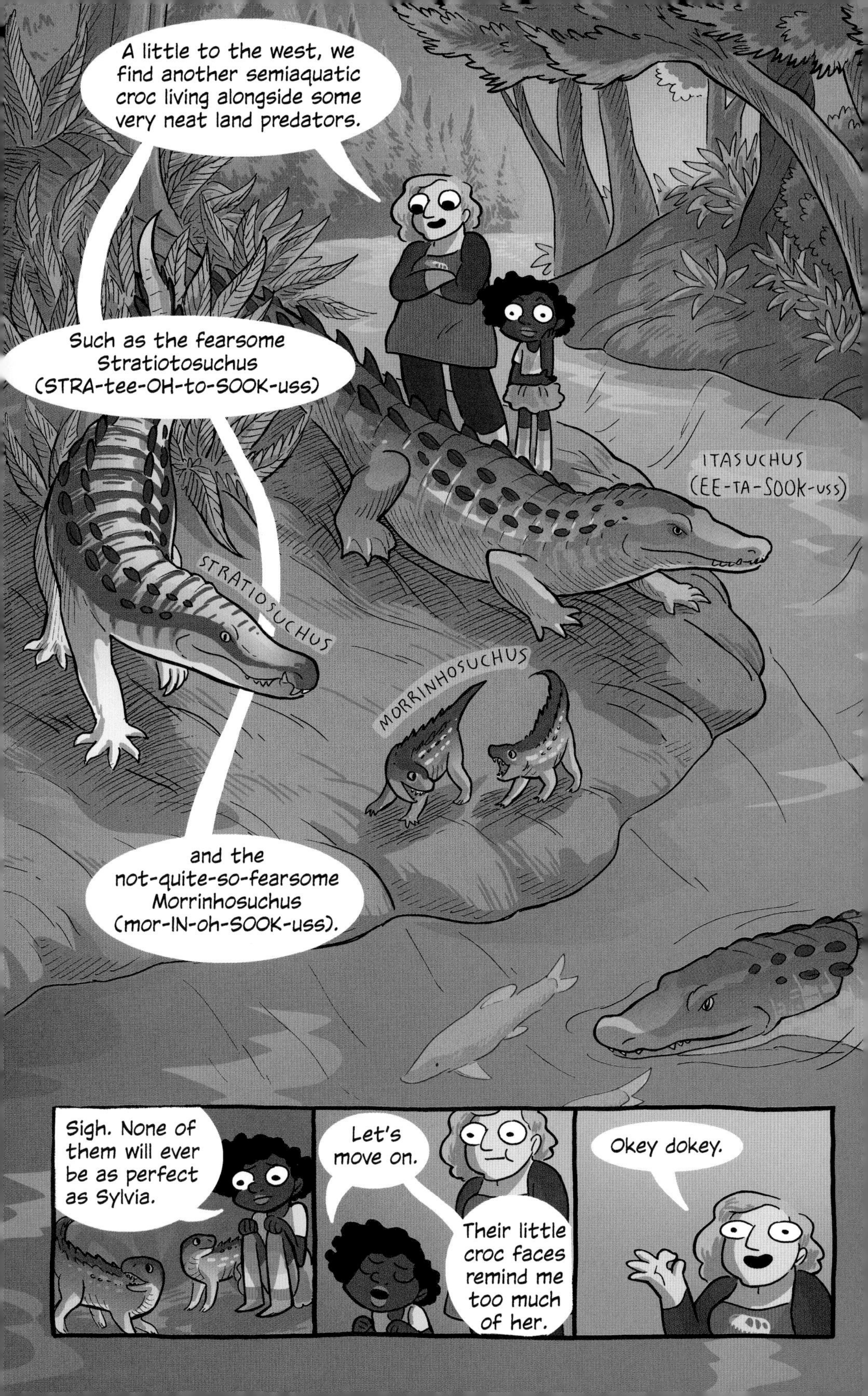
A little to the west, we find another semiaquatic croc living alongside some very neat land predators.
Such as the fearsome Stratiotosuchus (STRA-tee-OH-to-SOOK-uss)
and the not-quite-so-fearsome Morrinhosuchus (mor-IN-oh-SOOK-uss).
STRATIOSUCHUS
ITASUCHUS (EE-TA-SOOK-uss)
MORRINHOSUCHUS
Sigh. None of them will ever be as perfect as Sylvia.
Let's move on.
Their little croc faces remind me too much of her.
Okey dokey.

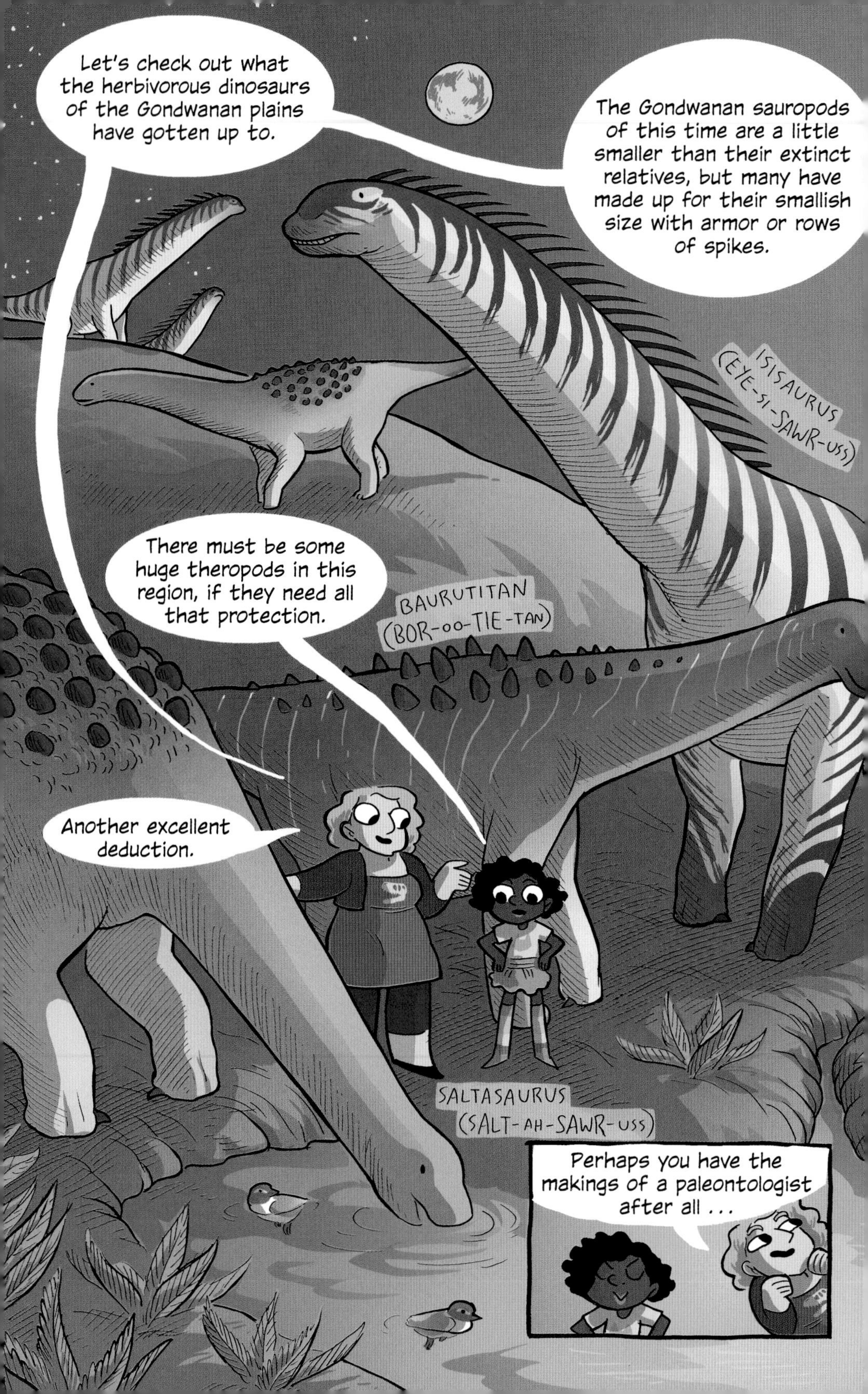
Let's check out what the herbivorous dinosaurs of the Gondwanan plains have gotten up to.
The Gondwanan sauropods of this time are a little smaller than their extinct relatives, but many have made up for their smallish size with armor or rows of spikes.
ISISAURUS (EYE-SI-SAWR-USS)
There must be some huge theropods in this region, if they need all that protection.
BAURUTITAN (BOR-OO-TIE-TAN)
Another excellent deduction.
SALTASAURUS (SALT-AH-SAWR-USS)
Perhaps you have the makings of a paleontologist after all . . .

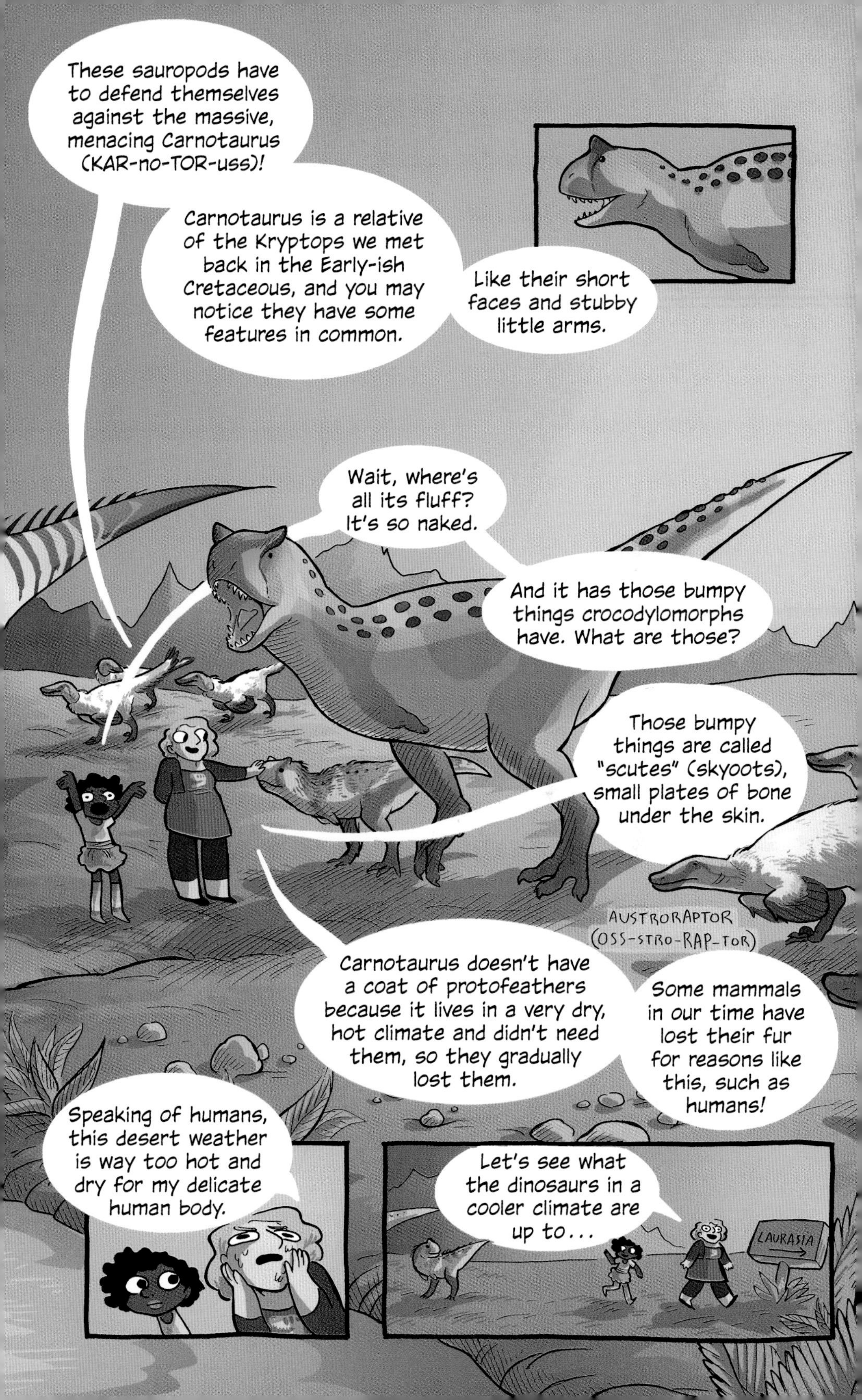
These sauropods have to defend themselves against the massive, menacing Carnotaurus (KAR-no-TOR-uss)!
Carnotaurus is a relative of the Kryptops we met back in the Early-ish Cretaceous, and you may notice they have some features in common.
Like their short faces and stubby little arms.
Wait, where's all its fluff? It's so naked.
And it has those bumpy things crocodylomorphs have. What are those?
Those bumpy things are called "scutes" (skyoots), small plates of bone under the skin.
AUSTRORAPTOR (OSS-STRO-RAP-TOR)
Carnotaurus doesn't have a coat of protofeathers because it lives in a very dry, hot climate and didn't need them, so they gradually lost them.
Some mammals in our time have lost their fur for reasons like this, such as humans!
Speaking of humans, this desert weather is way too hot and dry for my delicate human body.
Let's see what the dinosaurs in a cooler climate are up to...
LAURASIA

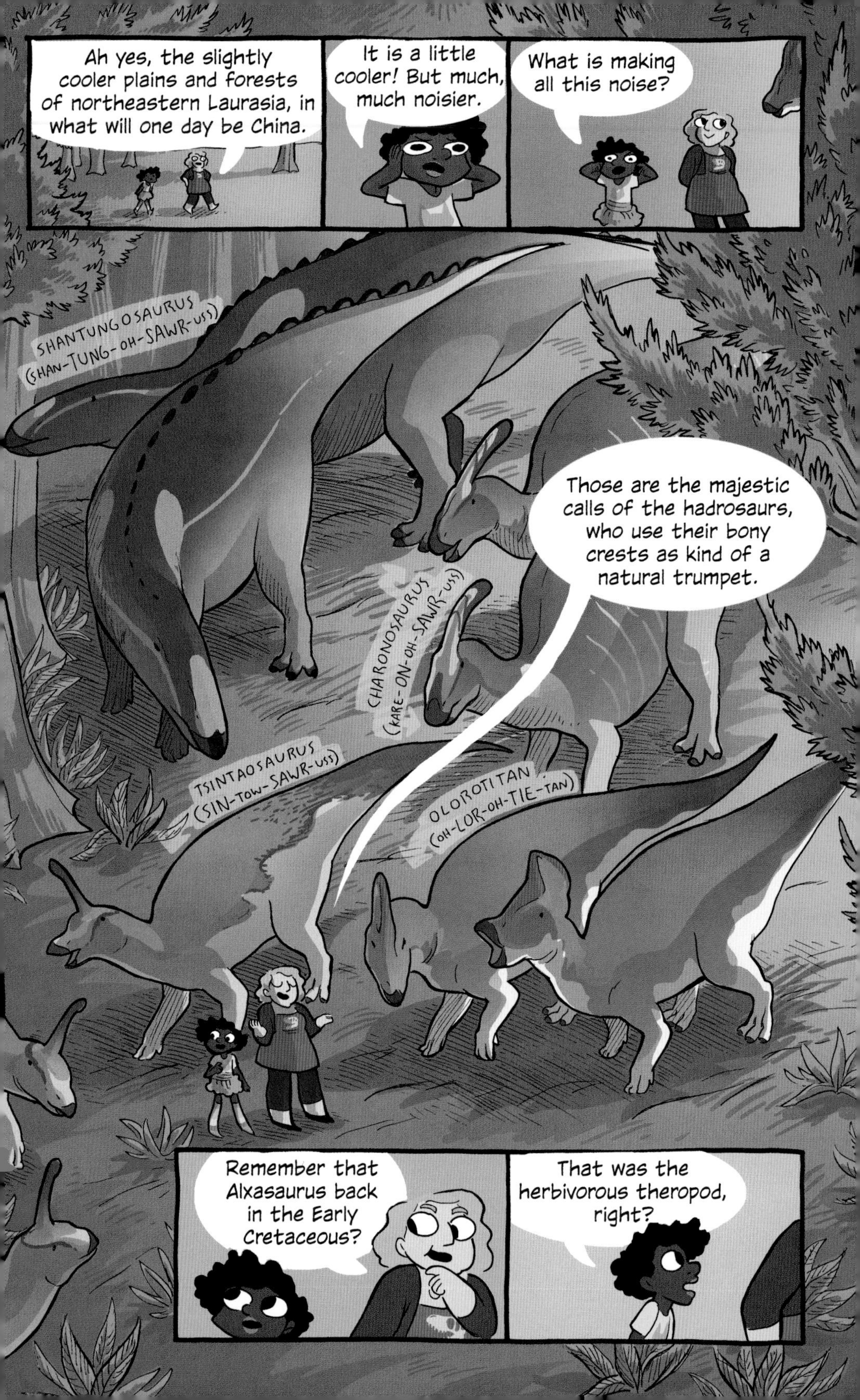

Ah yes, the slightly cooler plains and forests of northeastern Laurasia, in what will one day be China.
It is a little cooler! But much, much noisier.
What is making all this noise?
SHANTUNGOSAURUS (SHAN-TUNG-OH-SAWR-USS)
CHARONOSAURUS (KARE-ON-OH-SAWR-USS)
Those are the majestic calls of the hadrosaurs, who use their bony crests as kind of a natural trumpet.
TSINTAOSAURUS (SIN-TOW-SAWR-USS)
OLOROTITAN (OH-LOR-OH-TIE-TAN)
Remember that Alxasaurus back in the Early Cretaceous?
That was the herbivorous theropod, right?

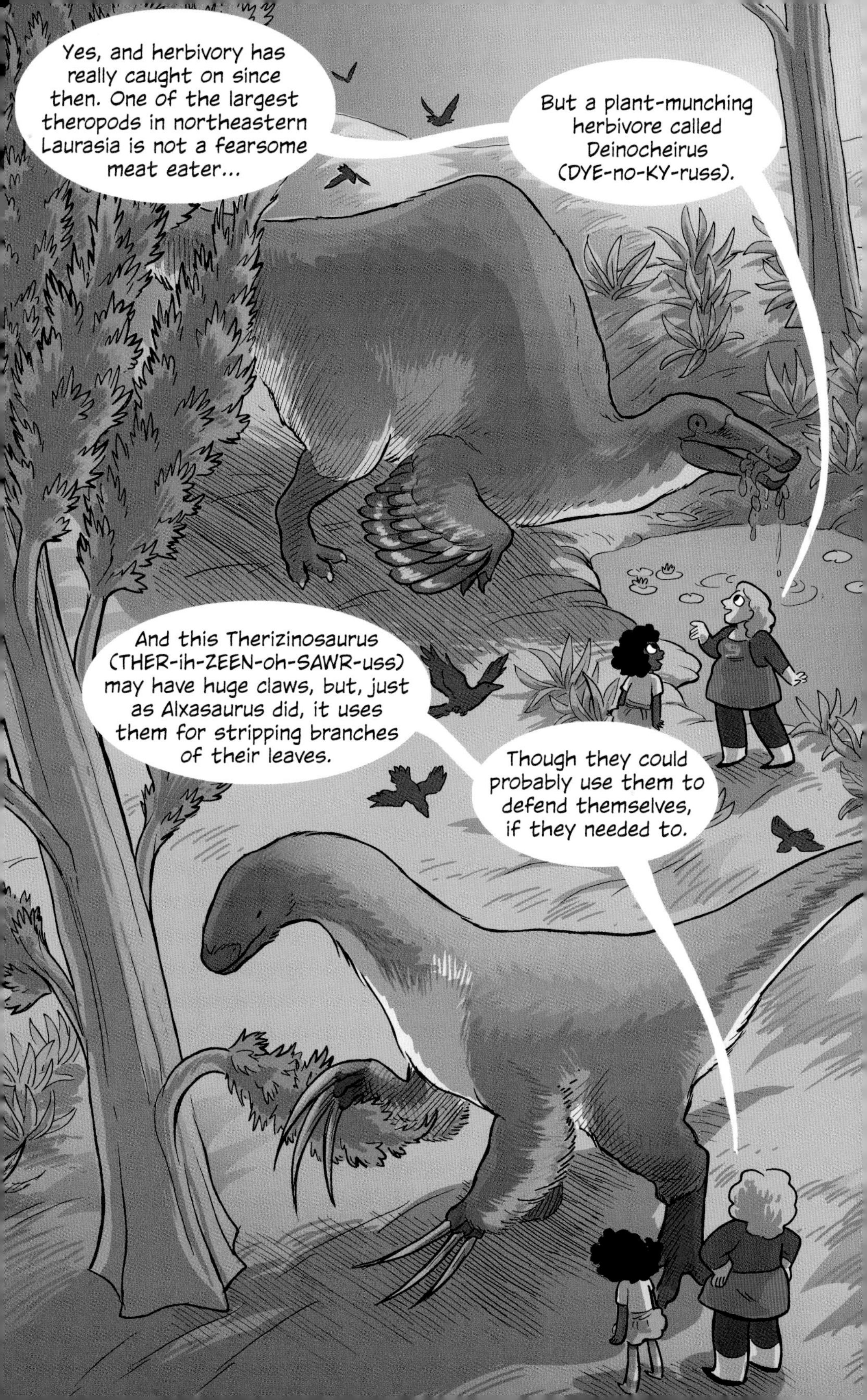
Yes, and herbivory has really caught on since then. One of the largest theropods in northeastern Laurasia is not a fearsome meat eater...
But a plant-munching herbivore called Deinocheirus (DYE-no-KY-russ).
And this Therizinosaurus (THER-ih-ZEEN-oh-SAWR-uss) may have huge claws, but, just as Alxasaurus did, it uses them for stripping branches of their leaves.
Though they could probably use them to defend themselves, if they needed to.

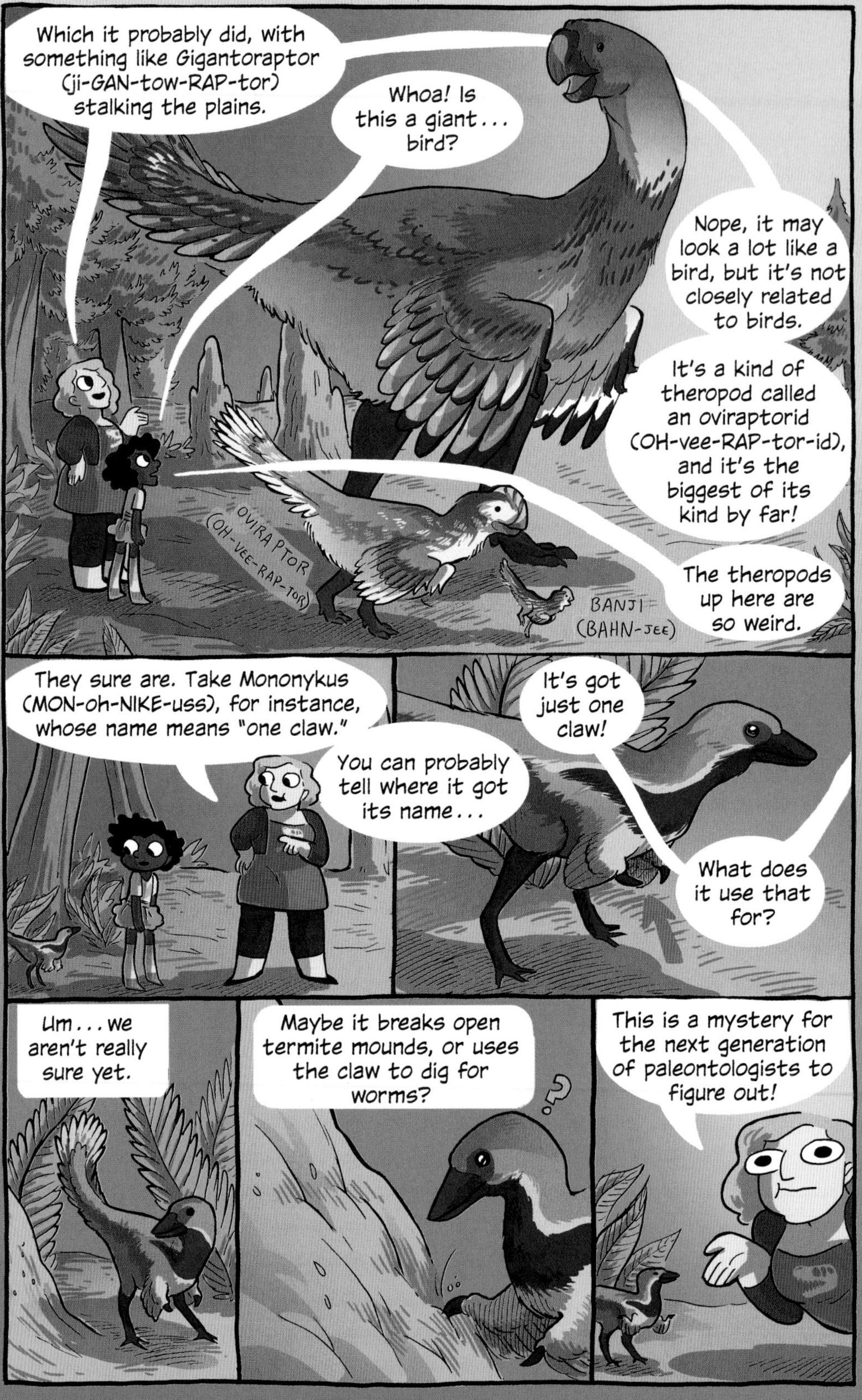
Which it probably did, with something like Gigantoraptor (ji-GAN-tow-RAP-tor) stalking the plains.
Whoa! Is this a giant... bird?
Nope, it may look a lot like a bird, but it's not closely related to birds.
It's a kind of theropod called an oviraptorid (OH-vee-RAP-tor-id), and it's the biggest of its kind by far!
OVIRAPTOR (OH-VEE-RAP-TOR)
BANJI (BAHN-JEE)
The theropods up here are so weird.
They sure are. Take Mononykus (MON-oh-NIKE-uss), for instance, whose name means "one claw."
You can probably tell where it got its name...
It's got just one claw!
What does it use that for?
Um... we aren't really sure yet.
Maybe it breaks open termite mounds, or uses the claw to dig for worms?
?
This is a mystery for the next generation of paleontologists to figure out!

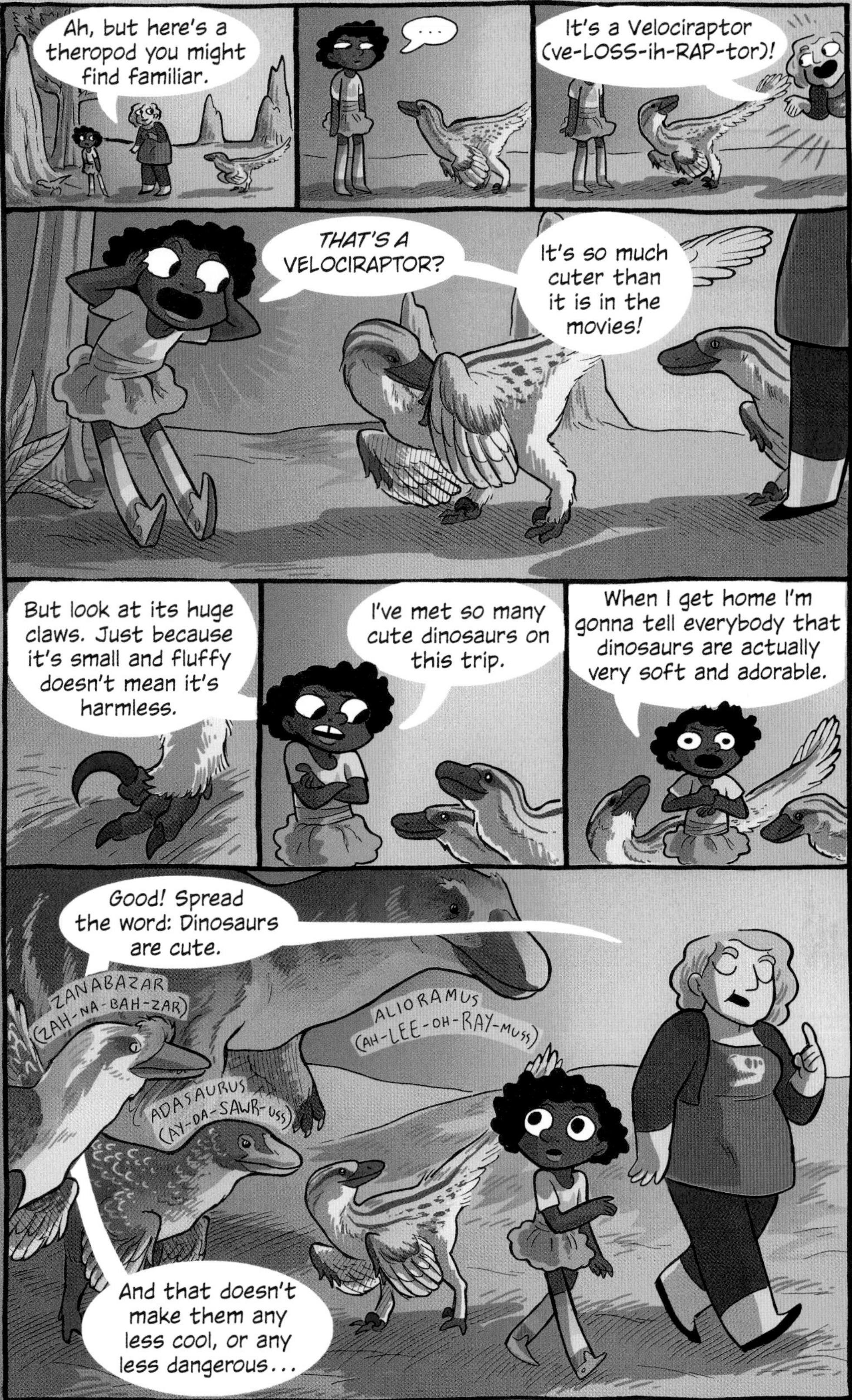
Ah, but here's a theropod you might find familiar.
. . .
It's a Velociraptor (ve-LOSS-ih-RAP-tor)!
THAT'S A VELOCIRAPTOR?
It's so much cuter than it is in the movies!
But look at its huge claws. Just because it's small and fluffy doesn't mean it's harmless.
I've met so many cute dinosaurs on this trip.
When I get home I'm gonna tell everybody that dinosaurs are actually very soft and adorable.
Good! Spread the word: Dinosaurs are cute.
ZANABAZAR (ZAH-NA-BAH-ZAR)
ALIORAMUS (AH-LEE-OH-RAY-MUSS)
ADASAURUS (AY-DA-SAWR-USS)
And that doesn't make them any less cool, or any less dangerous...

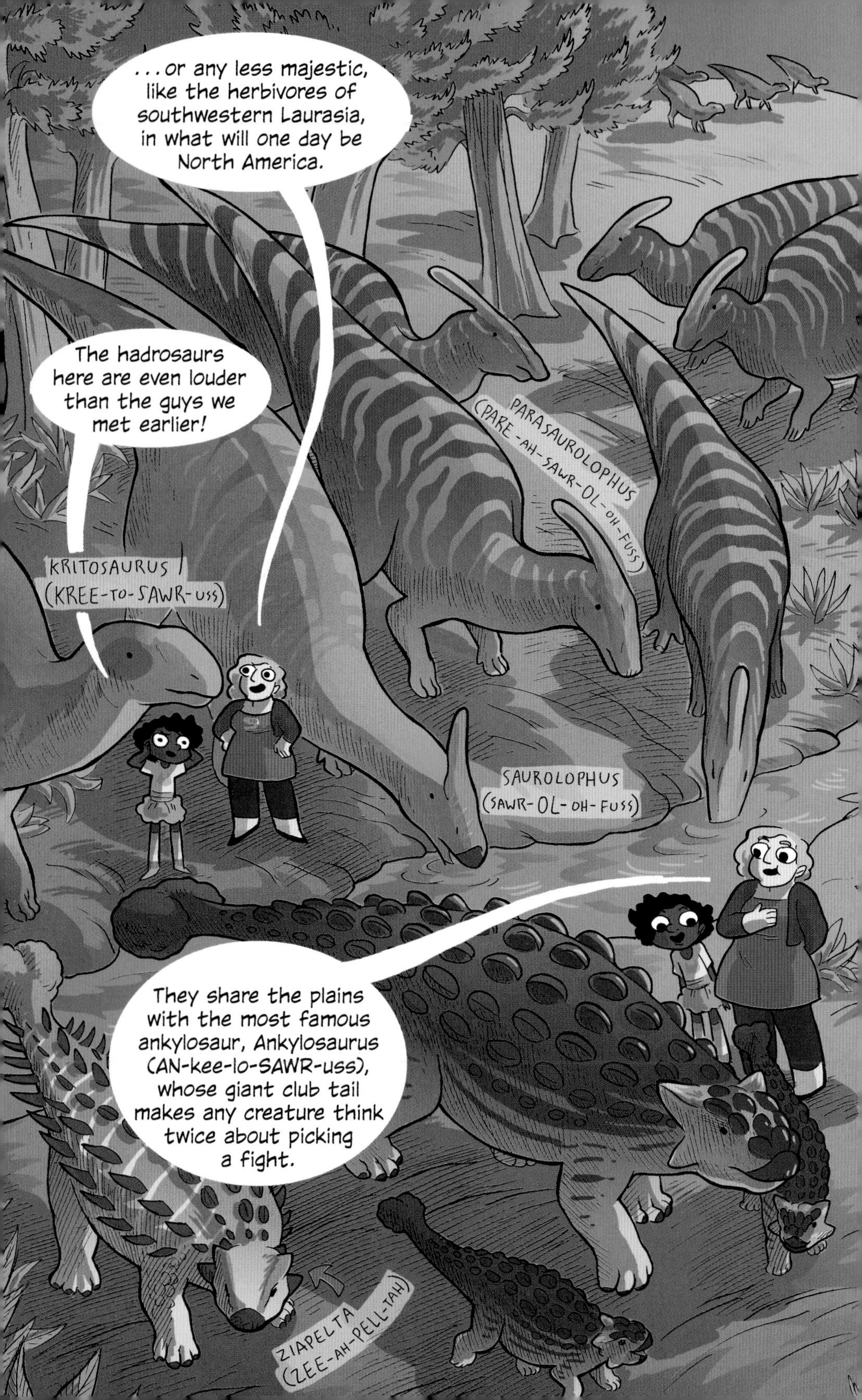

...or any less majestic, like the herbivores of southwestern Laurasia, in what will one day be North America.
The hadrosaurs here are even louder than the guys we met earlier!
PARASAUROLOPHUS (PARE-AH-SAWR-OL-OH-FUSS)
KRITOSAURUS (KREE-TO-SAWR-USS)
SAUROLOPHUS (SAWR-OL-OH-FUSS)
They share the plains with the most famous ankylosaur, Ankylosaurus (AN-kee-lo-SAWR-uss), whose giant club tail makes any creature think twice about picking a fight.
ZIAPELTA (ZEE-AH-PELL-TAH)

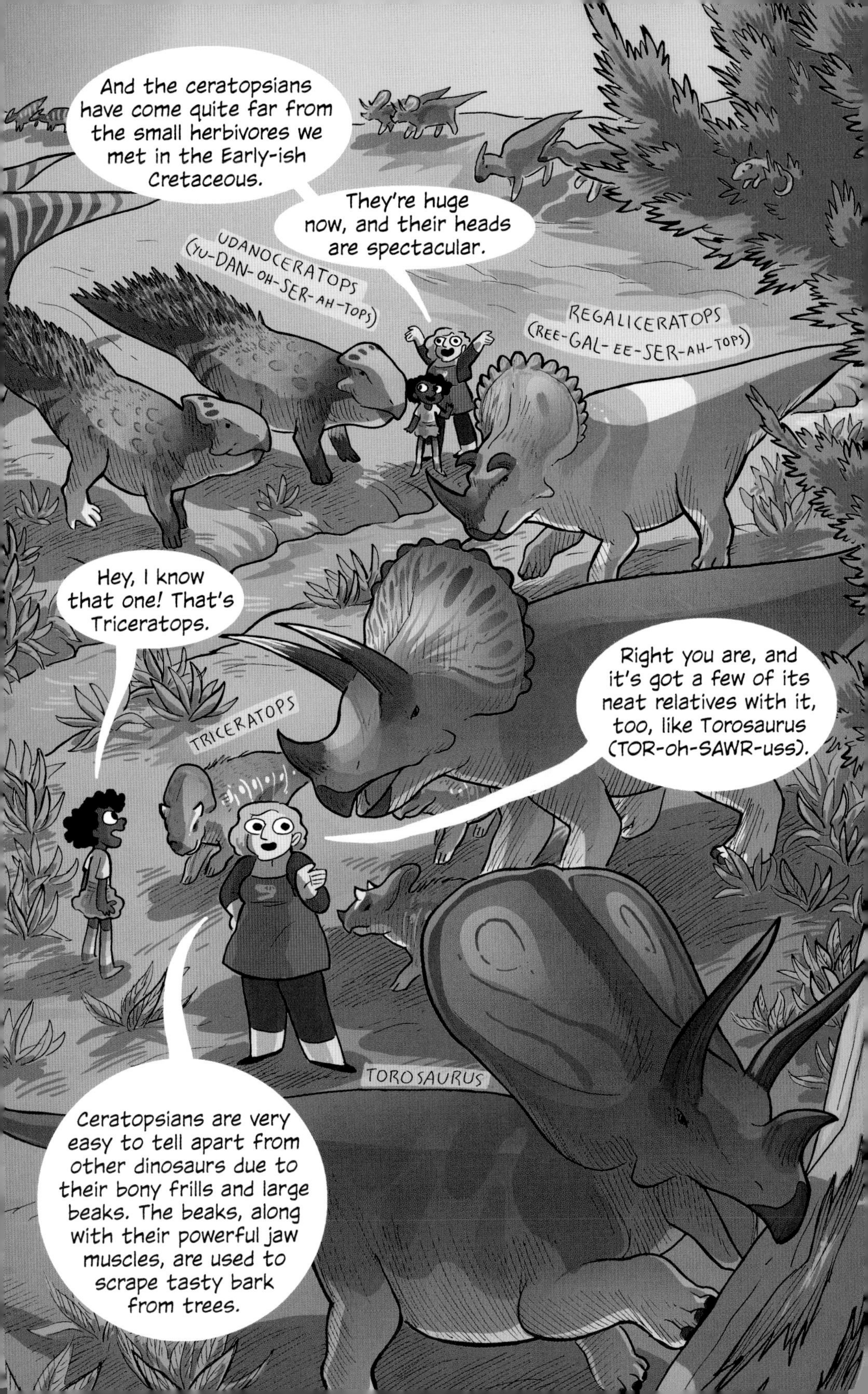
And the ceratopsians have come quite far from the small herbivores we met in the Early-ish Cretaceous.
They're huge now, and their heads are spectacular.
UDANOCERATOPS (YU-DAN-OH-SER-AH-TOPS)
REGALICERATOPS (REE-GAL-EE-SER-AH-TOPS)
Hey, I know that one! That's Triceratops.
TRICERATOPS
Right you are, and it's got a few of its neat relatives with it, too, like Torosaurus (TOR-oh-SAWR-uss).
TOROSAURUS
Ceratopsians are very easy to tell apart from other dinosaurs due to their bony frills and large beaks. The beaks, along with their powerful jaw muscles, are used to scrape tasty bark from trees.

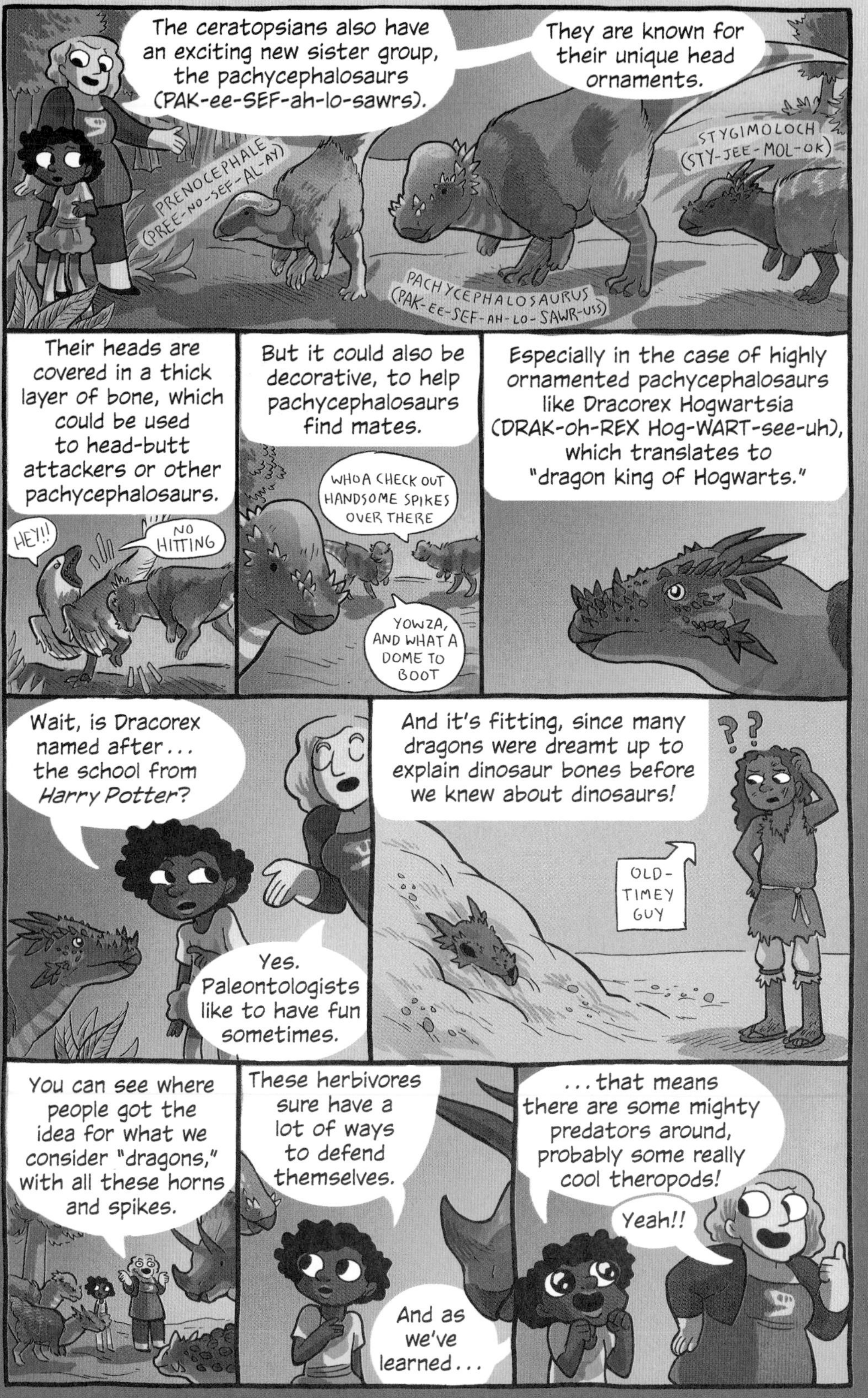
The ceratopsians also have an exciting new sister group, the pachycephalosaurs (PAK-ee-SEF-ah-lo-sawrs).
They are known for their unique head ornaments.
PRENOCEPHALE (PREE-NO-SEF-AL-AY)
PACHYCEPHALOSAURUS (PAK-EE-SEF-AH-LO-SAWR-USS)
STYGIMOLOCH (STY-JEE-MOL-OK)
Their heads are covered in a thick layer of bone, which could be used to head-butt attackers or other pachycephalosaurs.
HEY!!
NO HITTING
But it could also be decorative, to help pachycephalosaurs find mates.
WHOA CHECK OUT HANDSOME SPIKES OVER THERE
YOWZA, AND WHAT A DOME TO BOOT
Especially in the case of highly ornamented pachycephalosaurs like Dracorex Hogwartsia (DRAK-oh-REX Hog-WART-see-uh), which translates to "dragon king of Hogwarts."
Wait, is Dracorex named after . . . the school from *Harry Potter*?
Yes. Paleontologists like to have fun sometimes.
And it's fitting, since many dragons were dreamt up to explain dinosaur bones before we knew about dinosaurs!
??
OLD-TIMEY GUY
You can see where people got the idea for what we consider "dragons," with all these horns and spikes.
These herbivores sure have a lot of ways to defend themselves.
And as we've learned . . .
. . . that means there are some mighty predators around, probably some really cool theropods!
Yeah!!

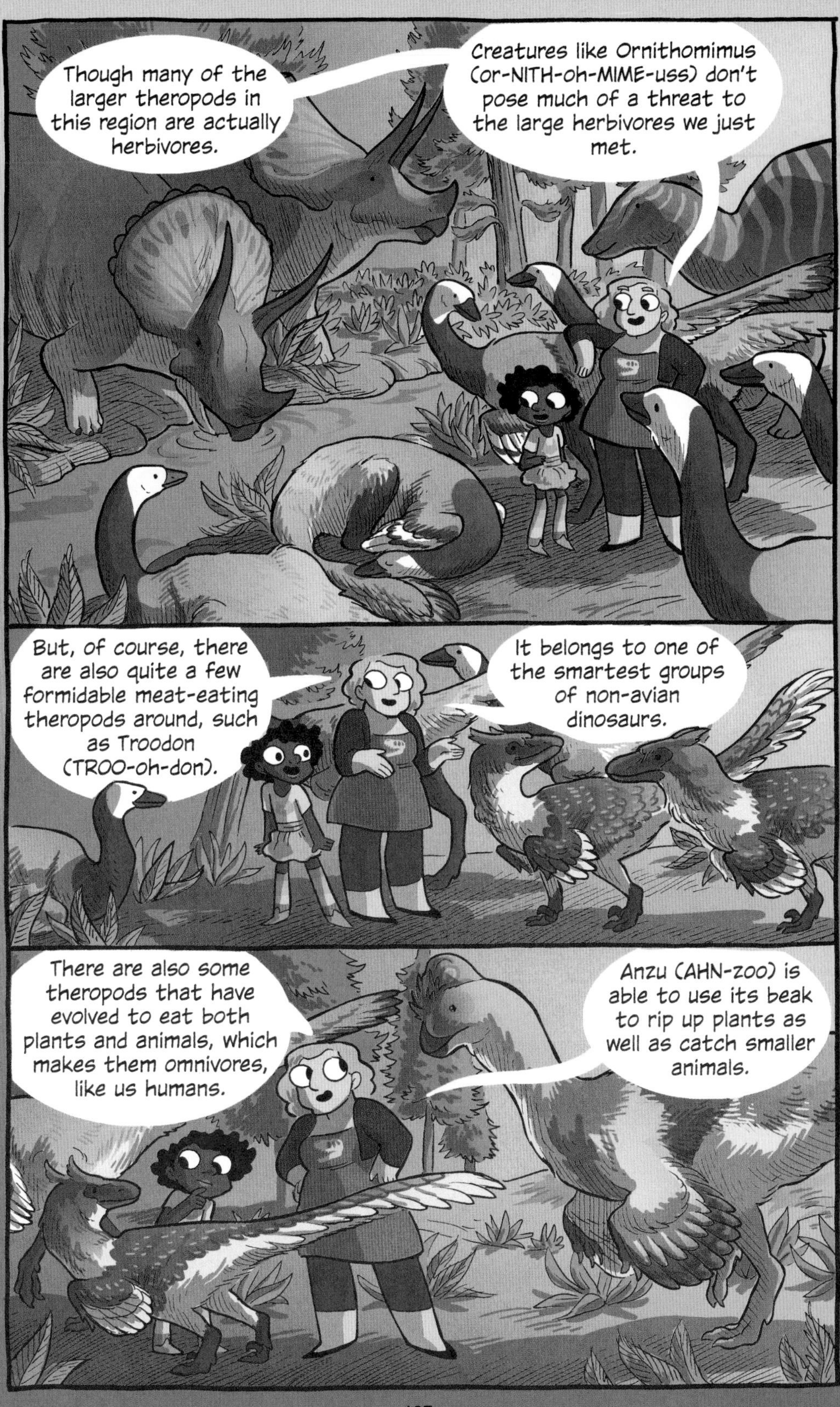
Though many of the larger theropods in this region are actually herbivores.
Creatures like Ornithomimus (or-NITH-oh-MIME-uss) don't pose much of a threat to the large herbivores we just met.
But, of course, there are also quite a few formidable meat-eating theropods around, such as Troodon (TROO-oh-don).
It belongs to one of the smartest groups of non-avian dinosaurs.
There are also some theropods that have evolved to eat both plants and animals, which makes them omnivores, like us humans.
Anzu (AHN-zoo) is able to use its beak to rip up plants as well as catch smaller animals.

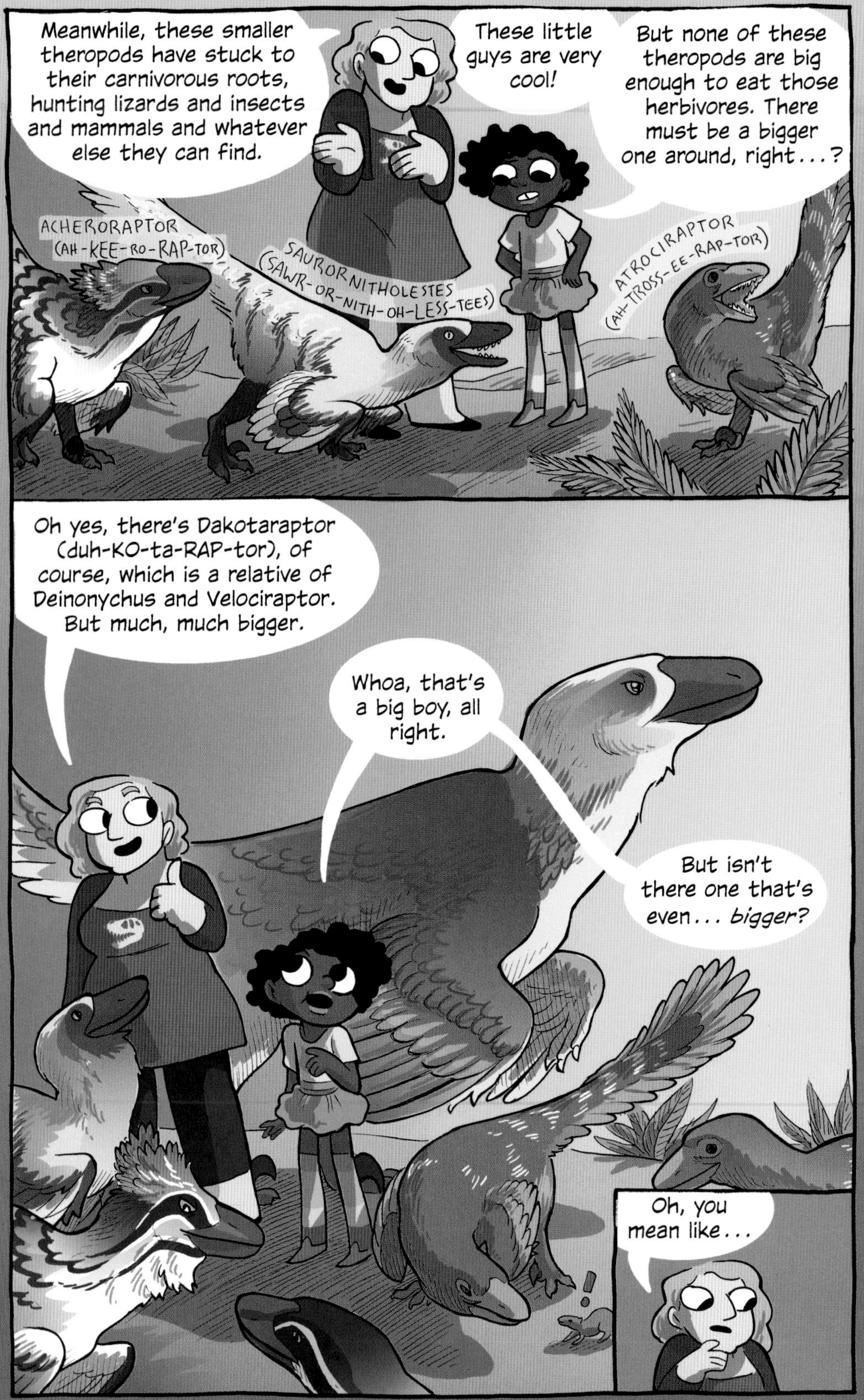
Meanwhile, these smaller theropods have stuck to their carnivorous roots, hunting lizards and insects and mammals and whatever else they can find.
These little guys are very cool!
But none of these theropods are big enough to eat those herbivores. There must be a bigger one around, right...?
ACHERORAPTOR (AH-KEE-RO-RAP-TOR)
SAURORNITHOLESTES (SAWR-OR-NITH-OH-LESS-TEES)
ATROCIRAPTOR (AH-TROSS-EE-RAP-TOR)
Oh yes, there's Dakotaraptor (duh-KO-ta-RAP-tor), of course, which is a relative of Deinonychus and Velociraptor. But much, much bigger.
Whoa, that's a big boy, all right.
But isn't there one that's even... *bigger*?
Oh, you mean like...
!

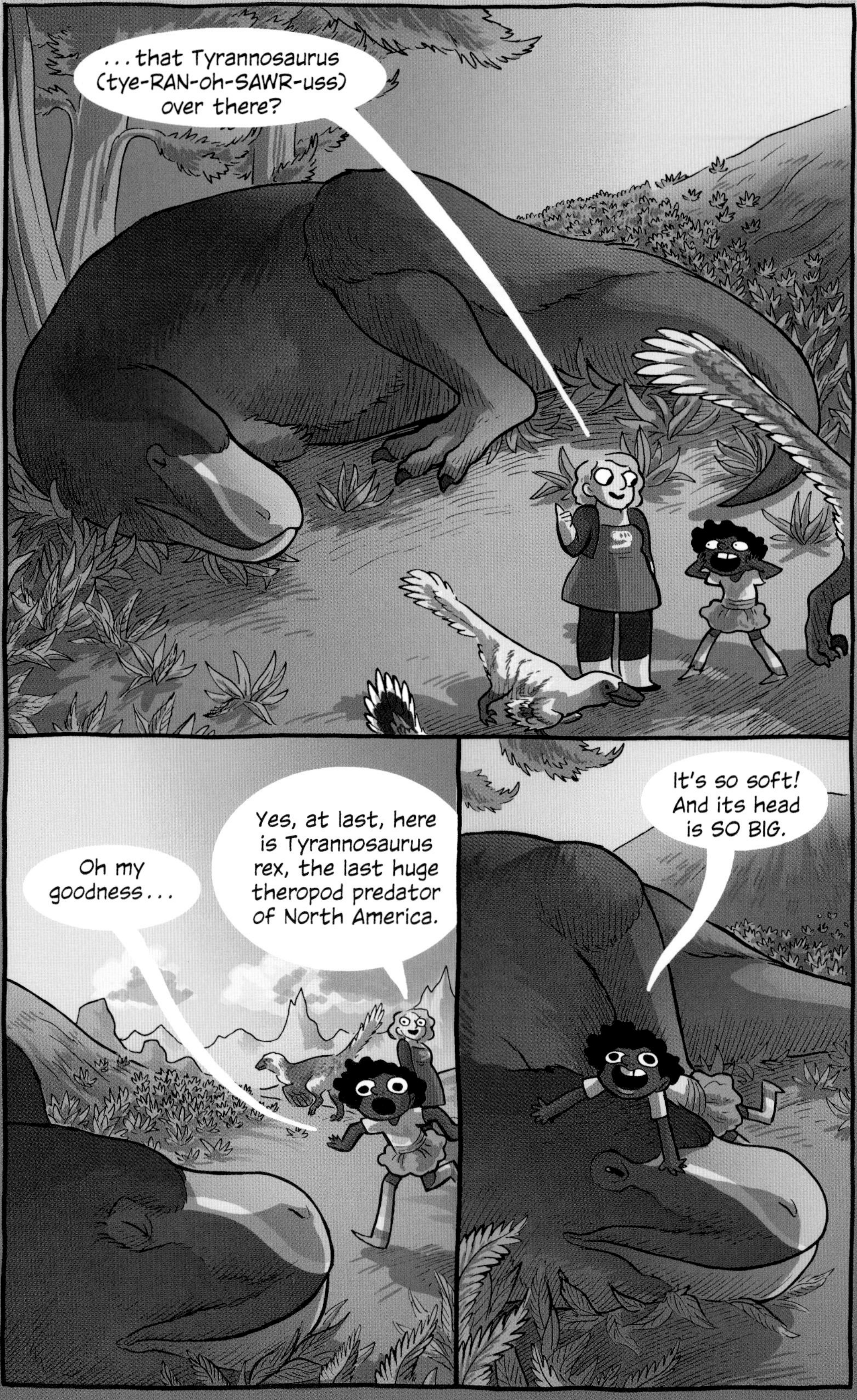
...that Tyrannosaurus (tye-RAN-oh-SAWR-uss) over there?
Oh my goodness...
Yes, at last, here is Tyrannosaurus rex, the last huge theropod predator of North America.
It's so soft! And its head is SO BIG.

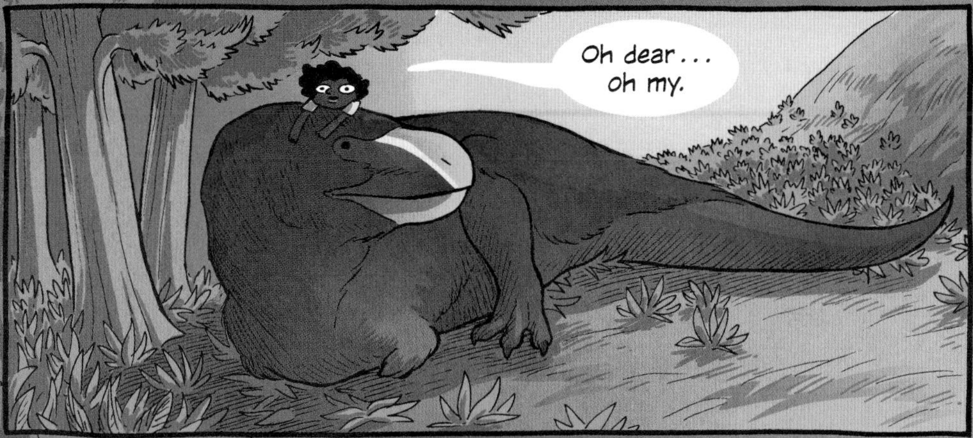
Oh dear . . .
oh my.

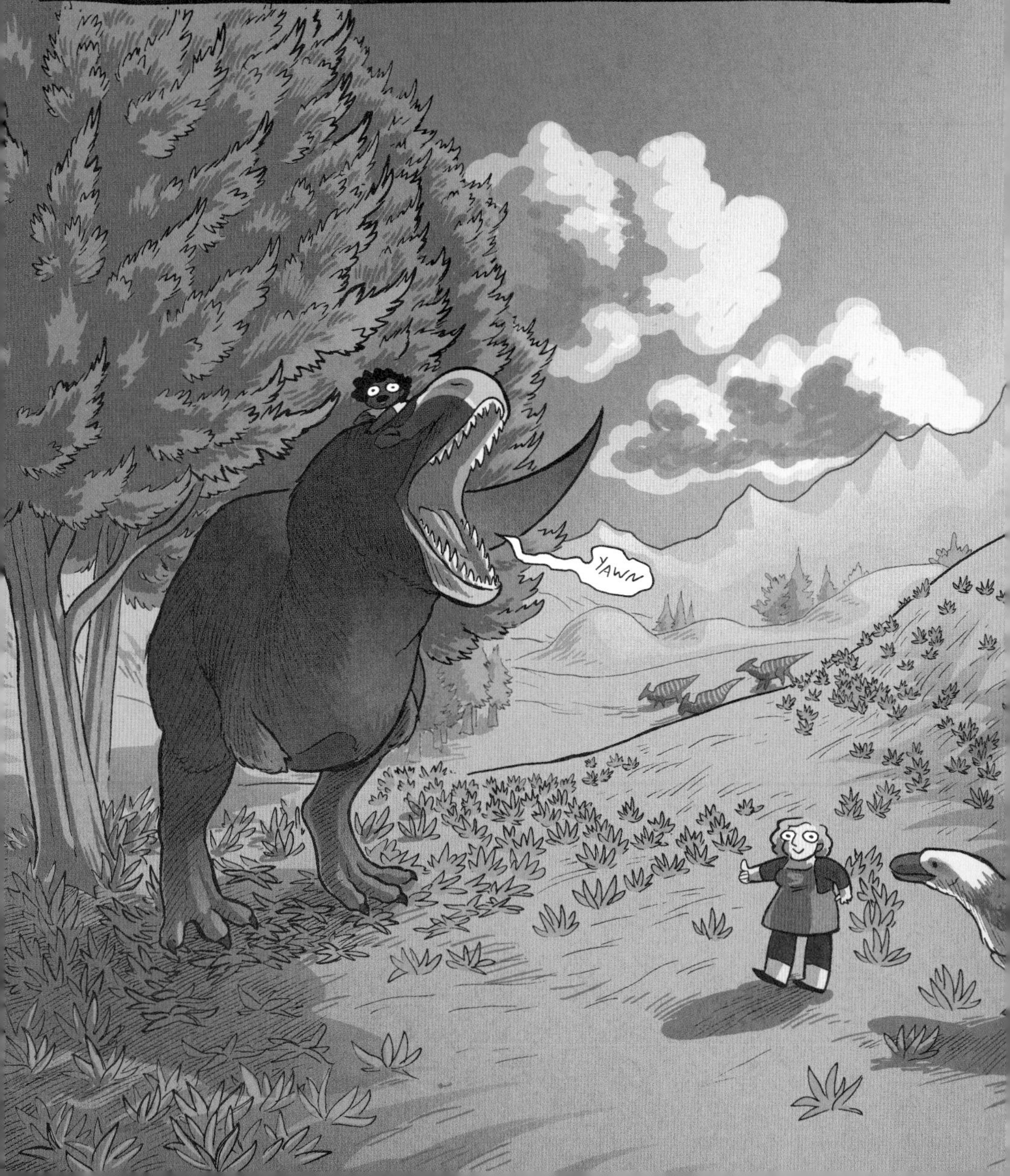
YAWN

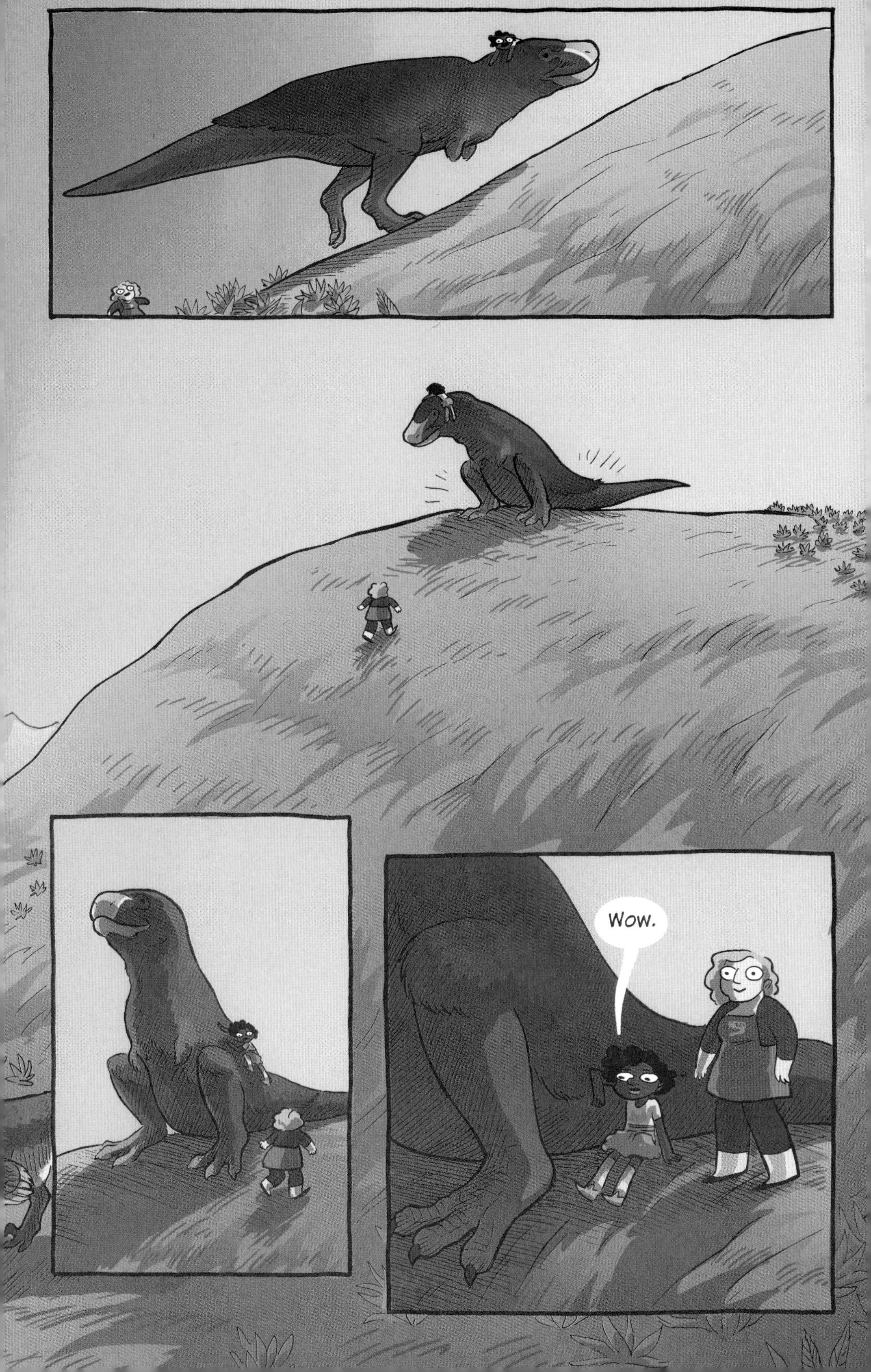
WOW.

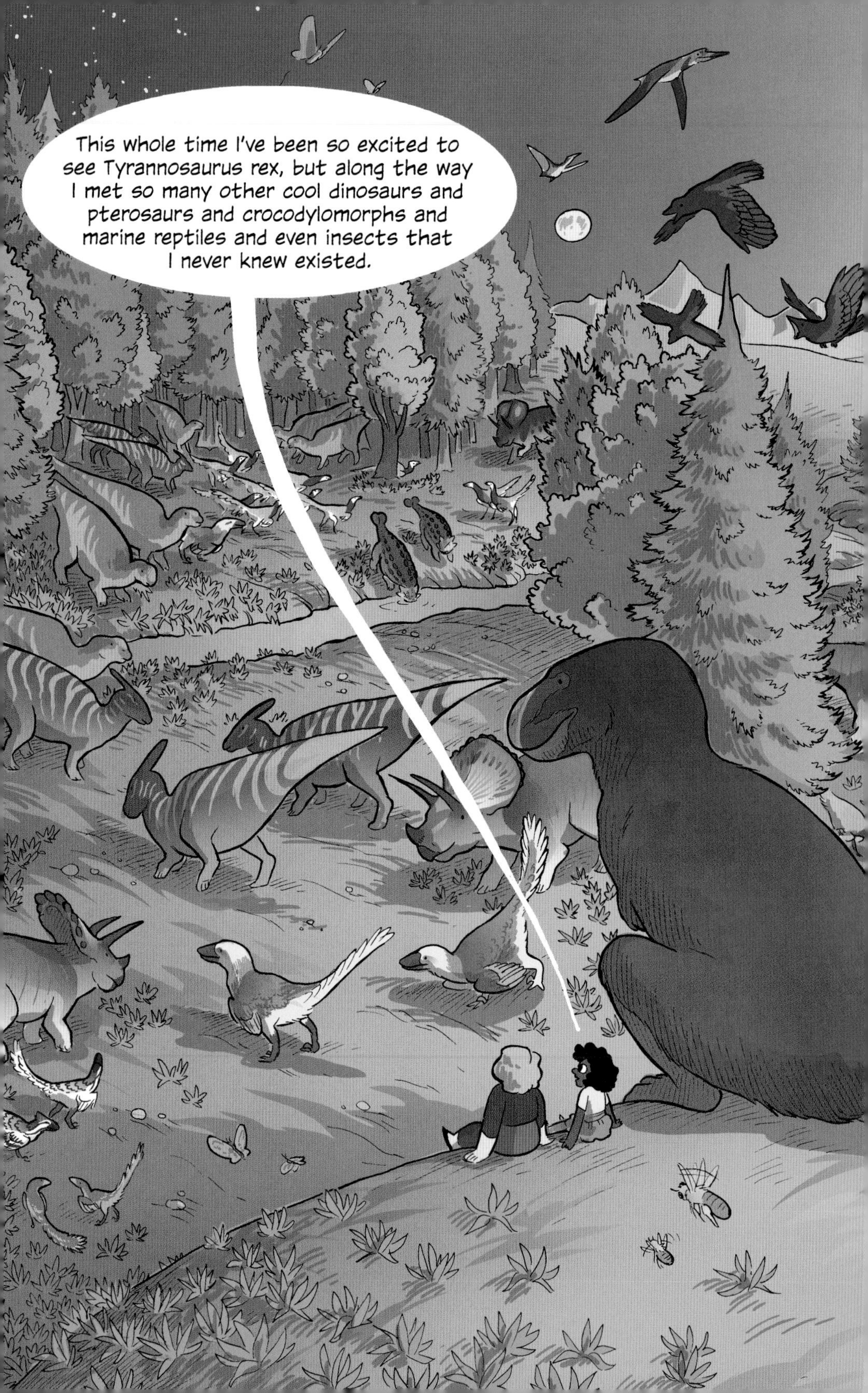
This whole time I've been so excited to see Tyrannosaurus rex, but along the way I met so many other cool dinosaurs and pterosaurs and crocodylomorphs and marine reptiles and even insects that I never knew existed.

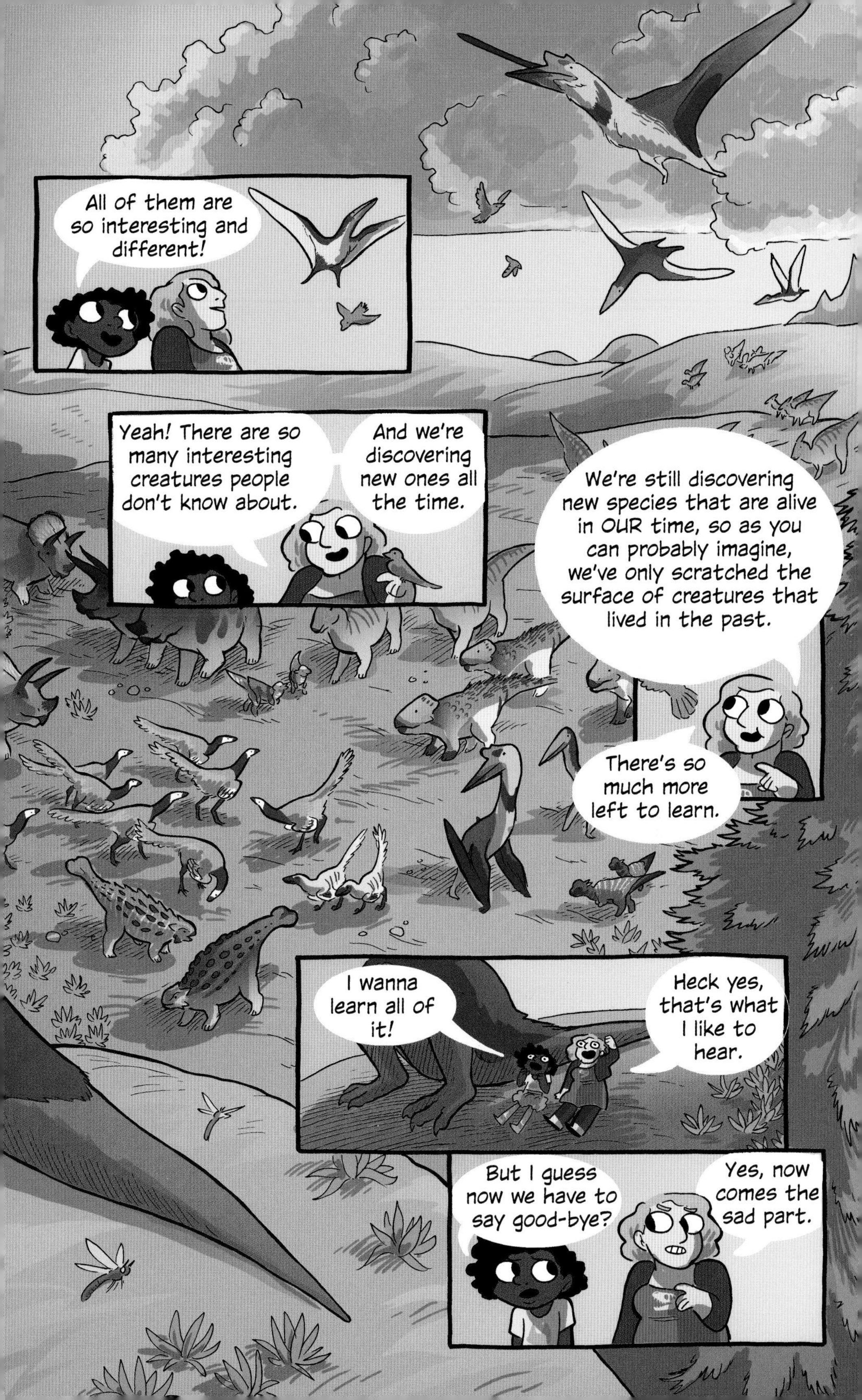
All of them are so interesting and different!
Yeah! There are so many interesting creatures people don't know about.
And we're discovering new ones all the time.
We're still discovering new species that are alive in OUR time, so as you can probably imagine, we've only scratched the surface of creatures that lived in the past.
There's so much more left to learn.
I wanna learn all of it!
Heck yes, that's what I like to hear.
But I guess now we have to say good-bye?
Yes, now comes the sad part.

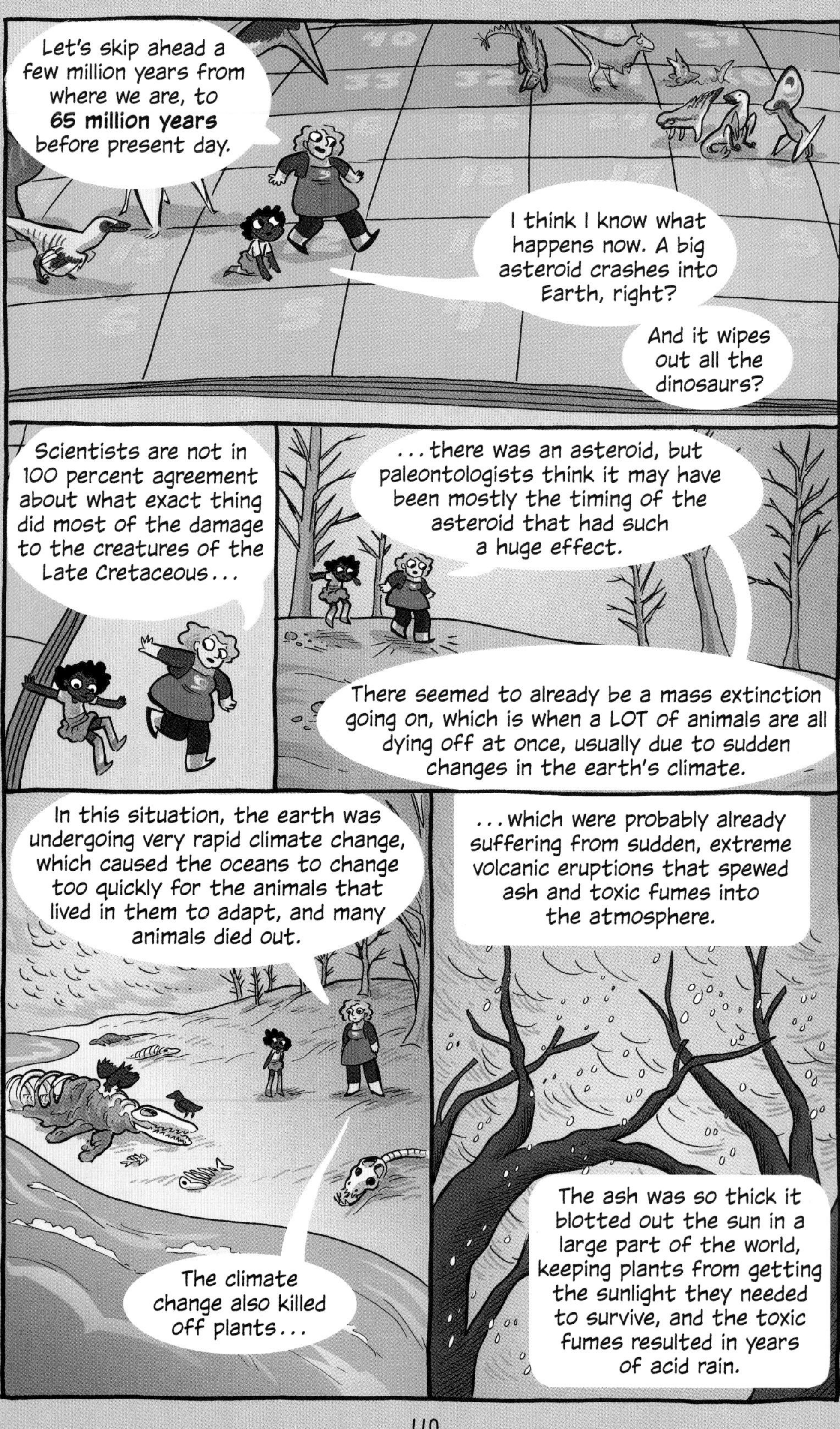
Let's skip ahead a few million years from where we are, to **65 million years** before present day.
I think I know what happens now. A big asteroid crashes into Earth, right?
And it wipes out all the dinosaurs?
Scientists are not in 100 percent agreement about what exact thing did most of the damage to the creatures of the Late Cretaceous...
...there was an asteroid, but paleontologists think it may have been mostly the timing of the asteroid that had such a huge effect.
There seemed to already be a mass extinction going on, which is when a LOT of animals are all dying off at once, usually due to sudden changes in the earth's climate.
In this situation, the earth was undergoing very rapid climate change, which caused the oceans to change too quickly for the animals that lived in them to adapt, and many animals died out.
The climate change also killed off plants...
...which were probably already suffering from sudden, extreme volcanic eruptions that spewed ash and toxic fumes into the atmosphere.
The ash was so thick it blotted out the sun in a large part of the world, keeping plants from getting the sunlight they needed to survive, and the toxic fumes resulted in years of acid rain.

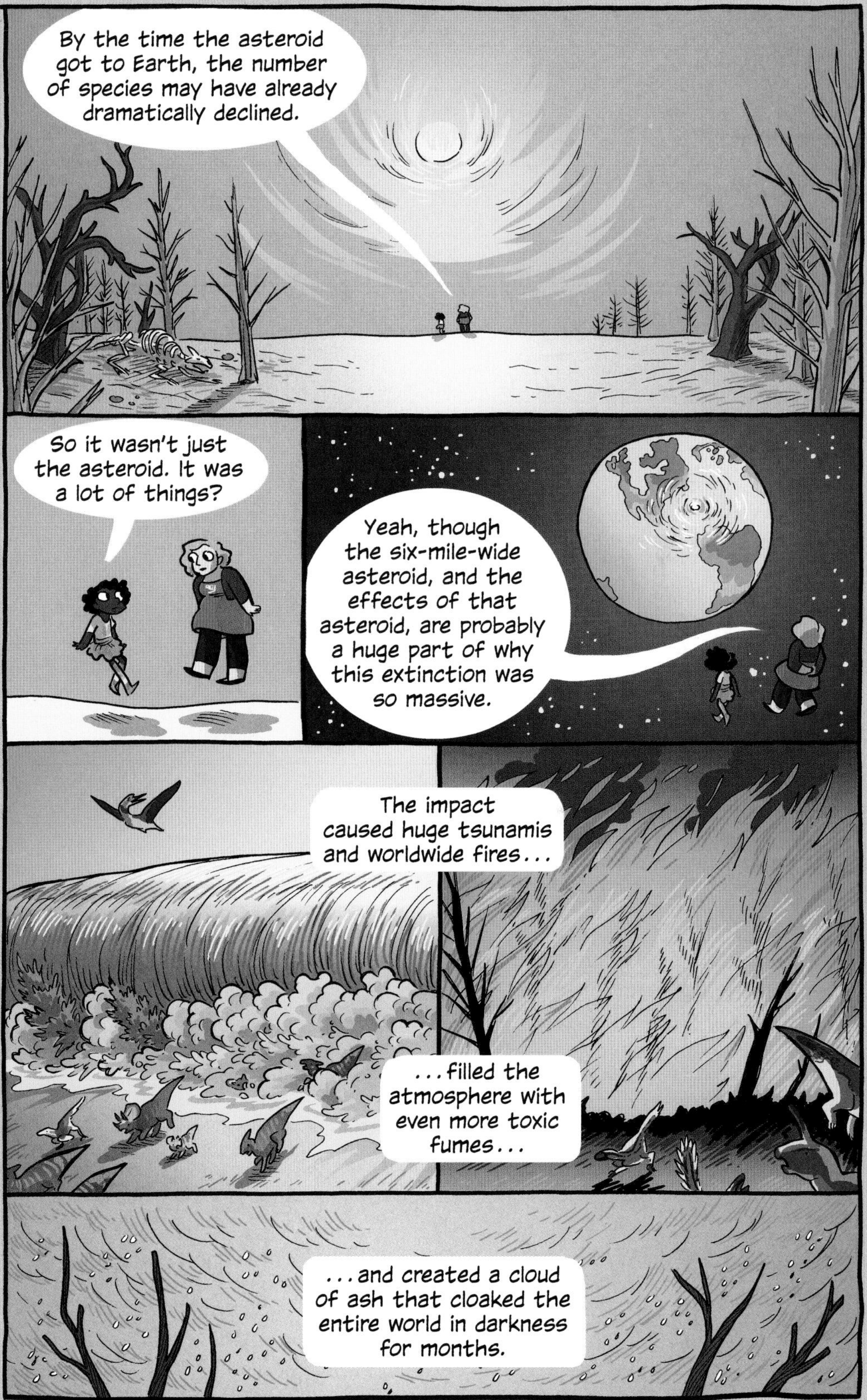
By the time the asteroid got to Earth, the number of species may have already dramatically declined.
So it wasn't just the asteroid. It was a lot of things?
Yeah, though the six-mile-wide asteroid, and the effects of that asteroid, are probably a huge part of why this extinction was so massive.
The impact caused huge tsunamis and worldwide fires...
...filled the atmosphere with even more toxic fumes...
...and created a cloud of ash that cloaked the entire world in darkness for months.

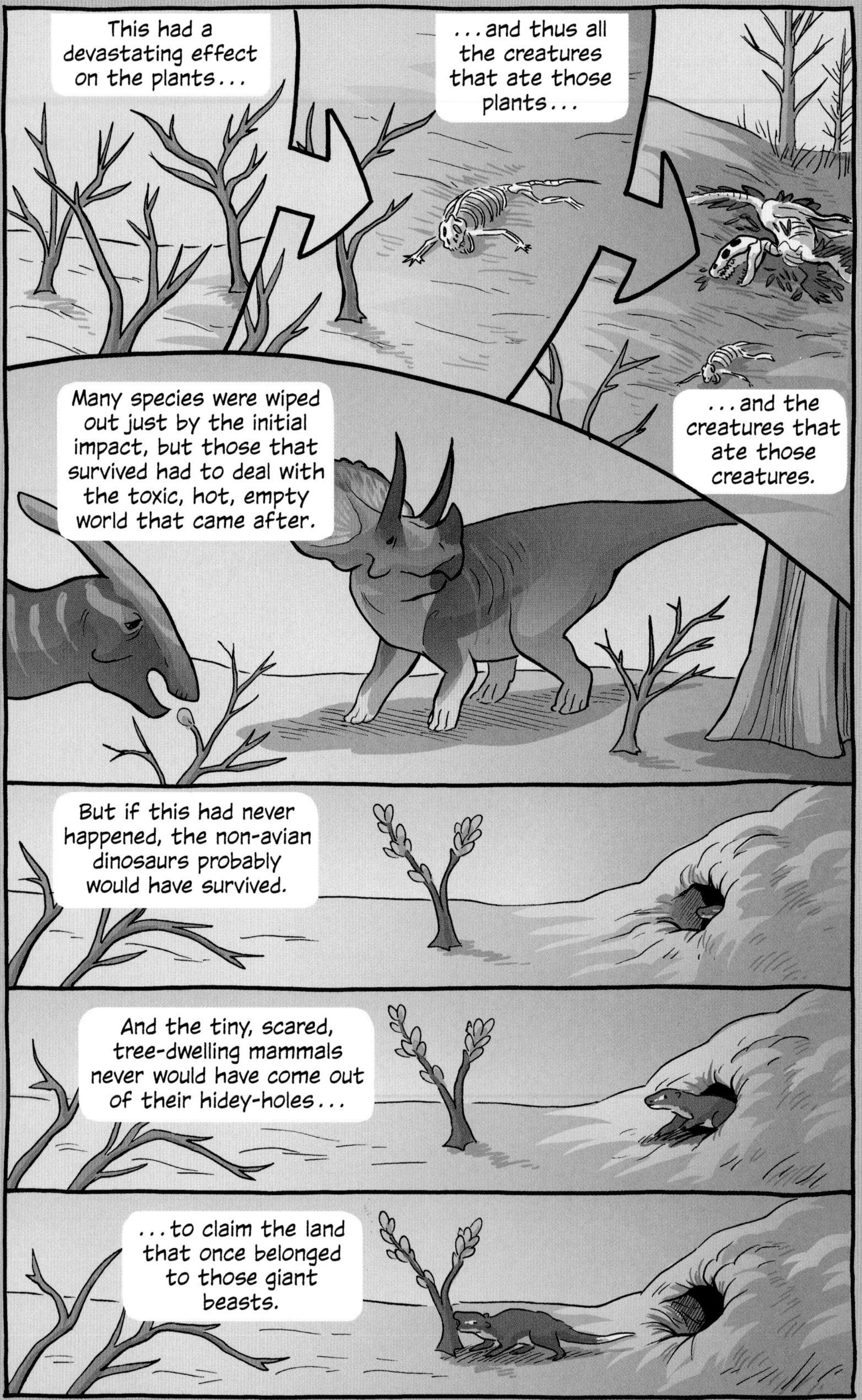
This had a devastating effect on the plants...
...and thus all the creatures that ate those plants...
...and the creatures that ate those creatures.
Many species were wiped out just by the initial impact, but those that survived had to deal with the toxic, hot, empty world that came after.
But if this had never happened, the non-avian dinosaurs probably would have survived.
And the tiny, scared, tree-dwelling mammals never would have come out of their hidey-holes...
...to claim the land that once belonged to those giant beasts.

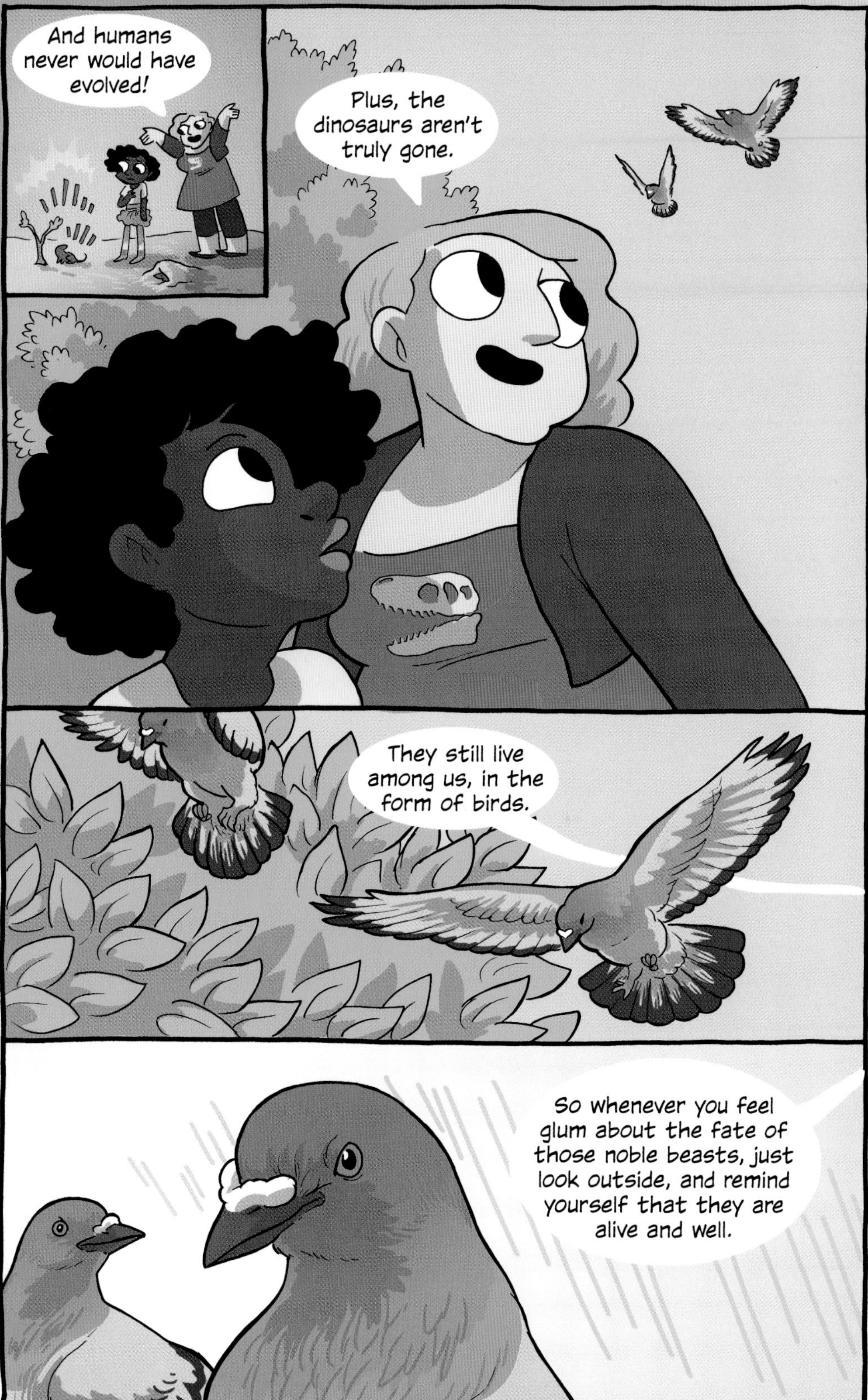
And humans never would have evolved!
Plus, the dinosaurs aren't truly gone.
They still live among us, in the form of birds.
So whenever you feel glum about the fate of those noble beasts, just look outside, and remind yourself that they are alive and well.

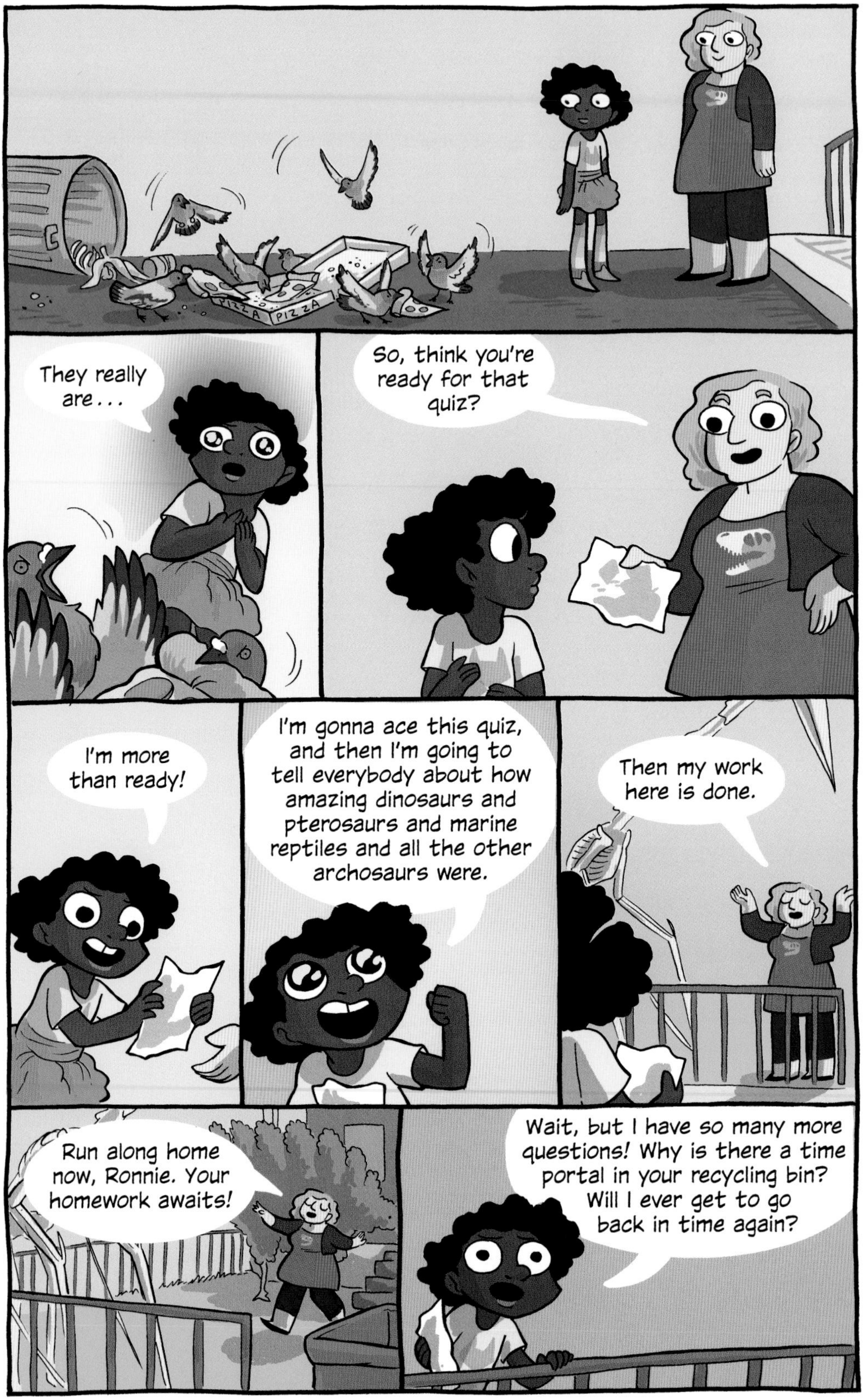

PIZZA
PIZZA
They really are...
So, think you're ready for that quiz?
I'm more than ready!
I'm gonna ace this quiz, and then I'm going to tell everybody about how amazing dinosaurs and pterosaurs and marine reptiles and all the other archosaurs were.
Then my work here is done.
Run along home now, Ronnie. Your homework awaits!
Wait, but I have so many more questions! Why is there a time portal in your recycling bin? Will I ever get to go back in time again?

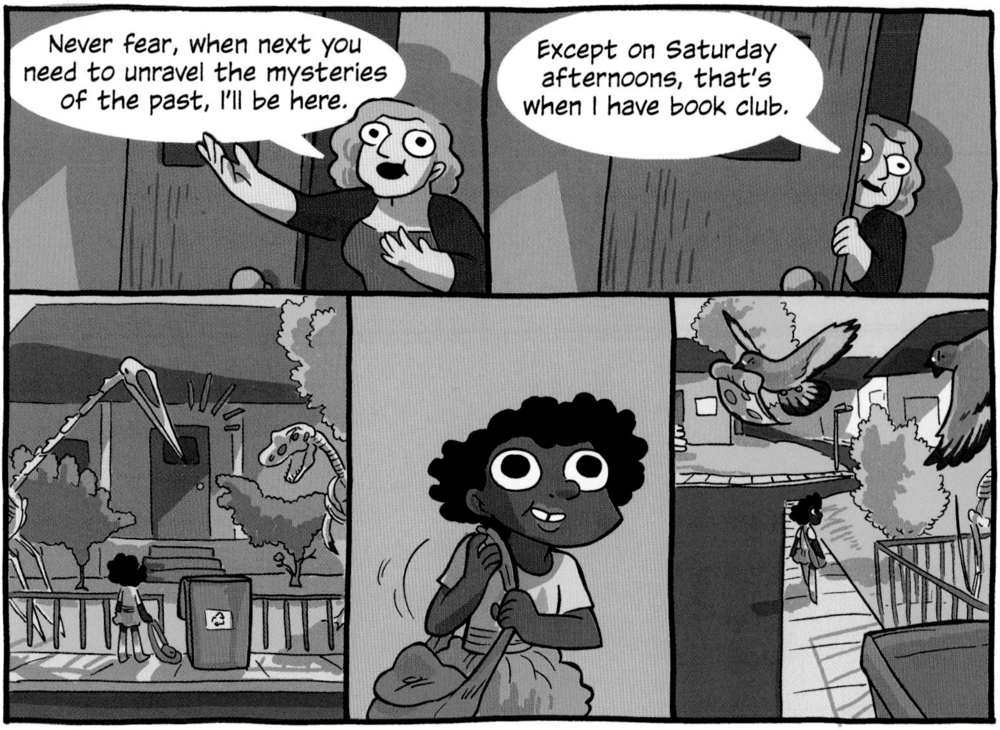
Never fear, when next you need to unravel the mysteries of the past, I'll be here.
Except on Saturday afternoons, that's when I have book club.

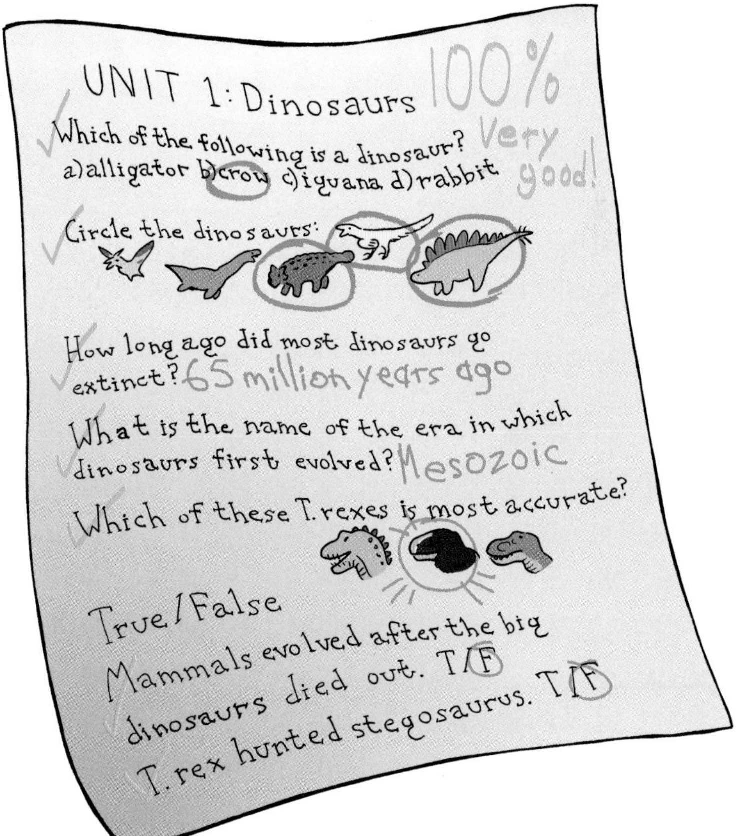
UNIT 1: Dinosaurs
100%
Very good!
Which of the following is a dinosaur?
a) alligator b) crow c) iguana d) rabbit
Circle the dinosaurs:
How long ago did most dinosaurs go extinct? 65 million years ago
What is the name of the era in which dinosaurs first evolved? Mesozoic
Which of these T. rexes is most accurate?
True/False
Mammals evolved after the big dinosaurs died out. T/F
T. rex hunted stegosaurus. T/F

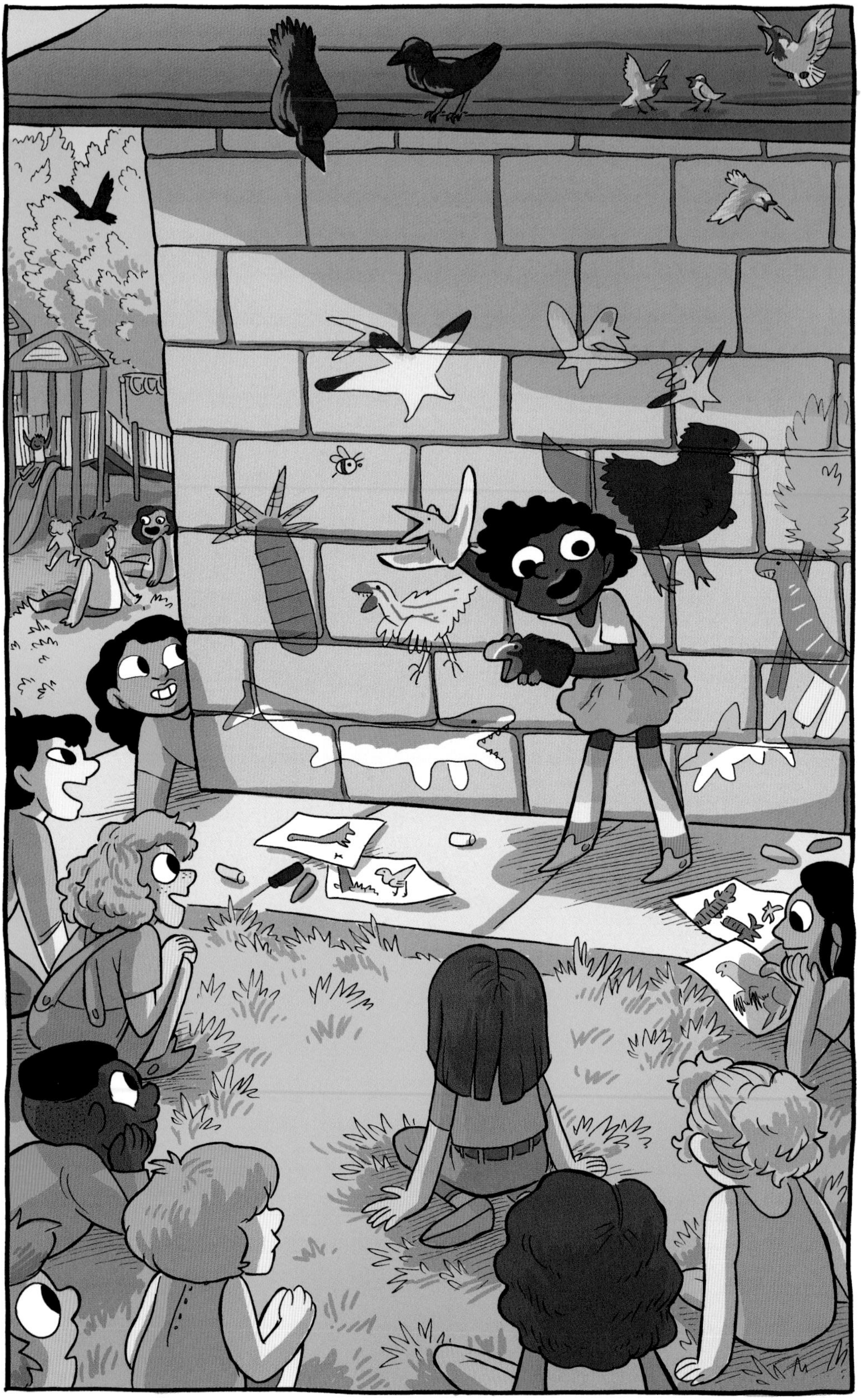

COOL ANIMALS FROM OTHER TIMES

MICRORAPTOR
(MIKE-RO-RAP-TOR)
LIVED
130-125 MYA
(MILLION YEARS AGO)

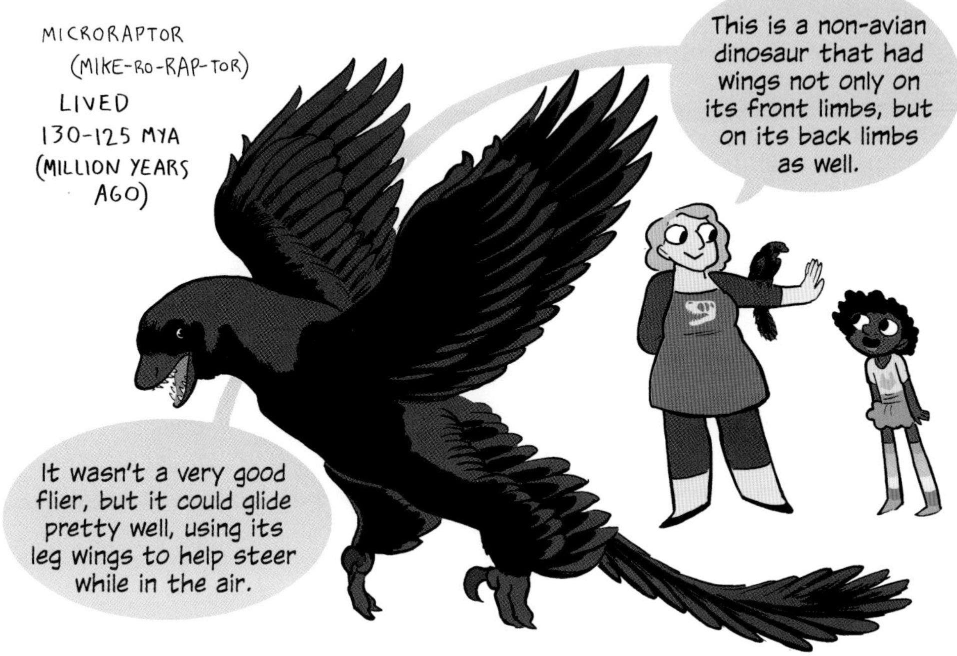
This is a non-avian dinosaur that had wings not only on its front limbs, but on its back limbs as well.
It wasn't a very good flier, but it could glide pretty well, using its leg wings to help steer while in the air.

UTAHRAPTOR
(YU-TAH-RAP-TOR)
LIVED 126 MYA

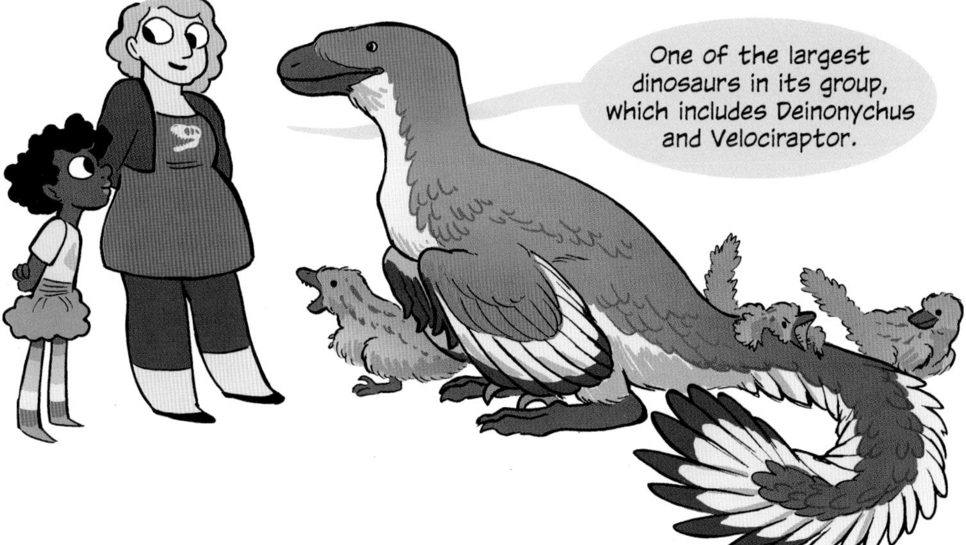
One of the largest dinosaurs in its group, which includes Deinonychus and Velociraptor.

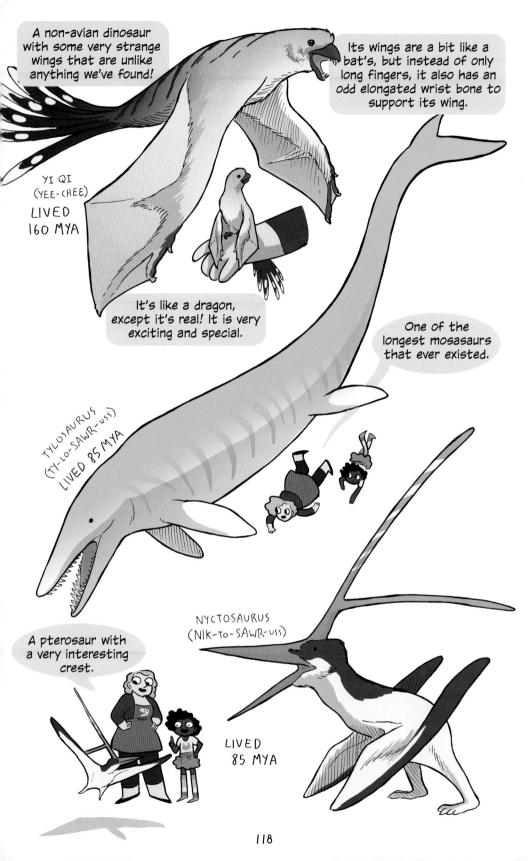

A non-avian dinosaur with some very strange wings that are unlike anything we've found!

Its wings are a bit like a bat's, but instead of only long fingers, it also has an odd elongated wrist bone to support its wing.

YI QI
(YEE-CHEE)
LIVED 160 MYA

It's like a dragon, except it's real! It is very exciting and special.

One of the longest mosasaurs that ever existed.

TYLOSAURUS
(TY-LO-SAWR-uss)
LIVED 85 MYA

NYCTOSAURUS
(NIK-TO-SAWR-uss)

A pterosaur with a very interesting crest.

LIVED 85 MYA

118

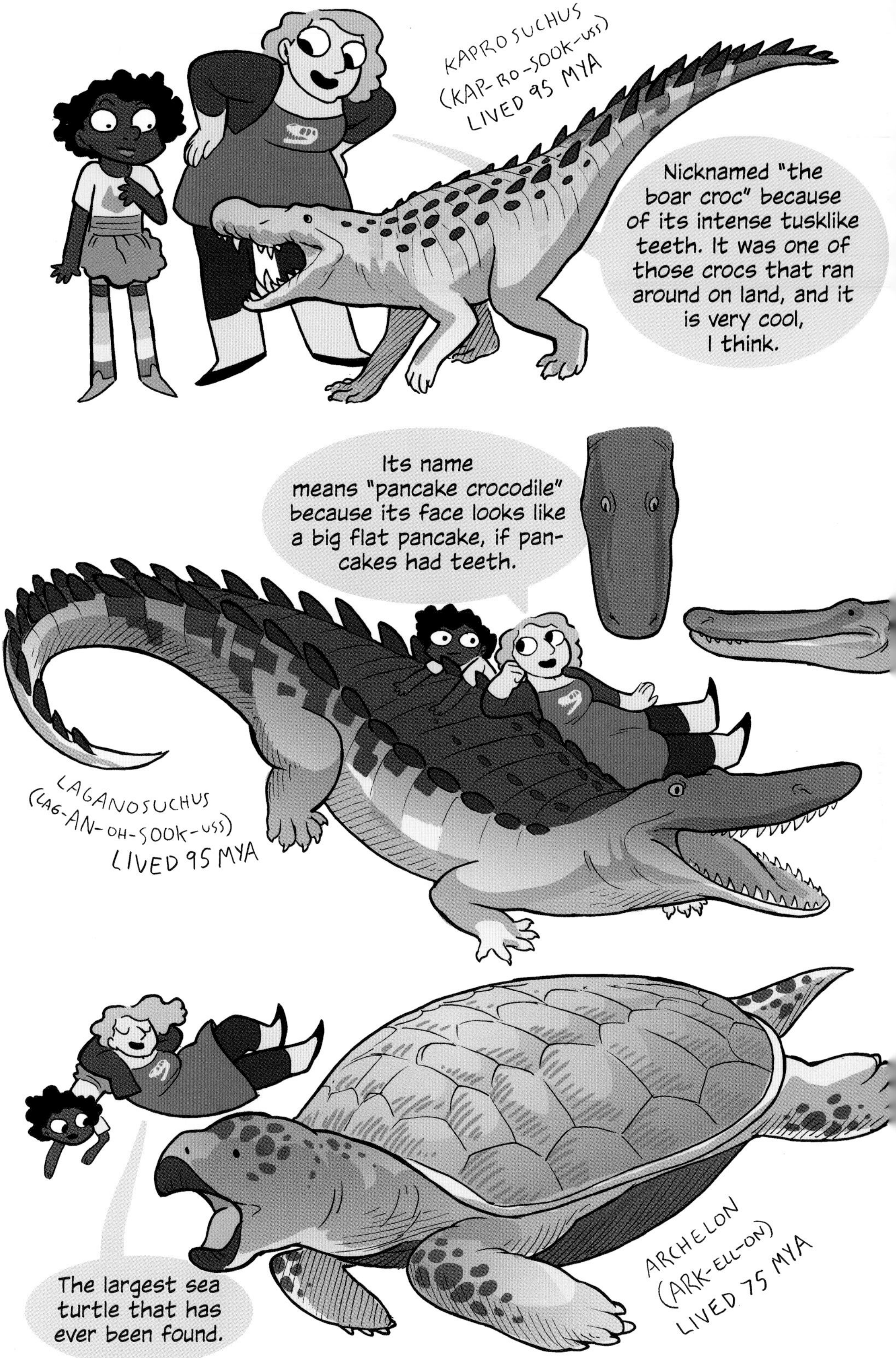

KAPROSUCHUS
(KAP-RO-SOOK-USS)
LIVED 95 MYA
Nicknamed "the boar croc" because of its intense tusklike teeth. It was one of those crocs that ran around on land, and it is very cool, I think.
Its name means "pancake crocodile" because its face looks like a big flat pancake, if pancakes had teeth.
LAGANOSUCHUS
(LAG-AN-OH-SOOK-USS)
LIVED 95 MYA
The largest sea turtle that has ever been found.
ARCHELON
(ARK-ELL-ON)
LIVED 75 MYA

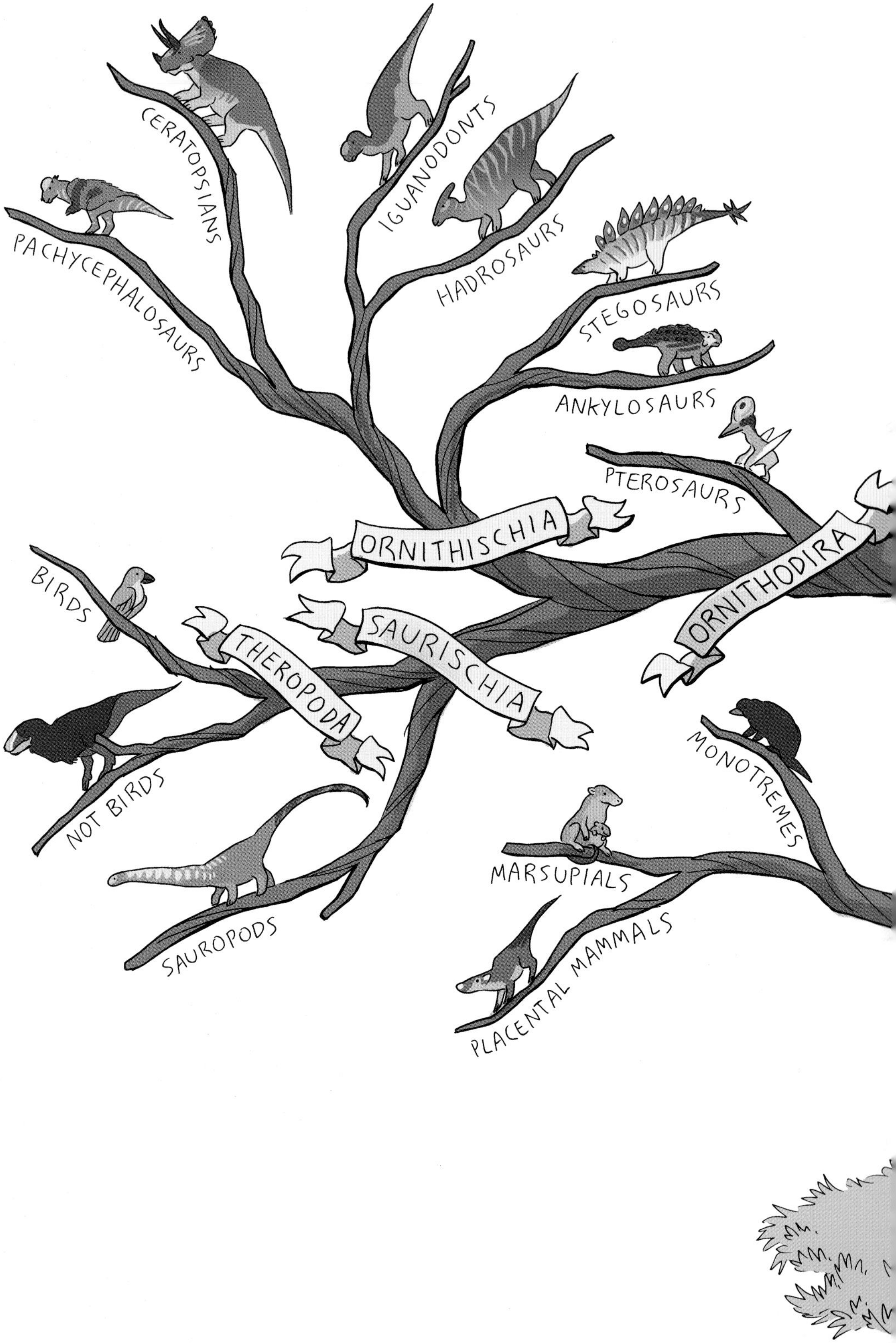
CERATOPSIANS
IGUANODONTS
PACHYCEPHALOSAURS
HADROSAURS
STEGOSAURS
ANKYLOSAURS
PTEROSAURS
ORNITHISCHIA
ORNITHODIRA
BIRDS
THEROPODA
SAURISCHIA
NOT BIRDS
MONOTREMES
MARSUPIALS
SAUROPODS
PLACENTAL MAMMALS

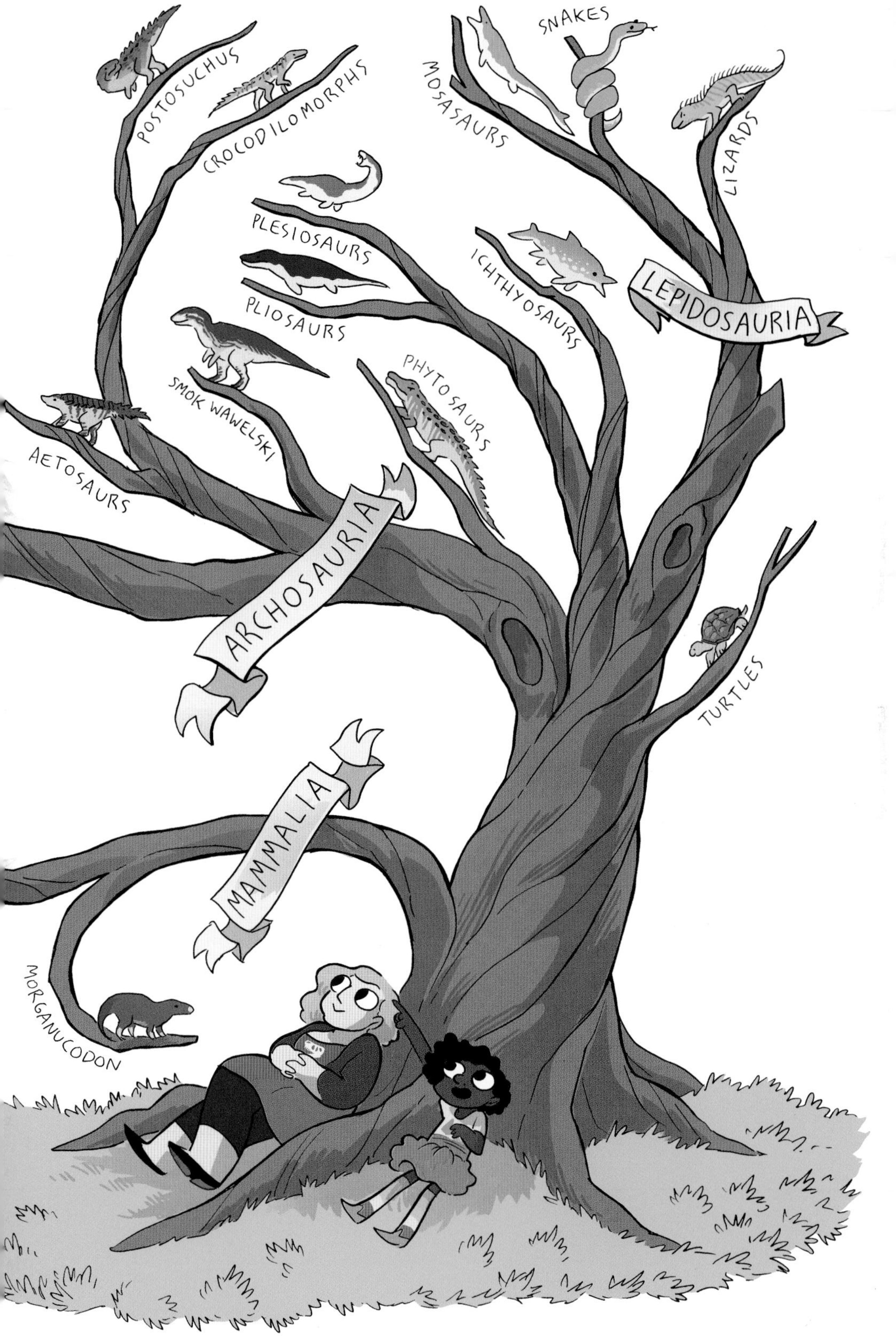
POSTOSUCHUS
CROCODILOMORPHS
MOSASAURS
SNAKES
LIZARDS
PLESIOSAURS
PLIOSAURS
ICHTHYOSAURS
LEPIDOSAURIA
SMOK WAWELSKI
PHYTOSAURS
AETOSAURS
ARCHOSAURIA
TURTLES
MAMMALIA
MORGANUCODON

GLOSSARY

Amphibian: Cold-blooded animals whose eggs don't have thick shells and must be laid in water to keep from dehydrating.

Bird: A kind of dinosaur with a toothless beak and a short tail.

Carnivore: "Carn-" means meat and "-vore" means eat, so a carnivore is a creature that eats meat, such as Tyrannosaurus rex.

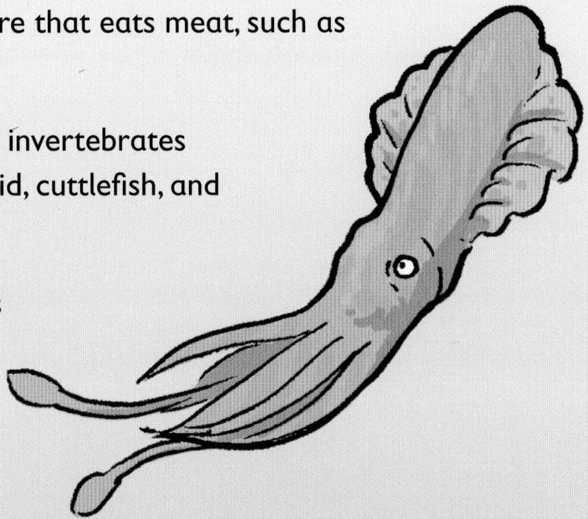

Cephalopod: A group of invertebrates that includes octopus, squid, cuttlefish, and nautilus.

Cold-blooded: Creatures that don't produce their own heat and rely on the sun for warmth.

Common ancestor: A creature that evolved into different groups of creatures. These groups have an ancestor in common.

Coniferous: Plants with needle-like leaves.

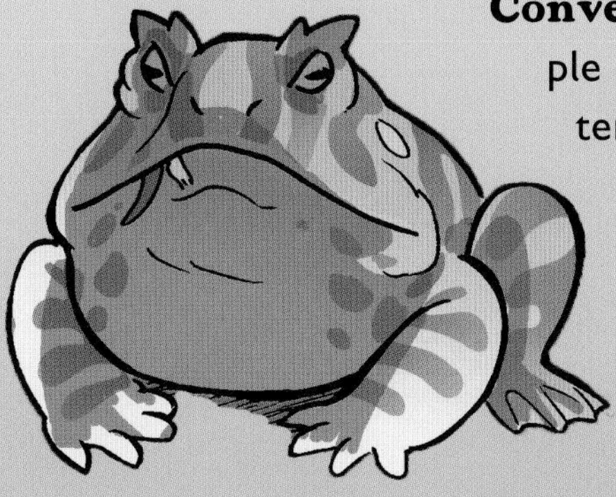

Convergent evolution: When multiple creatures evolve similar characteristics, despite not being related. For example, dolphins and sharks look very similar, even though one is a mammal and one is a fish.

Deciduous: Plants that shed their leaves as the seasons change.

Ecological niche: Where a creature lives, what it eats, and what eats it.

Evolution: When creatures develop new traits that help them survive and have babies.

Flowering plants: Plants that use flowers to transport their pollen to other plants.

Gondwana: A southern supercontinent containing Africa, India, South America, Australia, and Antarctica.

Herbivore: "Herb-" means plant and "-vore" means eat, so an herbivore is a creature that eats plants, such as Diplodocus.

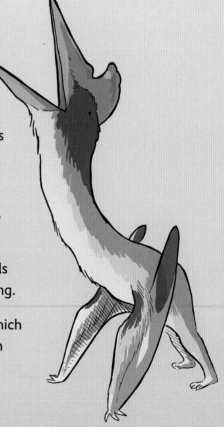

Ice caps: The frozen areas around the North and South poles that stay frozen all year round.

Laurasia: A northern supercontinent containing Europe, North America, and Asia.

Mammal: Warm-blooded animals that produce milk for their offspring.

Mass extinction: An event in which a large percentage of life on Earth dies out.

Mesozoic: "Meso-" means middle, and "-zoic" means animals, so "Mesozoic" means "middle animals." It is the era in which non-avian dinosaurs lived and died, stretching from 252 million years ago to 66 million years ago.

Mutation: A change in the DNA of a creature that causes it to develop a new and different trait than its parents. Sometimes these mutations help the animal live long enough to have more babies than its non-mutated relatives, and the mutation spreads, which is how evolution happens.

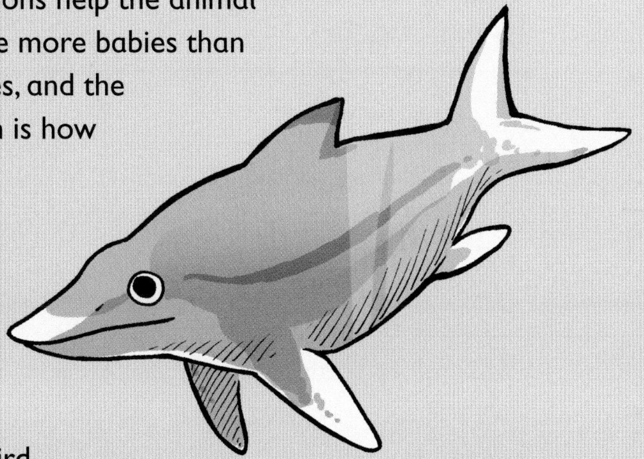

Non-avian dinosaur: "Avian" means "of or relating to birds," so a non-avian dinosaur is any dinosaur that is not a bird.

Omnivore: "Omni-" means all, so an omnivore is a creature that eats both meat and plants, such as Anzu.

Paleontologist: A person who studies fossils.

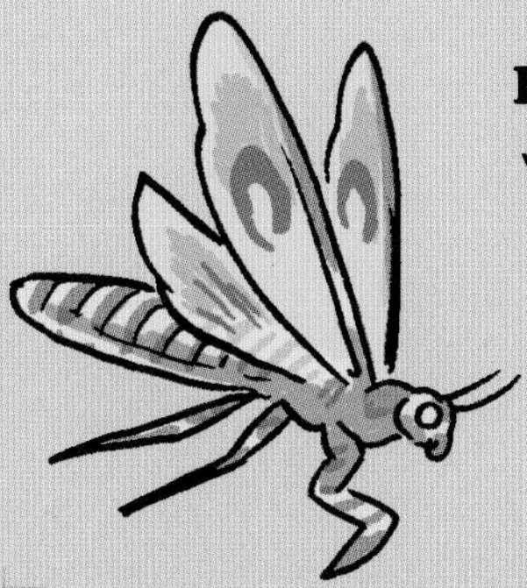

Phylogenetic tree: A branching map showing what creatures evolved from what other creatures, and how they are all related. It's a lot like a family tree.

Protofeather: A hairlike fiber that eventually evolved into feathers. "Proto-" means first, so "protofeathers" means "first feathers."

Supercontinent: A very large landmass composed of several groups of continental plates, which are the large sheets of rock that float across the earth's surface.

Vertebrate: An animal with a backbone. The bones in your spine are called vertebrae, so an animal with a spine is called a vertebrate.

Warm-blooded: Creatures that produce their own heat, such as humans.

ABOUT THE AUTHOR

Abby Howard is a full-time cartoonist living in Boston with her cat and snake. She loves dinosaurs, pterosaurs, and all their extinct friends, and would go back in time in a heartbeat—even if it meant she was eaten or stepped on immediately.